REPUTATIONS

D1296928

NIXON

Iwan Morgan

*Professor of American History
London Guildhall University*

A member of the Hodder Headline Group
LONDON
Co-published in the United States of America by
Oxford University Press Inc., New York

*To My Students
Past, Present and Future*

First published in Great Britain in 2002 by
Arnold, a member of the Hodder Headline Group,
338 Euston Road, London NW1 3BH

http://www.arnoldpublishers.com

Co-published in the United States of America by
Oxford University Press Inc.,
198 Madison Avenue, New York, NY10016

British Library Cataloguing in Publication Data
A catalogue record for this book is available from the British Library

Library of Congress Cataloging-in-Publication Data
A catalog record for this book is available from the Library of Congress

ISBN 0 340 76031 1 (hb)
ISBN 0 340 76032 X (pb)

1 2 3 4 5 6 7 8 9 10

Production Editor: Rada Radojicic
Production Controller: Iain McWilliams
Cover Design: Terry Griffiths

Typeset in 10 on 12 pt Sabon by Phoenix Photosetting, Chatham, Kent
Printed and bound in Great Britain by MPG Books, Bodmin, Cornwall

What do you think about this book? Or any other Arnold title?
Please send your comments to feedback.arnold@hodder.co.uk

Contents

General editorial preface

Hero or villain? Charlatan or true prophet? Sinner or saint? The volumes in the Reputations series examine the reputations of some of history's most conspicuous, powerful, and influential individuals, considering a range of representations, some of striking incompatibility. The aim is not merely to demonstrate that history is indeed, in Pieter Geyl's phrase, 'argument without end' but that the study even of contradictory conceptions can be fruitful: that the jettisoning of one thesis or presentation leaves behind something of value.

In Iago's self-serving denunciation of it, reputation is 'an idle and most false imposition; oft got without merit, and lost without deserving', but a more generous definition would allow its use as one of the principal currencies of historical understanding. In seeking to analyse the cultivation, creation, and deconstruction of reputation we can understand better the well-springs of action, the workings out of competing claims to power, the different purposes of rival ideologies — in short, see more clearly ways in which the past becomes History.

There is a commitment in each volume to showing how understanding of an individual develops (sometimes in uneven and divergent ways), whether in response to fresh evidence, the emergence or waning of dominant ideologies, changing attitudes and preoccupations of the age in which an author writes, or the creation of new historical paradigms. Will Hitler ever seem *quite* the same after the evidence of a recent study revealing the extent of his Jewish connections during the Vienna years? Reassessment of Lenin and Stalin has been given fresh impetus by the collapse of the Soviet Union and the opening of many of its archives; and the end of the Cold War and of its attendant assumptions must alter our views of Eisenhower and Kennedy. How will our perceptions of Elizabeth I change in the presence of a new awareness of 'gendered history'?

There is more to the series than illumination of ways in which recent discoveries or trends have refashioned identities or given actions new meaning — though that is an important part. The corresponding aim is to provide readers with a strong sense of the channels and course of debate from the outset: not a Cook's Tour of the historiography, but identification of the key interpretative issues and guidance as to how commentators of different eras and persuasions have tackled them.

Preface

I began my academic career in October 1973 when Watergate dominated the news. Part of my job was to teach a course on American politics, something I approached with trepidation since my graduate work had been in nineteenth-century international history. 'Don't worry', my head of department told me, 'just get the students talking about Nixon. They won't stop'. So it proved. For my own part, the more I learned about American politics and contemporary history through teaching it, the more fascinated I became with the subject. Before long it had become my primary area of interest rather than an unwanted responsibility to be shed as soon as possible. Since I owed this change of interest in large part to Richard Nixon, I am grateful for the opportunity to contribute this book on him to the *Reputations* series.

Nixon presents a particular challenge for any biographer. While it is important to keep the lens of history focused on his misdeeds, this should not preclude recognition of his substantial accomplishments. Nixon was arguably *the* major figure in American politics in the third quarter of the twentieth century. We are still living in the world that he helped to shape. What I have tried to write is an assessment of Nixon's role in history to show that he merits remembrance for more than just Watergate. In doing so, I have been conscious of the way that Richard Nixon tried to rebuild his reputation in the eyes of history during his final twenty years of life. As a historian, I have tried to guard against unquestioning rejection of his rehabilitation as much as against unquestioning acceptance of it. But while I would not count myself a Nixon hater, I suspect that Nixon would have hated this book. In the end, my estimation of him differs substantially from his own revisionism.

The best place to begin the assessment of Nixon's reputation is with his own campaign to reconstruct it (chapter 1). Since Nixon has been a favorite subject of psychobiographers, consideration of his unusual character is essential to understand what drove him (chapter 2). However, Nixon cannot be understood separately from his times and from the institutions in which he operated. For most of Nixon's political career, the Republican Party was the minority party in American politics and his efforts to change this state of affairs is an important part of his story (chapter 3). Conventionally viewed as conservative, Nixon deserves to be reconsidered for amassing one of the most significant records of domestic reform of any president since Franklin D. Roosevelt (chapter 4). Nixon was the leading anti-Communist of the early Cold War. His role in America's global struggle with Communism from the late 1940s through to his efforts as president to find 'peace with honor' in Vietnam is a critical element in his own and his nation's history (chapter 5). The militant Cold Warrior seemingly turned into man-of-peace in the early 1970s. Whether Nixon's claim to greatness has merit or not rests in large part on assessment of the significance of the foreign policy of détente with the Communist powers that he pursued as president (chapter 6). Finally, Nixon's presidential misconduct is considered in an effort to examine his personal abuse of power within the institutional context of the imperial presidency (chapter 7).

I am grateful to Christopher Wheeler, Director of Humanities Publishing at Arnold, for commissioning me to write about Nixon. As always I have to thank my family for putting up with my lonely obsession. My wife, Theresa, has borne an even more unfair share than usual of the parental and household management responsibilities for much of 2001. I am comforted when thinking of my relative neglect of Humphrey and Eleanor during this period that Richard Nixon's own children seemingly turned out well in spite of having limited call on his time! If I have added anything to the understanding of Nixon, it is due entirely to being able to draw on the work of others who have written about him. They are too numerous to mention here, but the notes testify to my obligations. Finally I would like to thank my students at City of London Polytechnic/London Guildhall University from 1973 to the present and beyond for sharing my interest in and helping my understanding of Richard Nixon and his times. It is to them that I dedicate this book.

|1|

Nixon and reputation

On 9 August 1974 Richard Milhous Nixon became the first American president to resign office, thereby avoiding certain impeachment by Congress. The chain of events that brought about Nixon's downfall began with the most famous burglary in history. On 17 June 1972 operatives of the Committee to Reelect the President had been caught breaking into the headquarters of the Democratic National Committee in the Watergate complex in Washington DC. For the next two years Nixon sought to cover up White House involvement in political espionage, but the investigations of journalists, the Justice Department, the Federal Bureau of Investigation, special prosecutors and Congress inexorably uncovered evidence of the President's obstruction of justice and abuse of power. The Watergate scandal, as it became known, destroyed the public career of one of the most important and most controversial political leaders of the twentieth century. Unmasked as a liar and a law-breaker, Richard Nixon departed the presidency with a villainous reputation unmatched by any other leader of a modern democracy.

Judging on the interest shown in Nixon since his resignation, there is more fascination with a sinner than a saint. The stream of biographies and other works about him shows no signs of diminishing. His presidency has become one of the most written about in American history. Nearly everyone – great and small – connected in some way with his administration or with the Watergate scandal has found a ready market for his or her memoirs. Moreover, Abraham Lincoln and John F. Kennedy apart, no other president has exercised such fascination for the cultural media. The link between these presidents, of course, is their status as tragic figures. Whereas Lincoln and Kennedy were inspirational leaders cut down by assassination, Nixon's tragedy was that of a leader capable of greatness but undone by his own weakness. As biographer Stephen Ambrose observed, he was 'Shakespearean like no other American politician'.[1]

Watergate completed the demonization of Nixon, but an uncommon level of notoriety had marked his political career from its start. He had acquired a reputation for fighting dirty long before he became president. The sobriquet 'Tricky Dick' clung to him for most of his political life. This was a small measure of revenge for Democrat Helen Douglas, who authored the name in retaliation for Nixon's red-baiting of her in the 1950 California Senate election. The Herblock cartoons in the *Washington Post* in the 1950s depicting Nixon as a sleazy politician risen from the sewer consolidated the negative perception of him. His physical characteristics reinforced his unsavory image. Photographs of the young Nixon show a man of fresh-faced if rather intense good looks who appears honest and unmenacing. By middle age, power had seemingly given Nixon an evil-looking face with ski-slope nose, heavy brows and jowls, deep eye-wells, and a tendency to 'five o'clock shadow'. All of this conveyed an image of untrustworthiness that a famous anti-Nixon poster exploited to the full with its accompanying caption – 'Would you buy a used car from this man?'

Nixon's misconduct as president signified that he did not simply look like a crook but had become one. His resignation left unanswered the question of whether he would face criminal prosecution. In March 1974 a Washington grand jury hearing the case of special prosecutor Leon Jaworski had indicted three of Nixon's former aides – H. R. Haldeman, John Ehrlichman and Charles Colson – and former Attorney General John Mitchell for participating in the Watergate cover-up. Though kept secret at the time, it had also named the President as an unindicted co-conspirator. Colson later pleaded guilty to obstructing justice and was sentenced to one to three years in prison. Haldeman, Ehrlichman and Mitchell went to trial and were found guilty on various charges of obstruction of justice, conspiracy and perjury. In 1975 they received sentences of two-and-a-half to eight years (later reduced to one to four years). 'For many', one historian observed, 'the verdict represented a conviction of the former president *in absentia*'.[2] Other lesser players in the Watergate scandal also went to prison for varying stretches. Nixon avoided this fate because his successor granted him a presidential pardon that gave immunity from prosecution.

Fearing that the nation's trauma would be prolonged indefinitely if Nixon went on trial, President Gerald Ford told the American people on 8 September 1974 that a pardon was the best way to end what he dubbed the 'American tragedy' and let the process of healing begin. However, this act of clemency aroused intense suspicion that Nixon had struck a secret deal to save himself before handing the presidency over to Ford. There is no evidence of such a deal, though Nixon certainly had tried to get one via his chief of staff Alexander Haig. A contrite Ford volunteered to explain his decision before a House Judiciary subcommittee, the first time that a president had testified in Congress since George Washington. Acknowledging misjudgment of the popular mood, he commented in his memoirs that the American people 'wanted to see him [Nixon] drawn and quartered publicly'.[3] Twenty-five years later, Bob Woodward, one of the journalists who helped to expose the Watergate conspiracy, avowed that Ford had been right to pardon Nixon but should have prepared the public, the media and Congress for his decision, especially by requiring the former President to sign a statement of guilt for release with the pardon. Ford himself still carries in his wallet a Supreme Court opinion in *Burdick* v *United States* (1915) that a pardon 'carries imputation of guilt, acceptance, a confession of it'.[4]

The unpopularity of Nixon's pardon contributed to Ford's narrow defeat by Jmmy Carter in the 1976 presidential election. It was a campaign in which the victor ran against Nixon as much as against Ford, as evidenced by his banner issue – a promise that he would never lie to the American people. Nixon was succeeded in office first by a healer and then by a moralist, roles preordained by the need to repair the damage that he had done. An acid quip by Senator Bob Dole of Kansas captured their historical relationship almost perfectly: 'See No Evil, Hear No Evil, and Evil.'[5]

Two months after Nixon had resigned, he fell ill with phlebitis and nearly died. Had this illness proved fatal, his obituaries in 1974 would have been universally negative because Watergate overshadowed everything that he had achieved in politics. At the time visitors to Madame Tussaud's in London voted Nixon the most 'hated and feared' figure in the waxworks. Such feelings were held even more strongly in the United States. A joke by comedian Jackie Mason summed up the mood of national bitterness towards Nixon: 'They say he is a sick man and that he's got phlebitis. He doesn't have phlebitis. He's got syphilis. You don't screw 200 million people and get phlebitis.'[6] Even the *Star Wars* movie, released in 1977, carried an anti-Nixon message. Though the film later became associated with Ronald Reagan's Cold War militance, writer-director George Lucas conceived its evil Emperor character as a metaphorical representation of Nixon.[7]

Nixon lived on for another twenty years after Watergate. Most of the obituaries that followed his death on 22 April 1994 were at least respectful and some went even further. Perhaps the most effusive praise came from *The Times* of London. Its editorial obituary, entitled 'President Nixon: Salute to a strategist whose skills are sadly missed today', avowed that in the post-Cold War disorder 'the need for such politicians stands out far more vividly than the memories of the absurdities and shame of Watergate'.[8] With only some exceptions, there was general recognition that, alongside its flaws, Nixon's record included many achievements that marked him out as one of the most significant American leaders of the twentieth century for positive reasons.

In contrast to every president since Abraham Lincoln, Nixon's body did not lie in state beneath the Capitol dome. To make sure that no one could deny him this honor, he had given instructions in old age that his remains should be flown directly to Yorba Linda, California, and buried beside his wife Pat in the shadow of his childhood home. However, the attendance at his funeral of Bill Clinton and all four living former presidents put the final seal on the rehabilitation that he had long sought. In his eulogy, Henry Kissinger quoted Shakespeare in assessing the leader he had once served: 'He was a man, take him for all in all. I shall not look upon his like again.' Perhaps moved by a concern that his own historical reputation might be overshadowed by scandal (Whitewatergate was his current preoccupation, Monicagate was still to come!), Bill Clinton also hailed Nixon's achievements. His tribute embodied the ethos of revisionism in proclaiming: 'May the day of judging President Nixon on anything less than his entire life and career come to a close'.[9]

Nixon's rehabilitation owed much to his last and in some ways greatest political campaign. In the depths of post-resignation depression and still weak from his phlebitis operation, he wrote in his diary on 7 December 1974, 'I simply have to pull myself together and start the long journey back.'[10] As scholar Michael Schudson put it, 'Metaphorically

Nixon died when he resigned the presidency and he has been his own survivor, entrusted to preserve and promote the reputation of the Nixon who died.'[11] By this he meant that Nixon aimed to preserve not the reputation Watergate had saddled him with but the one he wanted. As champion revisionist in his own cause, Nixon consciously emulated one of his heroes. 'What history says about this [Nixon] administration will depend upon who writes history', Nixon told David Frost in 1977. 'Winston Churchill once told one of his critics that history . . . would treat him well, and his critic said: "How do you know?" And he said, "Because I intend to write it."'[12]

The first step in Nixon's campaign to reconstruct his reputation was to write his memoirs, which took some three years of work and drew mainly on 10,000 pages of his hand-written diaries.[13] The 1,100-page *œuvre*, whose rights were sold for $2.5 million, ran up sales of 330,000 copies within six months of publication in 1978, despite unflattering reviews. A desperate need for cash to pay substantial and ongoing legal fees relating to Watergate compelled him to interrupt memoir-writing to record twenty-eight hours of television interviews with David Frost in March 1977 for a fee of $600,000.[14] The first of the four programs drew an estimated audience of 50 million in the US, making it the most watched interview in television history. Nixon got the chance to remind Americans of his achievements but was occasionally discomfited by Frost's probing on Watergate. The experience enhanced his determination to refocus attention away from his sins and onto his successes. In November 1978, he told students at the Oxford University Union: 'Some people say I didn't handle it (Watergate) properly, and they're right. I screwed it up and I paid the price. *Mea culpa*. But let's get on to my achievements. You'll be here in the year 2000 and we'll see how I'm regarded then.'[15]

The achievements that Nixon wanted his reputation judged on were those of his foreign policy. Through regular media appearances and public addresses and an outpouring of books – nine in total, most of them best-sellers – Nixon trumpeted the message that he had built a structure for world peace in opening up China and establishing détente with the Soviet Union. He portrayed himself as a foreign policy sage whose counsel could still help America meet the challenges of an uncertain world. Probably Nixon's most significant book in this regard was *The Real War*, a critique of American decline under Jimmy Carter in the face of

renewed Cold War.[16] This apocalyptic warning that the West was
in danger of losing the struggle with Communism became a best-
seller on both sides of the Atlantic. In a highly selective retelling
of history, Nixon put his own foreign policy record in the best
possible light, blamed liberals for the loss of Southeast Asia, and
explained that he had never conceived of détente as entente. His
advocacy of a twin-track approach of containment and détente –
whereby the US manifested its will and power to deter Soviet
aggression while showing itself willing to cooperate in areas of
mutual interest – found ready listeners within the incoming
Reagan administration. The book also won plaudits from some
of Nixon's critics in the media. In 1974 *Time*'s Hugh Sidey had
accused Nixon of 'charting himself a course straight into the
sloughs of history' but ten years later pronounced him 'a strategic genius' after reading *The Real War* and its 1984 sequel, *Real
Peace*.[17]

Nixon's effort to reconstruct his reputation also entailed insistence that he was guilty only of misjudgment not criminal misconduct over Watergate. Even his acceptance of a pardon was
not accompanied by any substantial expression of contrition. All
he would agree to say was that he was 'wrong in not acting more
decisively and more forthrightly', and that he had made 'mistakes
and misjudgments' that might lead people to think that he had
acted illegally.[18] In the final moments of the first Frost interview,
a moist-eyed Nixon came the closest he ever would to saying
sorry: 'I let down my friends. I let down the country. I let down
our system of government and the dreams of all those young
people that ought to get into government but think it's all too
corrupt and the rest. . . . I let the American people down. And I
have to carry that burden for the rest of my life.'[19] Thereafter he
perfected a more upbeat message. In 1988, on *Meet the Press*,
Nixon admitted the cover-up was 'a great mistake' but claimed
that the break-in itself was 'a small thing . . . and break-ins have
occurred in other campaigns as well'.[20] In his final memoir, *In the
Arena*, published in 1990, he claimed that Watergate was 'one
part wrongdoing, one part blundering and one part political
vendetta (by my opponents)'.[21]

It is important in Nixon's case, however, to distinguish
between personal rehabilitation and reconstruction of reputation. He was successful in the first but not the second. During his
final twenty years he rehabilitated himself in the sense of emerging from disgrace to regain acceptance and restore esteem for his

abilities. The media that had once helped to destroy him played its part in his comeback by providing a forum for his pronouncements on foreign affairs. There was ironic symmetry in the *Newsweek* cover story of 19 May 1986 – 'He's Back – The Rehabilitation of Richard Nixon' – because the magazine was owned by Katherine Graham, publisher of his old nemesis, the *Washington Post*. Official Washington also welcomed him back. He was asked for foreign policy advice by the Ford, Carter and Reagan administrations but always behind the scenes (and initially under the code name 'The Wizard'), because of concern about negative media and popular reaction.[22] A more public expression of official acceptance came in July 1990 when all but one of his successors in office (Jimmy Carter was the sole recusant) attended the ceremony to open the Richard M. Nixon Presidential Library and Birthplace.

All this did not add up to the reconstruction of reputation. As one critic commented, 'How's he doing at the tidy-up, after the fuck-up and the cover-up? . . . So far, time's bulldozer and his have done a pretty good job – except for one item: Watergate.'[23] Nixon's reputation was not his to control. Reputation is a social construction based in part on the character and achievement of the subject but also on the groups making use of that reputation and the nature of the times in which they do so. Nixon's campaign to be remembered as he wanted encountered powerful opposition from opinion-makers who chose to remember him in a different way.

Perhaps because of his Shakespearean qualities, it was the cultural media that came closest to buying into the reconstruction of Nixon's reputation. Watergate-era novels, plays and films featuring Nixon or Nixon-like characters were uniformly hostile in their portrayal of him as conspiratorial, power-hungry and ruthless.[24] Perhaps the defining performance was that of Jason Robards as President Monckton in the 1977 television series *Washington behind Closed Doors* (based on former Nixon aide John Ehrlichman's 1976 novel *The Company*). Within a decade, however, a significant change had taken place in how Nixon was depicted. In 1987 *Nixon in China*, regarded as one of the best late-twentieth-century operas, presented its main character, brilliantly sung and acted by James Maddalena, as a romantic idealist intent on building world peace.[25] The most significant example of the cultural media's revisionism was Oliver Stone's 1995 movie *Nixon*. An Oscar-nominated performance by Anthony

Hopkin portrayed a man with the capacity for greatness but whose dark side was in conflict with his light side. At the end of the film an off-camera narrator implictly endorses Nixon's version of history: 'Nixon always maintained that if he had not been driven from office the North Vietnamese would not have overwhelmed the South in 1975. . . . Cambodian society was destroyed and mass genocide resulted. In his absence Russia and the United States returned to a decade of high-budget military expansion and near war.' The image which the viewer is left with is the tragedy of a great president undone by his flaws. Stone's left-wing politics and his penchant for conspiracy theories, trenchantly exemplified by his earlier film *JFK*, made his treatment of Nixon all the more remarkable. He even had him standing up to a fictional conspiracy of rich Texans to murder Kennedy!

In the case of the journalistic media, however, Watergate held a special place in its heart. If the press helped to rehabilitate Richard Nixon, it was in part because his presence served as a reminder of its finest hour. When the *Washington Post*'s Katherine Graham died in July 2001, she was lionized for 'having struck a blow for all time against the abuse of power' through her determination to press ahead in the face of fierce White House opposition first with publication of the Pentagon Papers in 1971 and then with the Bob Woodward–Carl Bernstein investigation of Watergate in 1972.[26] The role of journalism in the downfall of a president became part of the press's own mythology about its importance as the guardian of democracy, even though other agencies within government itself were arguably far more important in exposing the truth about Watergate.[27]

Moreover, Watergate would seemingly always be news rather than history for journalists. The memory of Nixon's misdeeds was kept alive for the news media by the misconduct of his successors. Whenever there was a presidential scandal, comparisons with Watergate were inevitable – not least because the suffix 'gate' was always tagged onto the name by which the scandal became known. Hence the Iran–Contra scandal became Ronald Reagan's Iran–Contragate, and the Monica Lewinsky scandal became Bill Clinton's Monicagate. In 1999 Clinton became only the second president in US history to undergo impeachment trial by the Senate when he faced charges of perjury and obstruction of justice in the investigation of his sexual relationship with the White House intern. Yet this only served to enhance memories of Nixon's villainy, as Clinton's lies and misconduct looked so puny and personal by comparison and his attempted impeachment appeared so political. As Bob Woodward commented of Monicagate, 'There was no conspiracy. . . . there were no orders . . . to lie or obstruct justice.'[28] Whereas the American public had wanted Nixon's blood in 1974, it was broadly in favor of Clinton's acquittal. One of Clinton's lawyers, Charles Ruff, later commented that the President had saved himself by making a public admission of his guilt and speculated that Nixon could have avoided his fate twenty-five years earlier by doing the same.[29]

If Nixon's place in the future is tied to the mythology of the press and to recurrent presidential scandal, his place in the past will be determined in the main by historians. As a group they have remained resolutely resistant to revisionism. Nixon's position in almost all the scholarly rankings of presidential greatness has remained stubbornly at or near the bottom, with only Ulysses S. Grant and Warren Harding – other scandal-hit presidents who had the further disadvantage of being weak leaders – for company.[30] Whatever he accomplished in office continues to be outweighed in the view of many scholars by his abuse of presidential power and betrayal of the American people's trust.

Nixon attributed his consistently poor standing with historians to their bias. In 1988, he predicted in a television interview, 'History will treat me fairly. Historians probably won't, because most historians are on the left.'[31] To Nixon the hostility of historians was yet another example of the enmity he had encountered from liberals throughout his political career. Long before Watergate, he wrote in 1990, he had 'more intractable enemies than any postwar President' because he had offended liberals by his aggressive investigation as a freshman congressman of the Alger Hiss case in 1948 and his prolongation of the Vietnam war as president to secure an honorable peace.[32]

If historians had become the latest members in his long list of enemies, it was not because of ideological prejudice. For them, Nixon revisionism posed fundamental questions about the meaning and making of reputation. If Nixon could be his own historian, it made history vulnerable to personal interest and manipulation. Nothing signaled this danger more clearly than the way that the Richard M. Nixon Presidential Library and Birthplace attempted to shape popular memory with a highly sanitized and edited depiction of Watergate. More a museum than a library, its theme is Nixon the world statesman, great president and man-of-peace. Some scholars regarded it as a continuation of the cover-up – the 'liebrary', as one acerbic critic dubbed it.[33]

Nixon also tried to cover up history in another way. For historians to evaluate the record of modern presidents, they require access to the presidential papers that are conventionally housed in presidential libraries. The privately funded Nixon library does not meet this need. It did not qualify as a presidential library under the terms of the 1955 Presidential Libraries Act, which authorized the National Archives to administer libraries containing presidential papers. The last thing Nixon wanted was to surrender control of his records that revealed the full extent of his involvement in Watergate. The Presidential Recordings and Materials Act of 1974, upheld by the Supreme Court three years later, had decreed that his presidential papers and records should be deposited in the National Archives, which would have sole authority to decide their use. Nixon and his lawyers fought a dogged and expensive battle that succeeded in blocking the release of any papers until 1987. Legal challenges to restrict access have continued ever since, with the Nixon estate taking up the cudgels after the former president's death.[34] Nevertheless more and more of Nixon's presidential records have steadily become available over time to enable historians to begin a proper assessment of his presidency.

In the year of Nixon's death historian Joan Hoff published the first major reconsideration of his presidency. In it she warned, 'If historians continue to repeat one another about Nixon only in the context of Watergate, they will not only be living down to his assessment of them, but they will also have failed the fundamental calling of their discipline: to reevaluate, not rehash, controversial historical events'.[35] Hitherto the Nixon presidency had been remembered most for Watergate, next for foreign policy and least for domestic reform. Hoff's path-breaking study argued that the order should be reversed. Making use of the available Nixon records, she advanced a persuasive case that his domestic measures were more significant than his much vaunted diplomatic achievements. Less successful was her effort to relegate Watergate to the background because she had to deal with the damage it did to Nixon's other policies throughout her study. Leaving aside the debate over the relative merits of Nixon's domestic and foreign policies, Hoff's study demonstrated two things conclusively: firstly, that Nixon's reputation could never be divorced from Watergate and, secondly, that there was far more to Nixon than Watergate.

It is further evident that there was more to Nixon than Nixon. Tempting though it may be to explain his conduct solely as the result of his character and psychology, he was also the product of his nation and his times. Nixon was a major American politician from the late 1940s to the mid-1970s. He shaped and was in turn shaped by this historical era. On the day he resigned office, *New York Times* journalist Anthony Lewis dubbed his period in public life as 'the age of Nixon in our politics'.[36] Without doubt he was at the center of many of the issues that defined the historical character of postwar America: McCarthyism; the quest for a new Republican majority; the working out of the New Deal legacy; the Cold War; Vietnam; the pursuit of peace; and the evolution of the imperial presidency. As such, Nixon can never be properly evaluated outside the context of his times.

As Nixon himself appreciated, his historical reputation rests largely on two things. In 1962 he said of the Hiss investigation, 'My name, my reputation and my career were ever to be linked with the decisions I made and the actions I took in that case, as a thirty-five year old freshman Congressman in 1948.'[37] In 1990, he said of Watergate that if one sentence would encapsulate his historical reputation as president, it would not be 'He went to China' but 'He resigned the office.'[38] Nevertheless Nixon's significance is far greater than the sum of these two episodes.

Anyone visiting the Vietnam Veterans' Memorial in Washington DC sees that some 20,500 of the over 58,000 names inscribed on it by date of death were killed while Nixon was president. Yet Vietnam is seemingly only a footnote in remembrance of him. While John Kennedy and Lyndon Johnson are celebrated as the liberal protagonists of African-American civil rights, the desegregation of Southern public schools occurred on Nixon's watch not theirs. With the Cold War now over, Nixon's role in first promoting and then helping to end it should surely feature as a cardinal element of his historical reputation. For a brief moment in 2001, the Republicans controlled the presidency and both houses of Congress for the first time since 1953–4 (until the assumption of independent status by one Republican senator allowed the Democrats to recapture the upper chamber). This was a goal that Richard Nixon had pursued for the bulk of his political career, so his role in its eventual achievement merits assessment.

It is not accepting Richard Nixon's version of history to assess his reputation on the basis of his whole legacy rather than just Watergate. The post-Watergate Nixon was a post-modern man who had abandoned deeds for images in his drive to reconstruct his personal reputation. The political Nixon of 1946 to 1974 had real and complex substance. What follows is an effort to understand that substance in its entirety.

|2|

The Nixon character

Any assessment of Richard Nixon's place in history must begin with an attempt to understand Nixon the man. This is no easy task, for Nixon's personality was a labyrinth that many chroniclers have found inpenetrable in their quest to explain his motivation. Journalist Theodore White admitted in 1984, 'I have spent the greatest portion of my adult life writing about Richard Nixon and I still don't understand him.'[1] Nixon was full of contradictions that defy ready explanation. One of his major biographers has commented, 'As to questions of motive, of why he did what he did, I confess that I do not understand this complex man.'[2] Whether the 'real Nixon' can ever be discovered is a moot point, but the search has to be attempted.

The second of Frank and Hannah Nixon's five sons, Richard Nixon was born on 9 January 1913 in Yorba Linda, a small agricultural community in Orange County near Los Angeles. His memoirs open with a brief but telling sentence – 'I was born in a house my father built'[3] – a statement that evinces his strong sense of family ties, his modest origins in a twentieth-century equivalent of a log cabin, and his Horatio Alger-style rise from lowly status to the top. Scholars have poured over his formative years in Southern California to seek clues that help explain his later political conduct.

Much to Nixon's disgust, some psychobiographers claimed that his personality was warped by the conflicting personas of his mother and father, emotional deprivation from the refusal of a beloved mother to show him open affection, and resentment about his humble background.[4] Even if one does not admire Nixon, it is possible to sympathize with his exasperation on this score, because such analysis grossly undervalues the positive aspects of his upbringing. Viewed from an age when divorce, family break-ups and parent–children conflicts are relatively common, Nixon's family appears remarkably stable and mutually supportive, not to mention strong enough to cope with the tragic deaths of two sons. That said, there is no doubt that his parents were dominant influences on the shaping of his character.

Nixon's parents seemingly represented the attraction of opposites. Frank, born of Scotch–Irish ancestry in Ohio in 1878, was a rough-hewn character who endured a harsh and impoverished childhood, had little formal education, held passionate beliefs, was argumentative by nature and had a quick temper. By contrast, Hannah, who was born into a middle-class Quaker family of German and Irish stock in Indiana in 1885, was well educated, emotionally reserved, cerebral and deeply spiritual. As a father Frank was a strict disciplinarian who was sparing with words of approval but free with his sharp tongue and he often used a strap on the boys when his temper boiled over. The Nixon brothers turned to their mother for comfort and support but she could not always fulfil their emotional needs because her natural reserve and Quaker calm precluded displays of physical affection. Hannah's three-year absence nursing older brother Harold through tuberculosis in the dry climate of Arizona in the late 1920s also weighed heavily on Richard, who had earlier been away from her for a six-month stay with relatives to study music in 1925.

Former aide Bryce Harlow told journalist Tom Wicker of his conviction that as a young man Nixon 'was hurt very deeply by somebody . . . he deeply trusted. Hurt so badly he never got over it and never trusted anybody again.'[5] However, no evidence has ever been unearthed to support this or any other speculation about emotional hurt inflicted by his parents (or anyone else). Frank's outbursts were soon over and quickly forgotten without abiding resentments on either side. Nixon himself later testified that he feared the quietly spoken rebukes of his mother more than his father's strap. He acknowledged that he had never heard Hannah say to him 'I love you', but claimed there had been no need for her to do so. As Nixon put it, 'Her eyes expressed the love and warmth no words could possibly convey.'[6]

The love and respect that Nixon in turn felt for his parents were manifest throughout his adulthood and were frequently displayed in his speeches. In his 1968 presidential nomination acceptance speech, he spoke of Hannah's 'passionate concern for peace' in an address that foreshadowed the opening of new relations with the Communist world.[7] Most famously, he referred at length to both parents – Frank as a 'great man' and Hannah as 'a saint' – and the struggles the family had endured in his farewell remarks as president to White House staff on 9 August 1974. At the time many commentators decried this as mawkish and a contrived effort to win sympathy and deflect attention from his wrongdoings, for which he offered no apology in the address. Even Henry Kissinger remarked, 'It was as if having kept himself in check all these years he had to put on display all the demons and dreams that had driven him.'[8] In today's less heated atmosphere Nixon's words can also be seen as those of a man under great emotional stress who wanted to pay tribute to his parents' inspiration and sacrifice in what he knew would be his last public address in office.

Many biographers believe there was an inner struggle within Nixon between the different traits inherited from his saint-like mother and his domineering father, described by one as 'the broodying, bullying, politically minded Irishman'.[9] According to Jonathan Aitken, Hannah's death in 1967 and Nixon's misconduct as president were not unconnected. 'As long as Hannah was alive', he claimed, 'the dark side of Nixon was rarely in the ascendant. She was the sheet anchor of his morality . . .'[10] In similar vein, Herbert Parmet contends that Nixon's 'everlasting misfortune was to be split almost right down the line between Hannah and Frank, to behave as the one while wishing the world to believe he was the other'.[11]

Such judgments have to be treated with caution. It is true that Nixon's better qualities – his idealism (however shrouded), his openness to new ideas and his intellect – owed more to Hannah than to Frank. He aspired to emulate Hannah's serenity, her intellect and her compassion, but his idealized vision of her was an impossible model for anyone in the American political arena. Most obviously he did not live up to her Quaker beliefs – he enlisted to fight in World War II, he was a hard-line Cold Warrior, and one of his most controversial acts as president was to order the Christmas bombing of Hanoi in 1972. In truth Nixon would not have advanced in politics – perhaps not in any career – had he lived by Hannah's ideals. If his occasionally visionary politics – as demonstrated during his presidency in the pursuit of détente to promote international peace and of welfare reform to alleviate poverty – derived from Hannah, he needed Frank's qualities as a scrapper to win power and retain it. As

Merle West, one of Hannah's relatives, put it, 'some of that Nixon blood . . . did him a lot of good, too. He needed both'.[12]

Arguably what was most important in shaping Nixon's character was not Frank and Hannah's differences but their shared determination that he should achieve success. The Nixon brothers were fully aware of their parents' expectations of them. 'There was a drive to succeed', Nixon later told journalist Stewart Alsop. 'My mother and father instilled in us the desire to get going to be good not just at one single thing but at everything'.[13] Though not ambitious for themselves, Frank and Hannah set an example for their children by working long hours to make ends meet in the grocery store they set up in 1925 in Whittier, another small town near Los Angeles, to where the Nixon family had moved three years earlier. Equally important, they never gave in to setbacks, such as the failure in 1919 of their Yorba Linda lemon orchard or the deaths of two children – 7-year-old Arthur from meningitis in 1925 and 23-year-old Harold, the eldest son, after a prolonged battle with tuberculosis in 1933. Doubtless, too, Frank and Hannah transferred their main expectations of filial success onto Richard after Harold died.

Keenly aware that their lower-middle-class background afforded few privileges, the parents constantly urged their children – in adulthood as well as youth – never to give in to adversity. Frank's last words to Nixon on his deathbed in 1956 were 'Dick, *you* keep fighting.' In 1962, when defeat in California's gubernatorial election seemingly signaled the end of Nixon's political career, Hannah sternly chided him: 'Richard, don't *you* give up. Don't let anyone tell you you are through.'[14] In his memoirs, Nixon noted that his father had imbued him with 'the will to keep fighting no matter what the odds', while his mother's legacy had been 'the determination never to despair'.[15] This was important in sustaining a career that had its fair share of downs as well as ups. Nixon lived up to his own oft-voiced maxim: 'No politician is dead until he admits it.'[16]

Nixon's career bears testimony that the twin drives to succeed and to triumph over adversity were the most important traits that his parents ingrained in him. He always had the sense of having to struggle to prove his worth. Interviewed in retirement by former aide Ken Clawson, Nixon commented: 'What starts the process, really, are laughs and slights and snubs when you are a kid. But if you are reasonably intelligent and if your anger is deep

enough and strong enough, you learn you can change those attitudes by excellence, personal gut performance while those who
have everything are sitting on their fat butts.'[17]

Incompetence and indolence were never charges leveled at
Nixon by his many enemies. He worked hard to master the
details of public policy, even in areas in which his personal interest was not great. As president, Council of Economic Advisers
chair Paul McCracken commented, his attitude towards economic policy was 'somewhat like that of a little boy doing
required lessons'.[18] His work rate in every phase of his career was
immense. As a corporate lawyer in the 1960s, he was usually in
the office by 7.00 a.m. and rarely left before 6.00 p.m. He put in
long hours of intense preparation to give a polished, professional
and well-received argument in a privacy case, *Time, Inc.* v. *Hill*,
before the Supreme Court in 1966. Though Nixon lost the judgment by five votes to four, his performance earned plaudits and
Justice Abe Fortas, a Democratic appointee, commented that he
could develop into 'one of the great advocates of our times'.[19] As
president, he spent many hours working on his speeches and prepared for his 1969 inaugural address by reading every previous
inaugural address. He kept up a demanding routine of eleven-
hour days, seven days a week, for nearly three years to write the
memoirs that were the first step in his campaign for post-
Watergate rehabilitation.

But the need to succeed also drove Nixon to reach for power
any way he could. In his very first campaign for Congress in 1946
he used red smear tactics to defeat the incumbent Democrat,
Jerry Voorhis, whom he privately acknowledged had no
Communist sympathies. 'I had to win', he confided to one critic
of his conduct. 'That's the thing you don't understand. The
important thing is to win.'[20] This set a pattern of sharp practice
that ran through Nixon's time in politics and eventually escalated
into malpractice that went beyond the bounds of legality.

This points to the central paradox of Nixon's public life: he
regarded politics – in line with the idealism inherited from his
mother – as a means of doing good and serving his country, but
politics also brought out the worst in him. Toward the end of his
life, he avowed: 'A candidate's primary purpose in getting into
politics should never be self-interest. . . . But if he has a purpose
larger than himself and his personal ambitions that he wants to
pursue, he must not hesitate.'[21] However, his idealism was
entwined with darker sentiments. A sense of public mission and

the personal drive to succeed were indelibly fused in Nixon's view of politics as an arena where the only possible outcomes were victory or defeat. As amply recorded in his presidential tapes and various memoirs, 'fight', 'battle', 'enemies', 'victory' were recurrent words in his political vocabulary. In the 1950s he adopted the double-V sign with arms outstretched above his head as his symbolic political trademark. Since victory was necessary to fulfill his good intentions, Nixon could justify to himself his use of unsavory means to defeat opponents who stood in his way. It was as if doing bad could be excused as necessary to do good.

To Nixon's opponents, his good side was a sham to hide his bad self. In 1960 John F. Kennedy quipped, 'I feel sorry for Nixon because he does not know who he is, and at each stop he has to decide which Nixon he is at the moment, which must be very exhausting.'[22] However, a number of Nixon's presidential aides have suggested that both a 'light side' and a 'dark side' were ingrained elements of his character. Speechwriter Ray Price argued that his disciplined, rational side was in conflict with his emotional, angry side. It was the former that enabled him to pursue the carefully calculated and executed strategy of détente, while it was the latter that frequently got him into trouble.[23] Another speechwriter, William Safire, likened Nixon's personality to a marble cake, with its icing and many dark and light layers, which must be sliced vertically and not horizontally to get its true flavor.[24] In similar terms, H. R. 'Bob' Haldeman compared Nixon's character with a multifaceted quartz crystal, '(s)ome facets bright and shining, others dark and mysterious. . . . Some of them very deep and inpenetrable, others completely on the surface. Some smooth and polished, others crude, rough and sharp.'[25]

All three aides agreed that Nixon's light side was larger by far than his dark side and was the one he himself identified with. Haldeman also contended that 'the dark side grew mainly not out of Nixon's nature but out of his reaction to experience in public life'.[26] It was this side of him that was unveiled most often at election times. In his own memoirs, Nixon claimed that he 'played by the rules of politics as I found them'.[27] It is true that he was himself sometimes sinned against. Obvious examples include Democratic vote-rigging in the 1960 election and the use of federal agencies by the victorious Kennedys to audit his income taxes and financial affairs in the hope of uncovering wrongdoing.[28] However, no other major American politician of modern times has shown the same willingness to play dirty in pursuit of democracy's mandate.

In his 1946 campaign against Jerry Voorhis Nixon developed the technique of smearing an opponent while denying he was doing so. He perfected it for a lifetime's use when running for the Senate in 1950. Nixon promised in an early radio address: 'There will be no name-calling, no smears, no misrepresentations in this campaign.'[29] He then villified his Democratic opponent, Helen Gahagan Douglas, up and down the state of California as the 'Pink Lady' who 'follows the Communist Party line', a brazen lie in itself and an outrageous innuendo that she was herself a Communist.[30] In 1968, Nixon had no scruples about undermining a last-ditch Vietnam peace effort by the Johnson administration in his quest to become president. Four years later he got his come-uppance for a lifetime of dubious conduct. It was his insecurity about the final election that he would ever have to fight that led to the botched break-in for intelligence gathering in the Democratic National Committee headquarters.

For Nixon elections were life-or-death battles that he had to win in order to survive in politics. For most high-profile politicians electoral loss meant the end of their career in office rather than just a temporary setback. Relatively few had either the opportunity or the endurance to make a comeback. Nixon himself showed remarkable resilience in reviving his political star after two major defeats in 1960 and 1962. In most other professions, by contrast, setbacks were less public and less likely to be final, career prospects were more secure, and jobs were more plentiful. In a revealing passage in his final memoirs, Nixon commented: 'He [the politician] must be determined to win, but he must not be afraid to lose. . . . Those who are willing to risk all to gain all make the best candidates.'[31]

Significantly, Nixon had shown none of the ruthlessness that marked his life in politics during his initial career as a lawyer because the stakes of success and failure were not as high. In fact he had done little that marked him as being out of the ordinary. While a student at Duke Law School, he tried unsuccessfully to secure a position with several prestigious New York law firms. 'If they had offered me a position', he declared in 1958, 'I'm sure I would have been there today, a corporation lawyer instead of Vice-President.'[32] Instead, on graduation in 1937, he returned home to Whittier and a small town law practice that seemingly promised little more than comfortable obscurity. He even upheld the family tradition of failing in a business enterprise connected with fruit when the Citra-Frost company he had helped set up with two friends to market frozen orange juice went bust in 1941 as a result of technological and packaging problems. Nixon took this very hard because family and friends were among the many small investors who lost money.[33] After this setback, the man who would never give up in politics never again accepted an executive position in a business corporation, despite many attractive offers during the 1960s.

In politics, however, Nixon found his metier, a career that fully engaged his talents and in which he could do good through achieving success. Within six years he had risen meteorically from obscure first-term congressman to Vice-President. Nevertheless such rapid advance also had its drawbacks. It is arguable that Nixon rose too fast and came to power too early in his career for his own good. He never had real opportunity to learn the art of politics at the feet of more seasoned practitioners, to make mistakes and learn from them in relative obscurity, and to develop a stoic acceptance of minor setbacks that are the normal experience of politicians who climb the greasy pole to power at a more measured pace. Nixon's willingness to court controversy propelled him to the top, but it also made him a divisive figure and the object of widespread hatred among political opponents. After his early success, he was to find it much tougher to keep advancing toward the ultimate pinnacle of the presidency and had to contend with a host of adversaries eager to dig his grave and then dance on it.

It was not simply the threat of defeat that confronted Nixon from 1952 onward: he also experienced greater humiliations than any other modern American political leader. There were times when he was on the verge of falling as quickly as he had risen. Charges that his backers had kept a secret fund to pay his political expenses nearly led to him being dropped as vice-presidential candidate. To prove his integrity, he had to make a disclosure of his modest personal finances in the famous Checkers speech on national television. Both he and, in particular, his wife found this repugnant and humiliating – though publicly supportive, in private Pat Nixon had protested, 'Why do you have to tell people how little we have and how much we owe?'[34] Nixon faced further embarrassment from President Eisenhower's obvious reluctance to keep him as his running-mate in the 1956 election. In 1960 Nixon's experience in high office was his greatest asset against the relatively untried John Kennedy, but Eisenhower again wounded him by remarking in a press conference that he would require a week of thought to name one administration policy that originated from the Vice-President's initiative.

With defeat and humiliation ever constant threats, politics for Nixon became a matter of perseverance. It was significant that his first volume of memoirs focused on personal crises he had survived. Crisis, he wrote, 'is the exquisite agony which a man might not want to experience again – yet would not for the world have missed'.[35] Such a man could never enjoy life, not even when he reached the presidency. As one longtime aide commented, 'I do not recall a moment when I saw him completely lost in happiness.'[36] Nor could he be open and trusting. Instead, Nixon was driven in on himself to engage in secrecy and surprise throughout his political career. As another aide observed, 'he never showed his hand. He told no one the whole of his real plans or how he intended to proceed to realize them'.[37] Nixon also felt impelled to engage in constant risk-taking to achieve ever greater success. As he put it in 1990, 'The more you risk if you lose, the more you stand to gain if you win. Nothing great can be accomplished without taking great risks.'[38]

Yet the sweet taste of victory could never be fully savored because other challenges were waiting. Even reelection by a landslide in 1972, the Democrats' greatest defeat in popular-vote terms in a presidential election, induced only a sense of melancholy. In his memoirs, Nixon attributed this to a combination of factors – concern about Vietnam, fear about Watergate, disappointment that the Democrats had kept control of Congress, realization that he would never run for office again, and – somewhat banally – a painful tooth.[39] Henry Kissinger, by contrast, saw the darker forces of Nixon's resentments at work: 'It was as if victory was not an occasion for reconciliation but the opportunity to settle the scores of a political lifetime.'[40]

As Kissinger's words indicate, anger and vindictiveness were core elements of Nixon's political character. He thirsted for revenge against the enemies who threatened him with defeat and humiliation. Journalist Leo Katcher, who broke the slush-fund story in the *New York Post*, found himself the target of a Nixon-inspired FBI investigation into his personal finances and possible connections with Communist organizations. In *Six Crises*, Nixon tried to smear James Reston, the journalist he held responsible for the *New York Times* endorsement of Kennedy in

1960, by drawing attention to his previous friendship with Alger Hiss. Winning the ultimate prize of the presidency did nothing to make Nixon more magnanimous. In a secret memorandum, written on 30 November 1970, he ordered White House chief of staff H. R. Haldeman to compile a list of the administration's major opponents and to develop 'an intelligent program . . . to take them on'.[41] Zealous aides compiled lists with hundreds of names, including entertainers like Bill Cosby, Paul Newman and Barbara Streisand, journalists like Richard Rovere and Tom Wicker, academics like Kenneth Galbraith and Arthur Schlesinger Jr, and scores of Democrats. Whether Nixon ever saw any of these lists is unclear, but he was certainly well aware that the Internal Revenue Service was being used to investigate the finances of many of the people named on them.

At many of the crisis points of his career Nixon found himself at odds with what his enemies-list memorandum called the 'Eastern Establishment'. Nixon's supposed resentment of his humble origins has been used to explain his adversarial relationship with this elite. In private conversations with White House aides, Nixon often harked back to the hard times of his youth. From a young age he had helped out before and after school-time in the family grocery store and had held a succession of vacation jobs that involved physical labour, often in dirty conditions, to help the family make ends meet. According to friends and relatives, Nixon grew to hate working in the family store because he found it demeaning, but this was almost certainly a case of teenage angst about personal image and status rather than a psychological trauma that shaped his adult persona. Probably the greatest disappointment in the young Nixon's life was his failure to get into an Ivy League university. A gifted student, he had the grades and an award for entry to Yale, but his parents could not meet his travel and living expenses because of the cost of caring for Harold. Richard had to settle instead for a place in the local Whittier college.

Despite this, the Nixons were certainly not poor by the standards of the time. Frank Nixon may not have achieved the ultimate American Dream of great material riches, but through hard work he had risen from working-class to small-businessman status in his lifetime and earned the admiration of his son. Far from being resentful of his background, Nixon thought its hardships had taught him a valuable lesson. In an Oval Office conversation in April 1971, he avowed, 'It's a mistake to think that the way to greatness is to make it easy to get there'.[42] Late in life he similarly observed that if parents made life too easy, their children's 'inevitable realization as adults that life is a continuing struggle may find them unprepared for it'.[43]

Nixon's animosity towards the Eastern Establishment rested on more complex foundations than a sense of resentment about his social inferiority. To some extent he had inherited a populist streak from Frank, who had a lifelong anti-establishment outlook and was always willing to do battle against a world that he viewed as fundamentally hostile to him. As a personal protest against the growing power of oil companies, for example, he chose a smaller supplier in preference to Standard Oil for the gas station that was his initial business venture in Whittier. For his own part, Nixon saw himself as a representative of the material aspirations, cultural values and political concerns of ordinary Americans rather than of social, economic or intellectual elites.

Nixon's sense of rapport with this constituency came to his aid on several occasions. Faced with the slush-fund allegations that threatened to destroy him in 1952, he saved himself through a mawkish but highly effective appeal for popular support in the Checkers speech. This nationally televised address swayed public emotions with its canny references to – in Tom Wicker's words – 'his lack of affluence, his . . . genuine roots in republicanism with a small *r* and . . . his bond to the commonality of the people'.[44] Perhaps the most significant expression of his sense of identity with ordinary Americans as president was his so-called Silent Majority speech of 3 November 1969, which played on popular patriotism to rally public opinion in support of maintaining America's commitment to Vietnam and effectively depicted the anti-war movement as the preserve of a vocal, college-educated and youthful minority. Nixon's populist inclinations also informed his electoral strategy. Though a fervent supporter of free enterprise, he feared that the Republican Party's identification as the party of big business limited its popular appeal. Accordingly, one of his ambitions as president was to build a new Republican majority that included blue-collar, ethnic and suburban voters, whom he regarded as his natural constituency. As he put it in an interview in 1984, 'My source of strength was more Main Street than Wall Street.'[45]

Nevertheless Nixon recognized that the enmity of the Eastern Establishment could do him immense damage. His prominent

involvement in the late 1940s in the investigation of of Alger Hiss
as a suspected Soviet spy earned him the hostility of liberal elites.
Former New Dealers, Ivy League academics, liberal Democrats,
liberal journalists and many within the foreign policy establishment saw the Hiss case as the first significant manifestation of the
polluting effect of McCarthyism on American democracy. Nixon
then compounded his villainous reputation in their eyes by his
renewed use of red-smear tactics to defeat Helen Gahagan
Douglas in the 1950 senatorial election. An episode shortly afterwards underlined his pariah status: Averell Harriman, whose
public career spanned service to four Democratic presidents,
walked out of a Washington party when he found Nixon also
present and loudly declaimed, 'I will not break bread with that
man!'[46]

For the next quarter-century Nixon was alert to the enmity of
the Eastern Establishment and looked to do unto it before it
could do unto him. Even as president, he worried that his adversaries were plotting against him. One target of his animus was
the Brookings Institution, a liberal Washington think-tank,
which he suspected of holding secret foreign policy files of the
previous Democratic administration. Nixon thought that these
documents might contain embarrassing evidence about his predecessor's lies about Vietnam, but he also worried that they
might reveal his own intrigues against Johnson's 1968 Vietnam
peace initiative. On 1 July 1971 Nixon told Haldeman and
Kissinger, 'We're up against an enemy, a conspiracy. They're
using any means. *We are going to use any means.* Is that clear?'
The day before he had ordered aides to arrange a break-in to
steal the files, but none of the madcap schemes devised to this end
was implemented.[47]

Nixon also regarded the Northeastern media as an adjunct of
the Eastern Establishment. In his supposedly last press conference after his 1962 California defeat, he launched into a diatribe
against what he regarded as the unfair treatment he had long
received from sections of the print media. In his memoirs, he
charged that the Hiss investigation had poisoned many journalists against him, but this claim does not ring true. In reality
Nixon's role in that case had earned him a very good press, which
was instrumental in bringing him to national prominence. It was
only during the slush-fund crisis that some sections of the Eastern
metropolitan press turned on Nixon, but even these afforded him
respectful coverage during his vice-presidency. Nevertheless,

from that point Nixon believed that liberal journalists from the nationally influential New York/Washington-based media were out to get him. In the 1960 election, he led Kennedy in national editorial endorsements by 54 percent to 15 percent, yet was outraged by the decision of the *New York Times*, which had backed Eisenhower in 1952 and 1956, to endorse his opponent. Political resurrection and victory in 1968 did nothing to assuage his bilious view of the press. In a 1969 memorandum to Bob Haldeman, he alleged that less than 35 percent of journalists were ethical and the 'rest have no intention whatever to be fair whenever they are able to get away with unfair coverage'.[48]

Aware that he was an outsider who could not be part of the old establishment, Nixon set his sights as president on creating a new establishment. An episode during his Whittier college days established a precedent for this. He did not join the Franklins, the well-established and socially eminent campus club for men, preferring instead to help found while a freshman and become the first president of the Orthogonian Society. Members of the new club were mainly athletes and men working their way through school and had their pictures taken for the college yearbook in open-necked shirts rather than the tuxedos favored by the Franklins. The latter, Nixon later told a friendly journalist, 'were the haves, and we were the have-nots, see?' With the support of Orthogonians, he gained his initial experience of political success, first winning office as vice-president of student government and then (broadening his appeal through a promise to win permission from college authorities for dances on campus) election as student-body president over a Franklin rival.[49]

Some forty years later, Nixon told close aides in March 1972 that his administration 'must build a new establishment'. This entailed boosting contacts with provincial newsmen and local editors, rather than the Northeastern metropolitan press, building close relations with corporate leaders who were not Ivy League graduates (such as Pepsi Cola chairman Donald Kendall), and giving preference to individuals who had risen from modest circumstances and lacked the Harvard–Yale pedigree when making appointments to the Cabinet and the top echelon of the federal bureaucracy.[50] Nixon's first Cabinet had only one Ivy League graduate (Secretary of Labor George Shultz was a Princeton man), the least of any modern administration. However, turnover in Cabinet personnel made it impossible to hold the line against the elite universities. Despite Nixon's determination to have 'No Goddamn *Harvard* men', he would end up appointing seven in total.[51] Even Nixon's electoral strategy aimed to build a new Republican majority in opposition to the old establishment. According to aide Kevin Phillips, the goal was to win the support of the new middle classes of the Sunbelt and the suburbs who were in revolt against 'the caste, policies and taxation of the mandarins of Establishment liberalism'.[52]

Though Nixon was at the center stage of American politics for more than a quarter-century, there is broad agreement among friend and foe that he kept his real self hidden from public view. In 1956 Adlai Stevenson commented, 'This is a man of many masks; who can say they have seen his real face?'[53] According to some, Nixon was in essence a performer who calculated precisely what impression he wanted to make. His success in high-school and college debate team contests in which he had to argue the merits of a proposition regardless of his own belief and his youthful hobby of amateur dramatics are seen as significant harbingers of this. 'Throughout his public career', complained conservative activist Howard Phillips in 1974, 'Mr Nixon has always tried to please his audience, seeking their confidence and admiration by becoming the man he thinks they want him to be'.[54]

Nixon himself sometimes recognized that he came across as lacking sincerity, such as when he was bested by Kennedy in the first presidential debate in 1960. Recalling his preparations for the second debate in *Six Crises*, he declared, 'In the final analysis, I knew what was most important was that I must be myself.'[55] This passage reveals far more than Nixon intended: an effort to be sincere belies the nature of sincerity, which has to be natural, and implies a concern that one is basically insincere. A decade later and now president, Nixon worried that he was not coming across as sincere in his domestic policy addresses. 'He feels we need to get into his speeches more of a sense of conviction', Haldeman recorded in his diary on 30 July 1971, 'not just mouthing the stuff that we are now'.[56]

To critics, Nixon's fundamental lack of sincerity found its most extreme expression in the mendacity that ran through his career in politics. As James Reston observed in 1962, he 'never seemed to understand the difference between news and truth. To him what he said was "news" and should be left there'.[57] Nixon lied to defeat opponents, such as the red-smearing of Voorhis and Douglas, whom he knew had no Communist sympathies. He lied to establish his credibility: contrary to what he claimed in the

Checkers speech, his slush-fund donors had received political favors. He betrayed the trust of the American people by telling lies – both little and large – as president. One of his small lies was to have aides announce that he had watched the Apollo space launch on 26 July 1971 with great interest, when in reality he had slept through the event.[58] He lied most vehemently to deny that he was lying. On 22 May 1973, he issued a 4,000-word statement denying any involvement in the Watergate cover-up, which included seven categorical statements of innocence – six of which new chief of staff Alexander Haig later admitted were bare-faced lies.[59]

Psychobiographers fix on the lies as evidence of Nixon's warped personality. To Fawn Brodie, the real question is 'not why he lied so much but why he did not learn to tell the truth'. She finds the answer in his upbringing – the fantasies encouraged by his parents (notably the myth, repeated in Nixon's final White House address, that oil was discovered on Frank's lemon orchard after he sold it, so the family lost its chance to be rich), the difficulties of pleasing two such dominant yet different people as his father and mother, and the example of Hannah's secretiveness and manipulation to get her way without provoking Frank into one of his rages.[60] In essence Brodie portrays Nixon as a man for whom lying shored up a low self-esteem as he endeavoured to make himself lovable to others. Analysis of this kind can offer some insights, but has a tendency to be selective in using evidence that supports its case, to take things out of context, and to exaggerate the personality shortcomings of its subject.

Nixon's lying cannot be excused but needs to be better understood and contextualized. Firstly, he was not an inveterate liar. He was known for his honesty and trustworthiness in his school days and at Whittier College, even during his forays into student politics. Admittedly, he blotted his copybook in a small way at Duke University Law School: anxious about a delay in the announcement of their 1936 second-year grades, he and two friends sneaked into the Dean's office and opened his desk to locate the records without being discovered. Nixon revealed the episode to a friendly biographer, Bela Kornitzer, in 1959 and in the mid-1970s the episode was re-examined as his 'first breaking and entering'. Brodie claimed it had parallels with an episode in the Nixon presidency, recorded in H. R. Haldeman's memoirs. When presidential counsel John Dean was explaining the difficulties of accessing the tax files of hostile Democrats, Nixon reportedly responded, 'There are ways to do it. Goddamnit, sneak in in the middle of the night.'[61] This is a case of reading too much into the past through Watergate-colored lenses: there was no comparison between the Duke 'break-in' to find out the results of tests already sat and illegal political espionage.

Nor was there anything shady about Nixon's record as a small-town attorney. He made a good reputation as a trial lawyer and was made a partner of the Whittier firm of Wingert & Bewley within two years. Such was the respect for him in the local community that he became the youngest member of the Whittier College board of trustees. As a Navy lieutenant in World War II, Nixon served efficiently as a kind of quartermaster in charge of a small unit that loaded and unloaded planes on various air transport bases in the South Pacific in 1943–4. He won the respect, trust and loyalty of the men he commanded, many of whom told journalists after he became famous that they thought of him as a *Mr Roberts* character (a reference to the popular play and movie about a likeable junior naval officer, played by Henry Fonda). Nixon would sometimes claim to have been under air attack and in fox-holes more often than his experience warranted, particularly to friendly biographers around the time of the 1960 election when he was running against a real war hero. However, his exaggerations of his war record were small scale, particularly in comparison to those of Lyndon Johnson. Moreover, his famed success as a wartime poker player was achieved without any recourse to cheating. The truth is that most people who knew Nixon prior to 1946 would willingly have bought a used car from him!

Nixon's loyalty to the truth began to wilt when he crossed the threshold into national politics. Of course, other American leaders have been economical with the truth without being considered psychologically warped. Indeed, the encyclopedia of US presidential lies – if it were ever written – would include entries next to the names of virtually all of the great and the good. In 1999 the Watergate journalist Bob Woodward published a book detailing how all Nixon's successors sometimes lied or failed to tell the whole truth.[62] Paradoxically, the chain of events that led to Watergate was prompted by Nixon's outrage over the *New York Times* publication in 1971 of leaked classified documents known as the Pentagon Papers, which revealed how the Kennedy and Johnson administrations had deceived and misled the American public about Vietnam. However, it is the frequency of Nixon's lying that marks him out. According to Joan Hoff, he is best regarded not as *unprincipled*, in other words a person who consciously lacks moral scruples in knowingly violating standards, but as *aprincipled*, a person who has no remorse for trangressions because there is no awareness of ethics.[63] This fits well with Nixon's view of politics as an arena in which the truth was often a casualty in the battle for survival and success. As he once told aide Leonard Garment, 'You're never going to make it in politics, Len. You just don't know how to lie.'[64]

While Nixon's critics contend that he built his political career on the pretence of being better than he was, there is also a case that he felt obliged to pretend to be worse than he was. According to Tom Wicker, Nixon 'was an intellectual in a decidedly unintellectual business'.[65] This may seem a debatable contention in view of Nixon's oft-expressed disdain for intellectuals, whom he regarded as inherently leftist and associated with the Eastern Establishment. Moreover, Nixon felt unable to identify with the disinterested rationality that is the hallmark of the intellectual. His fascination was with the use of power. As he remarked in one of his books: 'A Professor can go off on flights into the stratosphere of the absurd. Those with power have to keep an eye firmly on the results, the impact, the effect.'[66]

A number of derogatory presidential comments about Jews recorded on the Watergate tapes and in Haldeman's diaries also suggested that Nixon's anti-intellectualism was tinged with anti-semitism. In May 1971, for example, he ruminated on 'the question of why all the Jews seem to be the ones that are for liberalizing the regulations on marijuana'.[67] In fact, Nixon had more top-level Jewish advisers (for example, Arthur Burns, Leonard Garment, Henry Kissinger, William Safire and Herbert Stein) than any other president and many of these felt he was comfortable with Jews because he identified with them as an outsider. It is therefore difficult to portray Nixon as a conventional anti-semite. His defenders claim that his real animus was against left-wing intellectuals, not Jews *per se*, and that his pro-Israel stance in foreign policy was proof of his lack of prejudice. So why was he more vituperative about Jews than any other ethnic intellectuals and why did his derogatory comments extend to Jewish journalists, civil servants and Democrats? We can only guess at the answer. It may have been that he resented fellow outsiders who had seemingly been accepted into the Eastern Establishment that barred its doors to him.

In spite of his disdain for intellectuals, there was a cerebral side to Nixon that shone through at times. Arthur Burns, a former Columbia University economics professor who served in the Eisenhower administration and later in Nixon's, concluded soon after they met that he 'could have held down a chair in political science or law in any of our major universities and would have served with great distinction'.[68] Nixon's intellect was more intricately engaged in his work than was usual for a politician. Nowhere was this better demonstrated than in his sophisticated grasp of the geopolitics. Elliot Richardson, who held several positions in Nixon's administration, labeled him 'the conceptualist, the architect, the chief strategist of his own foreign policy'. Stephen Ambrose, the biographer of both presidents, concluded that Nixon 'thought on a larger scale' than Eisenhower in world affairs.[69] Nixon himself recognized that he had more in common in this regard with one of his perceived enemies. Asked in a 1968 interview whether he would as president behave like Eisenhower, he replied: 'I've more of a philosophical bent I suppose, in a way I'm probably much closer to the kind of politician that Adlai Stevenson was.'[70]

This was a rare public admission of his intellectual self, which Nixon usually kept hidden from view because he feared it would not play well with voters. In private, however, he was much more studious than he let on to the outside world. As a student at Duke his long hours of solo study had impressed classmates, one of whom commented, 'You've got an iron butt, and that's the secret of becoming a lawyer.'[71] Thirty years later Nixon told Theodore White that his habit of intensive solitary reading to understand an issue had been developed at Duke.[72] Nor were current affairs and position papers his only reading as president. He avidly consumed biographies and history books. On 4 December 1970, domestic policy aide and former Harvard professor Daniel Patrick Moynihan responded to Nixon's request for a list of 'the ten best political biographies'. Nixon claimed to have read them all within five weeks – a prodigious feat if true.[73] For a time he had a running debate with another former Harvard professor, Henry Kissinger, about the relative merits of World War II German generals, based on his reading of histories by Winston Churchill and others.[74] Nixon also had a sound knowledge of classical music. It is difficult to imagine any other president reviewing a Kennedy Center concert as he did for Haldeman on 9 September 1971: 'He would have chosen a different program, thought the orchestra was quite good, but that [Antal] Dorati was trying to show off by doing the Stravinski thing, that [Isaac] Stern was wasted on a Mozart chamber music piece, and the great chorus was wasted with an odd Schumann composition.'[75]

As his penchant for solitary study indicated, for someone who spent a lifetime in such a gregarious and public profession as politics, Nixon was a very private and introspective individual. He grew into young manhood showing the introversion, emotional reserve and lack of openness to others that would define his character as a mature adult. Bookish and shy, he stood apart from other youngsters and was not a popular child with playmates and schoolmates. He found his principal form of expression through hard work, whether in the family store, at his studies or in a variety of extra-curricular activities.

Much speculation has focused on the effect on him of the deaths of two brothers, particularly whether guilt feelings as a surviving sibling over the death of Arthur induced neurotic behavior and low esteem. There is no evidence to support this – it is more likely that Arthur's death made Nixon, 12 at the time, more determined to work harder and be successful in order to make up the loss to his parents. Five years after the funeral he wrote that he would think of Arthur whenever 'I am tired and worried, and am almost ready to quit trying to live as I should'.[76] Older brother Harold died when Nixon was in his junior year at Whittier College. One biographer has speculated that this event may have been the turning-point in his life because the obligation of carrying his parent's expectation as the eldest son gave him new drive and determination.[77] Yet Richard's thirst for success had been manifest long before. It is more likely that Harold's death affected him in another way. The debonair, cheerful and high-spirited Harold was a much loved older brother who, in the words of another biographer, represented Nixon's 'best chance at establishing an open, trusting, honest, loving, adult relationship with another human being'.[78]

In his memoirs, Nixon declared, 'Three words describe my life in Whittier: family, church and school.'[79] Probably Nixon's shyness was simply natural to him, but his religious background may have enhanced it. Quaker meetings – sitting silently together, trusting to an Inward Light to lead one to one's own experience of God, the lack of rites – encouraged reserve and introspection. Everything was directed inward and there were no communal prayers or hymn-singing to release emotion. The essentially

personal and private nature of Quakerism rubbed off on Nixon's
later political rhetoric. Even though evangelist Billy Graham was
a highly public supporter, Nixon rarely quoted the Bible in his
presidential addresses. In the Cold War atmosphere of the 1950s,
Eisenhower had urged him to refer to God from time to time in
his speeches, but he never felt comfortable doing so.[80] On the
other hand, the Quaker church provided Nixon with an education in public speaking. Members were encouraged to stand up
and speak or pray before the congregation in a rational rather
than emotional manner, so that what was said was more a speech
than a personal disclosure. The Quaker aversion to public touch-
ing and embracing also remained with Nixon all his life. The first
time that he shook hands with Bob Haldeman, the man closest to
him during his presidency, was at the highly emotional moment
that he asked him to resign over the Watergate cover-up on 29
April 1973.[81]

The philosophical as opposed to the cultural influences of
Quakerism on Nixon appear less significant. Though a Quaker
institution, Whittier College had a dissenting tradition that
rubbed off on him. Philosophy classes taught by J. Herschel
Coffin provided Nixon with the chance to reconcile his spiritual
beliefs with what he knew about the rational world. An essay
written in October 1933 showed that he had rejected the Quaker
teaching about the infallibility and literal correctness of the Bible.
Nixon continued his church activities and still taught Sunday
school, but from that point on he was able to balance his beliefs
in 'the life and teachings of Jesus' with what he learned about life.
Without doubt, his most decisive break with Quaker philosophy
came with his decision to enlist in the Navy in the summer of
1942. Nixon was no pacificist. In his memoirs he stated bluntly
that he never considered seeking deferment as a conscientious
objector. In a further move away from his Quaker heritage,
which saw gambling as a sin, he became a very proficient poker
player during his service in the South Pacific and other players'
estimates of his total winnings ranged from $3,000 to $10,000.[82]

While he was working out the nature of his Quakerism, Nixon
enlarged his mind in other ways at Whittier College. In spite of its
relative obscurity, Whittier was an exacting institution of higher
learning with justifiable pride in its standards. Nixon found
inspiration in Paul Smith's history classes, Coffin's philosophy
classes and Albert Upton's English classes. These teachers
appealed to and nurtured his cerebral side. At Upton's behest, he

spent a summer reading Tolstoy, a moving experience which he told biographer Jonathan Aitken had instilled in him a 'Tolstoyan . . . belief in the individual and his importance, a belief in freedom, but particularly a passion for peace'.[83] Nixon was a very good student who graduated second in his class, but he was not truly outstanding. His history teacher, who found his papers concise and comprehensive but too brief, commented that he had 'an analytic mind rather than a philosophical mind' and was spreading himself too thin because of his other ambitions.[84]

Nixon's extra-curricular activities included debating, dramatics, organizing the Orthogonian club and football, all of which helped him to electoral success in student politics. The Whittier football coach, Wallace 'Chief' Newman, was a lifelong mentor, whose philosophy about the all-importance of winning (such as 'Show me a good loser, and I'll show you a loser') had a deep impact on Nixon. When his team did lose, Newman had a fallback philosophy about never giving up, and forty years later Nixon would again seek his advice about how to fight back from depression after resigning the presidency.[85]

Involvement in these group activities and his evident determination to do his best in whatever task he undertook won Nixon the respect of fellow students. Lacking the physical size and coordination to be a good footballer, he never made the first string but served as a talisman for the team because of his tenacity and loyalty to its cause and his willingness to be the butt of other players' jokes. Nevertheless, as had been the case in his school days, he did not interact closely on a one-to-one basis with any student. Even his one steady girl-friend, Ola Florence Welsh, found him an enigma. The pattern that would characterize his life in politics had emerged by the time he graduated from Whittier in 1934 – he was rarely alone but he had no friends, he was comfortable before an audience but disliked intimacy and had no small talk for individual situations, he was respected rather than loved, and he had obvious leadership ability but remained introspective. Above all, he had honed the political qualities on which he would depend more than any others – a fierce drive, a determination to win and a hunger for success.

Nixon made few friendships with people of like age in his formative years in school and college and none of these survived into his period of fame. At Duke, where he was elected president of the Student Bar Association, he relaxed only very occasionally and kept iron control over his emotions. He did come out of himself during wartime service, but true to form he never sustained these friendships in peacetime. His most significant relationships tended to be with older people, particularly teachers, whose counsel could help to advance him. In his political life, he would develop similar relationships with men like Herman Perry, the local banker who promoted his congressional candidacy in 1946, and Elmer Bobst, the businessman who helped resurrect his political career after 1962.

The youthful Nixon's sense that he was not popular with his schoolmates induced him to read Dale Carnegie's *How to Win Friends and Influence People*, but it is doubtful that he still craved friendship in mature adulthood. Indeed he treasured solitude and privacy as president and would often shut himself away in isolation in the Oval Office or a hideaway in the Executive Office Building to work on speeches. As the Watergate tapes show, he could blow off steam and engage in locker-room language in the company of his closest aides, but with almost everybody else he was shy and reserved. One of Bob Haldeman's jobs as chief of staff was to keep a tight rein over who got to see the President in order to shield him from having to make small talk with other members of his administration. Nixon's best friend during his political career was Charles G. 'Bebe' Rebozo, a Florida banker and land developer whom he first met in 1951. But Rebozo was not a confidant – his primary attraction appeared to be an endless capacity for silently listening to Nixon's monologues over the issues facing him and his proposals for dealing with them. Believing that his boss needed a real confidant, Haldeman decided to find a friend from his California past and settled on a Los Angeles oil executive who was given a job in the Executive Office where he could come into contact with Nixon. The scheme was a predictable flop.[86] In contrast to most other modern presidents, who have liked to relax and gossip with home-state cronies, Richard Nixon had a Garboesque preference to be alone.

What Haldeman failed to understand was not only that Richard Nixon had never had real friends in California but also that he felt no real attachment to his home state. Though he was the first (and to date, only) native-born Californian to be president, Nixon always associated success with the East. His life was the reverse of Horace Greeley's nineteenth-century exhortation that young men should go West to make their fortune. California became America's America, attracting generations of migrants like Nixon's own parents in pursuit of a better life than was their lot in the East or Midwest. Nixon, by contrast, always looked eastward – in spite of his disdain for the Eastern Establishment, he regarded the New York–Washington axis as the locus of real power within the nation and where he had to be to make a success of himself, whether as a politician, lawyer or ex-president trying to rebuild his reputation. 'This is where the action is', he reportedly declared after moving to New York in 1963, 'not with those peasants in California'.[87] Nixon lived in the nation's capital for over twenty years (parts of 1942 and 1945, 1947–60, 1969–74) and in the New York–New Jersey area for another twenty years (part of 1945, 1963–8, 1980–94). After six years 'exile' in his San Clemente, California, residence following his resignation as president, he moved back East permanently in 1980 better to promote his rehabilitation.

Barry Goldwater once commented that Nixon could be 'really a wonderful fellow' when drunk, a condition he had seen him in twice, and expressed the wish that he done more drinking as president to break down his reserve.[88] In a recent biography, however, journalist Anthony Summers charges that Nixon was often in his cups before and during his presidency.[89] Yet the man who knew Nixon best, Bob Haldeman, has stated flatly, 'In all my years with [Nixon] as candidate or as President, I never saw him intoxicated.' So what is the truth? There is no evidence that Nixon was dependent on alcohol. He did drink – usually in limited amounts – to relieve stress and tension, but he had low tolerance of booze, particularly when tired, and could quickly appear to be drunk. As Haldeman commented, 'The fact is Nixon *couldn't* drink when he was tired. One beer would transform his normal speech into the rambling elocution of a Bowery wino'.[90]

Nixon's relationship with his own family further attests to the complexity of his personal character. It was a case of love at first sight – for him at least – when he met his future wife at an amateur drama group in January 1938. Though he rarely did anything on impulse, he told Pat at their third meeting, 'Some day I'm going to marry you', and two years later he did. In spite of such a romantic beginning to their relationship, Nixon rarely if ever showed his wife physical signs of affection in public during his political career. A shy and reticent woman, Pat became increasingly disenchanted with the grind of political campaigns and having to live in the public eye. She tried to extract from her husband a promise that he would not run for office again after he lost the California gubernatorial election. There were rumours that the marriage was in trouble in the early 1960s and only survived thereafter as a loveless sham. Robert Pierpoint, a White House correspondent who had known Pat a long time, commented of their relationship in the White House: 'They tried to play the game of being the perfect husband and wife, but it came through as transparent. It looked so phony, so unrealistic.'[91]

More damagingly, Anthony Summers's recent biography made sensational charges that Nixon was possibly a wife-beater, but these are not convincingly documented. One specific instance of assault allegedly occurred the day Nixon lost the California gubernatorial election in 1962. The evidence cited for this is indirect oral testimony repeated to the author by those who claimed to have heard others – now dead – voice these concerns. Significantly, Nixon's long-serving and still-living press secretary Herb Klein has gone on record saying that he was with his boss for most of that day and no beating could have occurred. Another instance supposedly occurred in the White House in late 1973 (no specific date is mentioned), but it is hard to believe that this could have been hushed up in the investigatory climate of the time.[92] It is also difficult to reconcile Pat Nixon's conduct with that of a battered wife. She was tenacious in supporting her husband throughout the Watergate investigation and ministered lovingly to him after his phlebitis operation (when a weakened Nixon thought he was going to die following a post-operative cardiovascular shock, he spent two hours dictating what he feared might be his last reflections on his career to Pat).[93]

Looked at more positively, there is plenty of evidence that the Nixons' marriage was built on solid foundations and was strong enough to endure. In contrast to other presidents, notably Franklin D. Roosevelt, Kennedy, Johnson and Bill Clinton, Nixon never had an extra-marital affair. To a large extent he honored his promise made to Pat when he first entered politics in 1946 that he would not bring his work home with him (though he was rarely home). He and Pat raised two well-adjusted and happy daughters, no small accomplishment for any parents. Whatever the claims of psychobiographers and of journalists looking in from the outside, the probability is that Nixon loved his wife and his children deeply in his own fashion. After Pat's death in 1992, he went into deep depression from which he never recovered. What Nixon did not give his family was time, but this

did not make him unusual among successful men in all walks
of life.

What consumed Richard Nixon's life after 1946 was his fierce
determination to succeed in the political arena. Everything else
took second place to this ambition. The strengths and weaknesses of his personality were fully revealed as he struggled over
the next three decades to make his mark on American public life.
Nixon's many strengths – his intelligence, his boldness of vision,
his capacity for hard work, his idealism, his rapport with ordinary Americans – marked him out as a leader of potential greatness. In the end, however, the flaws in his character – his
mendacity, his lack of moral scruple in pursuit of his ambition,
his obsession with defeating his enemies – proved his undoing.
Leonard Garment described him as 'perhaps the last pure example of early twentieth-century political man, [who] found his
techniques and psychological postures, then stuck with them'.[94]
Nixon made the mistake of behaving in the presidency in the
same way as he had in his climb to power. He could not rise
above his shortcomings. As he himself reflected to Kenneth
Clawson, 'It's a piece of cake until you get to the top. You find
you can't stop playing the game the way you've always played it
because it is part of you and you need it as much as an arm
or leg.'[95]

|3|

Elephant man

Richard Nixon's political star was inextricably entwined with the Republican Party's for more than a quarter-century. In many respects he was the 'Mr Republican' of the postwar political generation in the way that Senator Robert Taft of Ohio had been for the preceding generation. But whereas Taft tried to make time stand still, Nixon preferred to move with the times. He entered politics when the Grand Old Party (GOP) was the minority party and left with it in a position of near parity with the Democrats. He did much to bring this transformation about. His rapid rise was largely due to his effectiveness in exploiting the Communists-in-government issue that was the Achilles heel of the Democratic Party after its New Deal heyday. Nevertheless, Nixon quickly realized that his own prospects and those of his party depended on accommodation with the New Deal's legacy. The centrist positions he adopted from the mid-1950s onward induced media stories about a new Nixon but were broadly consistent with the values that he had developed in the 1930s. Seeing the middle way as the only viable route to power, Nixon tried to steer the Republican elephant along this course but found its hind quarters had a constant tendency to turn right. When defeat in the California gubernatorial election seemingly spelled the end of his career, he appeared destined to be an 'also-ran' who had promised much but failed to leave any legacy as a politician and party leader. By 1968, however, Nixon's star had risen again because the political circumstances now favored his middle-way Republicanism.

From early in his political career, Nixon was saddled with a reputation as a right-winger, but his leadership role within the Republican Party was fundamentally that of a centrist. His involvement in the Alger Hiss investigation and his vehement anti-Communist rhetoric in the early Cold War distorted his ideological image in the eyes of liberal Democrats for years to come. However, Patrick Buchanan, a Nixon presidential speechwriter who later became a fervent protagonist of the American right, complained that his boss was 'the least ideological statesman' he had ever known.[1] William Safire, another conservative speechwriter, suggested that Nixon's heart may have been on the right but 'his head was, with FDR, slightly left of center'.[2]

Years earlier his Whittier teachers and classmates had identified similar traits in Nixon. In oral history interviews conducted in 1970, a number of former students described his views in the early 1930s as 'liberal', though it is evident from additional comments that they were using this term loosely and mainly to emphasize that he was not conservative.[3] In conversation with an early biographer, Nixon classified himself in similar fashion as a 'liberal' but 'not a flaming liberal' during his college days.[4] He described himself as a believer in *'practical* liberalism' as the best antidote against 'New Deal idealism' when making the first speech of his political career in 1945.[5] This remained his political position for the next thirty years. Whereas Ronald Reagan started out, in his own words, 'a near-hopeless hemophilic liberal' who followed FDR 'blindly' before his experience of high taxes and Communist unions in late 1940s Hollywood resulted in conversion to conservatism, Nixon's political ideology remained firmly rooted in the broad center of American politics throughout his life.[6]

Writing at the start of the Nixon presidency, cultural historian Gary Wills claimed: 'Nixon is a postwar man. Politically, he does not preexist the year 1946. . . . For Nixon, the thirties seem not to have taken place.'[7] In his view, Nixon was too consumed with getting ahead to be affected by the political debates of the Depression era. This does not ring true. Nixon had developed a coherent but critical position on the New Deal in his student days at Whittier and Duke. In line with his father's populism and the progressivism of his Whittier teachers, Nixon recognized the need for programs such as work relief and social security to protect working people against unemployment and the economic problems of old age. He himself was a beneficiary of New Deal largesse – to supplement his meagre graduate school finances, he secured an assignment to research a criminal law problem that was financed to the tune of 35 cents an hour by the National Youth Administration. However, he grew concerned about the potential dangers of government control of the economy that the New Deal might spawn. In his memoirs, he noted that his reading into the relative benefits of a free economy and a managed economy, one of the topics he had to prepare for the Whittier debate team, left him 'thoroughly persuaded of the superior merits' of the former.[8]

Nixon feared that governmental regulations and high taxes could undermine the ethos of individual initiative and responsibility that constituted the lifeblood of the American system. As he liked to put it to a fellow Duke student, 'Social Security is fine, but we need a certain amount of insecurity too'.[9] This did not mean that he was in favor of rolling back the New Deal. Though vehemently critical of FDR's efforts to pack the Supreme Court in 1937, he admired the progressive justices – Charles Evans Hughes, Benjamin Cardozo and Louis Brandeis – who accepted a larger role for the federal government than was explicitly specified in the Constitution.[10] In essence Nixon accepted the basic structure of the Roosveltian state but opposed its expansion into new domains.

Nixon began to contemplate a political career in the late 1930s. The law was his first ambition. In the highly competitive environment of a large graduate school, he worked harder than ever to be a success and endured a spartan lifestyle to graduate third in his class. Disappointed not to get a position with a New York law firm or the Federal Bureau of Investigation (FBI), he sought the guidance of Law School Dean Claude Horack. None of his classmates thought Nixon cut out for politics. One of them, Basil Whitener, who later became Democratic congressman for North Carolina, commented that he 'was not outward, but seemed shy'.[11] But Horack, another male authority figure cultivated by Nixon, was well aware from their frequent conversations that his interests lay in prestige, power and leadership, rather than wealth. 'If you're interested in politics, go home', Nixon remembered the Dean telling him. 'Practice law at home. You may not get as much money but that's the only way if you want to do anything in the political arena.'[12]

Given his views, it was natural for Nixon to register as a Republican, which he did in 1938. He cast his first presidential ballot in 1940 for Wendell Willkie. Meanwhile, he used his position with a Whittier law firm to lay the foundations for a career in politics. He was appointed assistant city attorney, which brought him into contact with local businessmen. One of these, banker Herman Perry, quickly assessed Nixon as a political comer whose advancement he began to promote. Nixon himself appears to have confided his ambition to become US president to some of his male friends on his return to Whittier. Three weeks after first meeting him in January 1938, Pat Ryan was also telling her friends that Nixon would become president one day.[13]

The war interrupted Nixon's career track but it was immensely significant for his political development. For eight months he had a job in the Office of Price Administration, a new agency charged with overseeing wartime rationing and price controls. This was Nixon's first real contact with not only the federal bureaucracy but also Eastern liberals, many of whom were drawn to serve in the agency by its New Dealish mission to defend the common man, in the person of the ordinary consumer, against price gouging and war profiteering. In later life he claimed that the experience made him more conservative: 'I . . . became greatly disillusioned about bureaucracy and about what the government could do because I saw the terrible paper work that people had to go through.' It also engendered a low opinion of civil servants that he held throughout his political career. In his eyes some OPA colleagues were mediocre and incompetent, concerned only to build little empires that would further their career, while others were positively dangerous. 'There were people in government . . . who actually had a passion to GET business and used their government jobs to that end', he declared. 'These were of course some of the remnants of the old, violent New Deal crowd.'[14]

Nixon left OPA to enlist as a Navy lieutenant in August 1942. Wartime military service was very important to his career. Firstly, veteran status was proof of patriotism and virtually a requirement for anyone entering national politics in the postwar era. Equally important it brought Nixon into contact with enlisted men from backgrounds he had never encountered. He was well liked and respected by those of his men who had been blue-collar workers, farm hands, or the like in civilian life and learned something that was invaluable to him as he rose through the ranks of politics. As Stephen Ambrose has indicated, 'It was here, in the Navy, that Nixon discovered he had a real rapport with working-class Americans. He and they understood each other, shared common values, liked pretty much the same things.'[15]

No one else in the leadership ranks of the postwar Republican Party matched Nixon's understanding of the ordinary Americans who were the natural constituents of the Democratic Party.

According to Jonathan Aitken, 'To many working people he [Nixon] looked and sounded like "one of us", even though he had the brains and vision of "one of them".'[16] His political image was certainly more populist than elitist. Nixon could articulate the aspirational values of the white working and lower middle classes who saw the opportunity for socioeconomic betterment in the prosperous postwar years. As Republican pollster Claude Robinson commented when analysing pre-election opinion data in 1956, 'Plain folks with grade and high school education who hew wood and draw water like Nixon.'[17]

Before the war Nixon had aspired to a state assembly seat as the first step in a political career, but a much bigger opportunity presented itself at the end of the war. He ran for Congress as the hand-picked candidate of the Committee of One Hundred, a group of bankers, businessmen and other eminent citizens who ran California's twelfth district Republican organization. These local leaders were anxious to defeat the incumbent congressman, Jerry Voorhis, a liberal Democrat whose views on monetary reform, anti-trust regulation of insurance companies and public power expansion marked him in their eyes as an extreme New Dealer. Addressing a meeting of the group in Whittier in November 1945, Nixon won the nomination with a speech avowing that what returning veterans wanted was not government controls and handouts but 'a respectable job in private industry where they will be recognized for what they produce, or . . . the opportunity to start their own business'.[18] In time the committee would be depicted as an all-powerful cabal who found their Manchurian candidate in Nixon. In reality their role was unremarkable and typical of the way that candidates were selected in many obscure congressional districts. Far more sinister was the interest taken by outsiders once it became evident after the primaries that Nixon could mount a credible campaign against Voorhis, a five-term congressman with an aura of electoral invincibility.

Nixon showed the Jekyll-and-Hyde sides of his character as a politician in his very first campaign. Having won the Republican nomination by presenting himself as the *Mr Roberts*-like spokesman of veterans, he entered into a faustian pact with the power of money to win the election. Nixon could best offset the massive advantage that incumbency gave his rival by outspending him on campaign publicity. The means to do so came from the oil industry, whom Voorhis had offended by investigating shady drilling-rights deals and taking a leading role in defeating the tidelands bill of 1945 that would have enhanced oil company access to offshore petroleum deposits. Nixon formally reported campaign expenses of $17,774 compared with $1,928 for Voorhis, but it is likely that unreported funds placed his spending in excess of $50,000 (about $450,000 in 2001 money).[19] This contrasted with Nixon's protestations that he was the David whose campaign was so poverty-stricken that he had used some of his own money to keep it afloat (which he had done only in its early stages) against a well-heeled Goliath with the financial backing of organized labor. As Roger Morris has observed, Nixon's 'furtive, mincing attitude towards political money, the gradual atrophy of ethics that ended so painfully thirty years later, began in the first campaign'.[20]

The other notorious aspect of Nixon's conduct in the 1946 election was his exploitation of the Communist issue. His use of this tactic was hardly exceptional, since it was a staple element in almost every Republican congressional campaign across the country. Nor did he imply that Voorhis was a traitor in the McCarthyite fashion that became his trademark after the Hiss case changed the political landscape. In 1946 Nixon's concern was to focus attention on the quality of life in postwar America at a time when reconversion to a peacetime economy was beset by a wave of strikes, inflation and shortages. Many voters blamed these problems on the trade unions affiliated to the Congress of Industrial Organizations (CIO), in which Communists were widely believed to have considerable influence. Mindful of this, Voorhis had informed the CIO's Political Action Committee (PAC) that he did not want its endorsement. Nixon's master stroke at the candidates' debate in Pasadena on 13 September was to highlight Voorhis's endorsement by the National Citizens PAC, a separate organization but one that had close ties to and the same leader (Sidney Hillman) as the CIO PAC. In effect he succeeded in portraying the two PACs as being one and the same. The point was rammed home in a subsequent campaign ad that 'a vote for Nixon is a vote against the Communist-dominated PAC with its gigantic slush fund'. Other ads distorted Voorhis's congressional record in claiming that he had backed the 'Communist-dominated PAC line' in 43 out of 46 legislative votes.[21]

The man often credited with masterminding Nixon's campaign was political consultant Murray Chotiner, whose golden rule was that elections were won through attack. Chotiner would work for every Nixon campaign through 1972, excepting for a brief hiatus from 1956 to 1960 when he was too hot to handle. In 1956 he appeared before a Senate subcommittee probing influence-peddling and racketeering to deny allegations that he had used his connections with Nixon to help his law firm's clients. To many, Chotiner was the Svengali who taught Nixon the dark arts and put him in thrall to the financial contributions of big business and organized crime. In reality, he played only a small part in the 1946 campaign. Indeed, the Chotiner–Nixon relationship was never that of master and pupil. While he valued Chotiner's advice, Nixon's own political instincts were always to go for the jugular and he called the shots on all his campaigns.[22]

Nixon's duel with Voorhis was not the progenitor of McCarthyism that it became in liberal legend. Nixon had not invented the Communist issue, only adopted it and in a more restrained manner than many of his fellow Republicans running for office in 1946. Nor was it what one biographer has called 'the blunt instrument most effective in felling Voorhis'.[23] In essence the Democrat lost because he was struggling against a national Republican tide, was more liberal than his largely rural constituency, and proved a poor campaigner – he had never faced such an able and well-financed candidate in his previous races and did not take Nixon seriously until it was too late. Of course, this does not excuse the deceitful way in which Voorhis was smeared. Nixon denied any wrongdoing on grounds that 'the question of which PAC had endorsed him was a distinction without a difference'.[24] But the two organizations were not the same and he had deliberately confused them to damage his opponent. This was the first example of what became his long-standing practice to level a dubious charge against an opponent while self-righteously denying he was doing so.

The smear tactics defined the historical image of Nixon's first campaign, overshadowing the progressive positions he adopted regarding the social responsibilities of government and in condemnation of racial bigotry. The centrist message that he would trumpet for the next thirty years was already in evidence. Nixon's speeches envisioned an America whose promise of prosperity for its people would become a reality through their hard work, initiative and enterprise and in which government's role was only to compensate for some of the flaws and omissions of the private economy. In his credo, government restrictions, overly powerful unions and Communist subversives posed a threat to this vision, but so did racial discrimination, poverty and the economic insecurity of old age.[25]

Although Nixon's unexpected victory over Voorhis gave him national visibility in the the Eightieth Congress, the first under Republican control since 1931, no one could have foreseen his meteoric rise to vice-president within six years. New congressmen had little power in the committee system and no prospect of enacting legislation with their name on it. However an unexpected career-making opportunity quickly presented itself. Appointment to the House Un-American Activities Committee (HUAC) did not appear a glittering prize because of its reputation as the bailiwick of extremists and bigots. It said much for Nixon's talent that he was the only member of this body ever to advance in politics through association with it. The making of his career was the role he played in the committee's investigations of Communists in government.

Testifying before HUAC in August 1948, Whittaker Chambers, an editor of *Time* magazine and a self-confessed former Communist, sensationally claimed that a ring of Communist sympathizers had infiltrated the Roosevelt administration. The most prominent member of this group, he avowed, was Alger Hiss, a former State Department official who had accompanied FDR to the Yalta conference of 1945 that determined the postwar settlement of Europe. In counter-testimony, the suave, elegant and well-connected ex-diplomat, now President of the prestigious Carnegie Endowment for International Peace, seemingly persuaded a majority of the committee of his innocence, but Nixon would not let go. Although he was being secretly leaked FBI information that pointed to Hiss's Communist links, Nixon was taking a considerable risk in backing Chambers. The latter had offered no proof in support of his allegations. When he finally did so in late November, it was in the form of copies of State Department documents that Hiss had supposedly passed on to him in the 1930s for despatch to a Russian agent. In essence Chambers now claimed that Hiss had spied for the Soviets but admitted having done so himself too, something he had previously denied in HUAC testimony. Fearing at one point that Chambers no longer had credibility, Nixon wailed, 'Oh, my God, this is the end of my political career'.[26] Eventually, however, the famous Pumpkin Papers – microfilmed State Department documents that Chambers had supposedly received from Hiss in

1937–8 and then hidden in a hollowed-out pumpkin – broke the case.

Nixon took full credit for being the man who had nailed the most important spy in the State Department's history. However, others had done far more to expose Hiss, particularly HUAC's special investigator Robert Stripling, who later described Nixon's self-glorifying account of the Hiss affair in *Six Crises* as 'pure bullshit'.[27] It was poetic justice that, having claimed the credit, Nixon would get the full blame from outraged liberals, who saw the Hiss affair as the first flowering of McCarthyism. In their view Nixon had cynically tarred an innocent man as a Communist traitor in order to advance his career. In fact Nixon had conducted himself in a responsible, legalistic manner throughout the investigation and had refrained from making reckless charges. Allen Weinstein, the most thorough analyst of the case, found 'no evidence that a demonic Dick Nixon partici-pated in an effort to frame Alger Hiss'.[28] Paradoxically, in view of his later conduct over Watergate, Nixon's real claim to fame in the affair was to have prevented a presidential cover-up – and done so with the aid of leaks!

In December 1948, shortly after his reelection, President Harry S. Truman tried to suppress the HUAC investigation by getting the case transferred to the Justice Department. As Nixon well knew, thanks to informants in this agency, the administration then planned to prosecute Chambers for perjury, on grounds that he had previously lied about his involvement in espionage. This would have destroyed the credibility of the chief witness against Hiss. Nixon showed considerable courage and great political savvy in taking on Truman. He went on the counter-attack in an effort to embarrass the administration into prosecuting Hiss not Chambers. An indictment of the latter, he charged, would be a 'Department of Justice whitewash which would give the greatest encouragement to the Communist conspiracy in this country'.[29] Called to surrender the Pumpkin Papers to the Justice Department, Nixon appeared in a federal court to argue that they were the property of the House of Representatives, so could only be released by order of Congress. In a compromise arrangement, he agreed to hand them over not to Justice Department officials but to the FBI, which he was confident would pursue the investi-gation vigorously. Within days FBI agents tracked down the type-writer Priscilla Hiss had used to transcribe the documents, which convinced a federal grand jury to indict her husband on two counts of perjury (the statute of limitations for espionage had expired). After his first trial resulted in a hung jury, Hiss was eventually found guilty by a federal court in 1950 and imprisoned for five years.

To Nixon, the Hiss case was proof of treason in high places, but he was dismayed that the Democrats refused to acknowledge this publicly. Journalist Bert Andrews had confidentially informed him that, on sight of the evidence implicating Hiss, Truman had paced the floor of the Oval Office saying over and over again, 'The son of a bitch – he betrayed his country.'[30] Yet when Hiss was convicted, the President refused in a press conference to withdraw his earlier remark that the HUAC investigation had been a politically motivated 'red herring'. Like other Republicans, Nixon was further angered that Secretary of State Dean Acheson avowed, 'I do not intend to turn my back on Alger Hiss', a pledge of continued friendship to a man found guilty of perjury about his role as a Soviet agent.[31]

In these circumstances the Hiss affair became enmeshed in extreme partisanship. Truman's conduct reflected his conviction that the HUAC investigation was intended to embarrass the Democrats. In common with many Republicans, Nixon deemed the President and his party guilty of playing politics with national security and fair game for all-out assault. He now entered the most controversial phase of his pre-presidential career to become an active participant in the politics of McCarthyism. His rhetoric may not have been as vitriolic as the Wisconsin senator whose name is associated with the Red Scare, but this was merely a matter of degree. If Nixon did not actually call Truman and the Democrats traitors, he as good as did so in his repeated accusations that they were refusing to investigate the existence of Communist agents in high places. A speech to Young Republicans in 1951 was typically vitriolic: 'Communists infiltrated the very highest councils of this Administration . . . [yet] our top Administration officials have refused time and time again to recognize the existence of the fifth column in this country and to take executive action to clean subversives out of the administrative branch of government.'[32] Adlai Stevenson spoke for many Democrats when he later called Nixon 'the white collar McCarthy', whose rhetoric was made to look moderate only by the latter's excess.[33]

This was also the phase of his career when Nixon was most closely associated with the Republican right. 1946 had proved a false dawn for the GOP revival. Truman's shock reelection and the Democratic recapture of Congress in 1948 showed the futility of a direct assault on the New Deal. Conservative Republicans were desperate for another avenue of offense, which the Hiss case provided. Their new battle-cry charged that liberalism had harbored Communists in government who were intent on selling out America abroad and socializing it at home. Nixon made common cause with conservatives in this attack. The middle-of-the-road positions that he had previously taken no longer featured in his rhetoric. Announcing his candidacy for the Senate, he decried the Democratic Party for its 'phony doctrines and ideology' and for offering 'the same old Socialist baloney'.[34]

On the strength of the Hiss case, Nixon won the GOP nomination to contest California's vacant Senate seat in 1950. As one biographer observed, his battle with Democrat Helen Gahagan Douglas became 'a spectral presence . . . a hoary ghost repeatedly exorcised but echoing in ironic allusions and sequels across the next quarter-century'.[35] A former Broadway actress and a leftish Los Angeles congresswoman, Douglas found herself the victim of the most vicious smear campaign that Nixon ever mounted. What he did to Voorhis was mild by comparison. He all but made Douglas out to be a supporter of Communism. In a typically disingenuous denial of any intent to smear, he claimed in his memoirs, 'I never questioned her patriotism.'[36]

Nixon embellished the claim previously made by her Democratic primary opponent that Douglas had consistently voted on the same side as Congressman Vito Marcantonio of New York, a reputed fellow-traveller. His infamous 'Pink Sheet', over half-a-million copies of which were distributed to voters, detailed 354 House votes in which she had taken the same side as 'the notorious Communist Party-liner'. It omitted the fact that most of these were straight Democratic votes, many on routine matters (Nixon himself had voted with Marcantonio 111 times). It completely distorted the reality that, in contrast to Marcantonio, Douglas had backed the Truman administration on every key measure of Cold War policy, excepting the 1947 bill providing economic aid to Greece and Turkey. Sexism merged with red-baiting when Nixon dubbed Douglas the 'Pink Lady', a term originally coined by her Democratic opponents, and avowed that she was 'pink right down to her underwear'.[37] The McCarthyite tactics did not stop there. Virtually every Nixon campaign speech linked Douglas to Hiss. 'If she had had her way', he intoned in one radio address, 'the Communist conspiracy in Washington would never have been exposed, and Alger Hiss instead of being a convicted perjurer would still be influencing the foreign policy of the United States'.[38]

As in 1946, secret oil money found its way into Nixon's coffers because Douglas opposed transferring tidelands oil deposits from federal to state jurisdiction. It has also been alleged that mobster Mickey Cohen raised $75,000 for Nixon from gambling interests. Estimates of Nixon's actual spending range between one and two million dollars, for the time a fabulous sum that funded a blitz of newspaper ads, billboards, and television and radio time far beyond what could have been afforded on his reported expenditure of $300,000.[39] Douglas, by contrast, was underfunded and suffered a news blackout by pro-Republican newspapers – the *Los Angeles Times*, in particular, printed Nixon's attacks on her but not her rebuttals. All this helped Nixon win by a landslide – his 59 percent share of the popular vote was the largest for any Republican Senate candidate in 1950.

Nixon's rising star now came into the orbit of the men promoting the presidential candidacy of Dwight D. Eisenhower. His selection as Ike's running-mate was largely engineered by the General's advisers, led by Governor Thomas E. Dewey of New York. They were impressed by his vigor, intelligence and speaking ability. He also gave balance to the ticket through his youth, partisan style, Western home-state and ties with the Republican right. Nixon got the nomination because he seemed the perfect foil for the non-partisan Ike: he represented in a friendly biographer's words 'a Republican meld of Paul Revere and Billy Sunday', who could warn of the Democratic threat and preach the party's gospel.[40]

Nixon's triumph soon turned sour. On 18 September the *New York Post* published a story headlined 'Secret Nixon Fund!' and 'Secret Rich Men's Trust Fund Keeps Nixon in Style Far Beyond His Salary'.[41] The ensuing outcry threatened to destroy Nixon and bring down the Republican ticket. Ironically, in a career littered with funny money, this was one of the few occasions that Nixon was not guilty of misconduct. Political slush-funds were commonplace. Democratic presidential candidate Adlai Stevenson himself had one. Nixon's fund, created in late 1950, held $18,000 in contributions from California businessmen to finance political operations necessary for his reelection as senator. None of the money was for private use. Although Nixon had

$70,000 a year from the government to run his office, this did not cover all mail costs, weekly radio reports, additional secretarial assistance and regular trips back to California. While wealthy politicians like John Kennedy could fund additional expenses themselves, Nixon could not make a salary of $12,500 plus some $6,500 in speaking honorariums stretch this far. The real issue was not the existence of the fund but whether contributors had bought influence. In spite of his denials, there is plenty of evidence that Nixon did help his backers in their dealings with government agencies, in matters such as oil drilling rights and tax rebates. Whether this was untoward is another matter. Helping constituents in this way was part of the congressional routine. It is unlikely that Nixon would have acted differently even if the individuals seeking help had not been contributors.

To protect Eisenhower, his advisers tried to get Nixon dumped from the ticket. On 20 September, the *New York Herald Tribune*, owned by prominent Eisenhower backer William Robinson, called on him to resign. Ike himself pointedly held back from supporting him in public and in private. Twice during the affair, an angry and humiliated Nixon considered resigning but was talked out of it by Pat Nixon and Murray Chotiner. Eventually he saved himself by going on national television on 23 September to make a half-hour address explaining the fund. Shortly before he left for the Los Angeles studio, Dewey telephoned from New York urging him to submit his resignation to Eisenhower at the conclusion of the broadcast. It was obvious that this was what Eisenhower himself wanted, so that he could make the final decision on Nixon's fate. According to Nixon, he weighed up the alternatives during the ride over to the studio and decided by the time he got there to stick with his original plan of letting the American people decide. At the end of his address, he said 'I am not a quitter' and asked viewers to write or wire the Republican National Committee as to whether he should stay on the ticket.[42]

Nixon's idealized self-portrayal as a common man of modest means struck a chord with many Americans. He made a clean breast of his finances, entailing a painful admission that he could barely support his family, talked proudly of Pat's 'Republican cloth coat' (a cunning allusion to the Democrats' 'mink coat' corruption scandal), and claimed that he had only ever accepted one gift from a political supporter – a cocker spaniel named Checkers – which he would never return because his two young daughters loved it so.[43] For the actor in Nixon, it was a performance to match James Stewart playing Jefferson Smith in *Mr Smith Goes to Washington*. Walter Lippmann, dean of liberal commentators, was so embarrassed by the corniness of the speech that he called it 'the most demeaning experience my country has ever had to bear'. Another columnist, Robert Ruark, evaluated it more shrewdly: 'This came closer to humanizing the Republican party than anything that has happened in my memory.'[44] Ordinary Americans thought so too. They deluged the Republican National Comittee with 160,000 telegrams and 250,000 letters urging Nixon's retention on the ticket. Eisenhower climbed on board the bandwagon. When the two men met at Wheeling airport, West Virginia, the following day, Ike rushed up the steps of Nixon's plane, hand outstretched, and told him, 'You're my boy!'[45] Nixon would learn that he was exactly that over the next eight years!

Having survived the crisis, Nixon returned to business-as-usual against the Democrats. His rhetoric did much to make the 1952 campaign the bitterest presidential election of the twenty-year period after World War II. For the first time in modern American history the suitability of a vice-presidential candidate became a major election issue. Nixon hammered away at the Truman administration's containment strategy as nothing more than the appeasement of Communism. In one speech he accused the President, Dean Acheson and Adlai Stevenson of being 'traitors to the high principles in which many of the nation's Democrats believe', a vicious slur on their patriotism. He repeatedly charged that the Democrats had tolerated Communists in government and accused Acheson of 'color blindness – a form of pink eye to the Communist threat in the United States'.[46] His attacks provoked furious Democrats to question his suitability for high office. Stevenson complained that Americans needed a campaign of 'elevating national discussion' not 'innuendo and accusations aimed at sowing the seeds of doubt and mistrust'.[47] Such fine words belied the fact that the Democratic National Committee was still digging in vain for further dirt on Nixon's finances.

On balance, Nixon's main contribution to the GOP ticket in 1952 was to have stayed on it. As Eisenhower himself had shrewdly acknowledged during the fund crisis, if Nixon was compelled to resign, 'we can't win'.[48] Beyond that, his partisan stridency shored up the Republican faithful but held little appeal to other voters whose support the GOP needed. Nixon could claim little credit for the biggest Republican victory since 1928, but neither could the Republican Party itself for that matter. Thanks to his unrivalled personal appeal as a war hero, Eisenhower won 55 percent of the popular vote and his coat-tails enabled the Republicans to recapture both houses of Congress, albeit narrowly. The Republicans also benefited as the 'out' party in 1952 from popular dissatisfaction with the Truman administration over Communism, corruption and the Korean War stalemate. They would now need a strong record in government if they were to wrest the mantle of majority party from the Democrats.

One weapon that the Republicans could no longer use was the charge that Communists were still being harbored in government. The trouble was that Senator Joseph McCarthy continued to make embarrassing allegations of Red infestation in the departments responsible for national security. Nixon had enjoyed good relations with McCarthy since his emergence into the limelight in early 1950. In his memoirs, he defended the Wisconsin senator's sincerity and adjudged his worst sin was gross exaggeration of the facts, so that 'McCarthy became the issue instead of communism'. By contrast, Eisenhower in his memoirs condemned McCarthy absolutely as the purveyor of reckless charges that did great damage.[49] Although the Democrats likened them to two peas in a pod, Nixon and McCarthy were different. Nixon was smarter so he never overstepped the mark in his allegations in the way that McCarthy almost always did. Also, Nixon's fortunes were tied to Eisenhower and the Republican Party, while McCarthy was a maverick with no loyalties except to himself. As such, Nixon recognized that McCarthy had to be muzzled, but his efforts to this end were ineffective.

The Wisconsin senator's reckless charges threatened to undermine the respectability of Republican anti-Communism. As a frustrated Eisenhower put it, 'McCarthy is probably [Soviet leader] Malenkov's best helper in the United States.'[50] Rather than directly challenge McCarthy, which would have alienated the Republican right, the President used Nixon as a go-between in a futile behind-the-scenes effort to restrain him. Eventually in April 1954 Nixon was delegated to make an oblique attack against the embarrassing maverick on national television. Though never mentioning McCarthy by name, he declared, 'When you go out to shoot rats, you have to shoot straight, because when you shoot wildly, it not only means that the rat may get away more easily, you make it easier on the rat.'[51] The message was clear: anti-Communist investigations were a good thing if practiced in Eisenhower's – and, of course, Nixon's – fair fashion rather than McCarthy's disreputable manner. None of this had any effect. In the end it was not administrations containment tactics but his own excess in looking for Reds in the US Army that undid McCarthy, whose censure for conduct unbecoming by the Senate in late 1954 signaled his downfall.

By then Nixon was engaged in a reappraisal of his own McCarthyite rhetoric. Arguably the 1954 election represented a turning point in his career as a Republican leader. It was the low-water mark of the vitriolic campaign style that he had employed in his climb to power, but his attacks were out of step with the public mood. America was no longer involved in a shooting war in Korea and popular revulsion with anti-Communist witch-hunts had grown as a result of McCarthy's embarrassing conduct in the nationally televised Army–McCarthy congressional hearings. The Republicans ended up losing eighteen seats in the House and four in the Senate, surrendering control of Congress that they would not regain until 1994 (a political famine partially broken only by a six-year Senate majority in the Reagan era). Nixon was left to ponder the need for a new approach that would better serve himself and the GOP.

With Eisenhower preferring to remain above the battle, Nixon deputized as party leader on the stump, visiting 95 cities and giving 204 speeches over a seven-week period. He set the tone of the Republican campaign by charging that the Truman administration had been blind to the Communist threat at home and abroad. He blamed the Democrats for the loss of China and subsequent Cold War setbacks in Asia. He repeatedly avowed without ever furnishing the proof that the incoming Eisenhower administration had found in the files of the outgoing Truman government 'a blueprint for socializing America'. With the Democrats exploiting the recent recession, Nixon also charged that Adlai Stevenson's criticisms of the US economy were akin to 'spreading pro-Communist propaganda'.[52]

As usual Nixon claimed in his memoirs that he only questioned the judgment of his opponents, not their patriotism: 'I categorically dissociated the administration from McCarthy's reckless charges that the Democratic Party was the party of treason'.[53] Yet his rhetoric made him once again a major issue in the campaign and the focus for Democratic counter-attacks. Adlai

Stevenson decried what he called Nixon's 'ill-will campaign'. In a telling riposte, he quipped, 'The President smiles while the Vice-President smears'. He also accused Nixon of turning the campaign into 'a cheap, sordid, ugly slugfest of slogans, charges and epithets'. This last remark so upset Nixon that he wired Stevenson to protest and then complained about being the victim of 'the big [Democratic] lie'![54]

Whether Nixon helped or hindered the Republican cause in 1954 is unclear. GOP reverses were consistent with the normal trend that the president's party loses ground in off-year elections when he is not on the ballot. As *Newsweek* observed, many Republicans were convinced that their party would have suffered a landslide if Nixon had not campaigned so energetically to bring out its habitual supporters.[55] On the other hand, the Republican Party could never win a national election without broadening its support beyond its core constituency of suburban middle classes, small town residents, rural dwellers and business. In February 1960, after eight years of Eisenhower-era peace and prosperity, a Gallup poll found that only 30 percent of voters classified themselves as Republicans, against 47 percent who were Democratic identifiers and 23 percent who were independent. According to Nixon's own estimate, this meant that he needed the support of virtually all the Republican voters, more than half of the independents, *and* five to six million Democratic identifiers to beat Kennedy.[56] This was the daunting problem of electoral arithmetic that he had to solve to realize his ambition of becoming president. How to expand the Republican voter base became one of his principal preoccupations from late 1954 onward.

Nixon's solution was to locate the Republican Party in what GOP intellectual Arthur Larson called the 'Authentic American Center'.[57] This was precisely where Eisenhower himself was trying to take it, but this was a challenging task. Admittedly, the Republican Party of the postwar era was neither as neatly nor as deeply divided as were the Democrats between their Northern-urban-liberal and Southern-states' rights-conservative wings. The GOP never suffered the kind of open rebellion that produced the Dixiecrat splinter of 1948 within Democratic ranks. Its fissures were more complex and imprecise on issues, but right-wingers in particular were so devoted to their beliefs that most of them preferred to fight for these than compromise to win office. In the bitter struggle for the 1952 presidential nomination, Nixon often heard conservatives avow that they would prefer to lose with Robert Taft heading the ticket than win under Eisenhower.[58]

There were three broadly identifiable GOP factions. Liberal Republicans advocated an activist state that would provide the social services required by an urban-industrial society and supported Cold War internationalism. The smallest faction, they included governors and congressmen with urban, primarily Northeastern constituencies. Their putative leaders were Thomas Dewey and later Nelson Rockefeller, both New York governors. The moderates, the largest faction, accepted a basic accommodation with the New Deal state but drew the line against significant expansion of federal responsibility. They enthusiastically supported Cold War internationalism but were more critical than their liberal kith of Democratic foreign policy failures. More sensitive to public opinion than their rivals, they had a strong base in both the national and state parties and regarded Eisenhower as their natural leader.

Finally, the conservatives – often dubbed the Old Guard – sought to roll back the New Deal in favor of limited government, low taxes and balanced budgets. In foreign policy they criticized containment as a sham, calling instead for the liberation of China and Eastern Europe from Communism. In a throwback to their prewar isolationism, they were skeptical of America's foreign aid and alliance programs as an instrument to combat Soviet expansion. The right drew its support from the rural Northeast, Midwest and West, but was out of touch with the needs of urban America, whose support the GOP needed to win national power. Led in succession by Senators Robert Taft of Ohio, William Knowland of California and Barry Goldwater of Arizona, the Republican right was powerful within Congress. In alliance with conservative Democrats, it could block the progressive initiatives of the Eisenhower administration. The Old Guard was also intent on recapturing control of the presidential wing of the party from the liberal-moderate alliance that had nominated every GOP candidate for the White House since 1940.[59]

In his first term of office, Eisenhower sought a new Republican middle way that avoided the extremes of Old Guard conservatism and Democratic liberalism. Modern Republicanism, as he dubbed it in 1956, was a somewhat imprecise philosophy that regarded private enterprise as the wellspring of American prosperity but recognized that government had some responsibility to

address societal problems over which individuals had no control.[60] Nixon's adherence to this centrist cause was not a case of
jumping on a bandwagon but a reaffirmation of core values that
had shaped his political outlook for twenty years, despite being
recently overshadowed by his strident anti-Communism.
Probably Eisenhower's clearest exposition of his Modern
Republican views was his nomination acceptance speech at the
1956 Republican convention, an address that had much in common with the values of 'practical liberalism' that Nixon had outlined back in 1945.

From 1955 onward Nixon consistently supported measures
more akin to the New Deal than to Republican traditions of limited government and worked hard, often in vain, to enact them.
He was particularly enthusiastic about Eisenhower's proposals to
develop the interstate highway system and to fund school construction. Roads and schools were smart politics, he told the
Cabinet, and by combining the two the Republican Party 'can
really go someplace'.[61] The Interstate Highway Act of 1956
established what is still the most expensive public works program
in American history. However, conservative Republicans and
Southern Democrats allied to defeat aid for school construction
as a federal intrusion into state jurisdiction.

Breaking with traditional Republican balanced-budget philosophy, Nixon also accepted the Keynesian legacy of the New Deal.
In 1958 recession sent unemployment above the five million
mark for the first time since the Depression. While Eisenhower
adopted a cautious approach out of concern about the rising
deficit, Nixon pleaded unsuccessfully for bolder compensatory
spending to avert heavy GOP losses in the forthcoming elections.
Moreover, in September 1958 he delivered a major speech at
Harvard University that foreshadowed the 'new economics' of
the Kennedy administration in its advocacy of tax reduction to
boost the economy. He declared, 'We must not allow the fear of
a temporary budget deficit to put us in a strait jacket which will
keep us from doing what we ought to do to insure economic
growth'.[62] Meanwhile, Nixon built bridges to organized labor by
steadfastly opposing the introduction of state right-to-work laws
whose aim of outlawing the closed shop was dear to conservative
hearts.

Though Nixon won the 1960 Republican presidential nomination with support from conservatives, he ignored Old Guard
preferences in writing the party platform. By contrast, he agreed

the so-called Compact of Fifth Avenue to avoid a convention battle with Nelson Rockefeller, who wanted stronger commitments on civil rights, social programs and increased defense spending. Wrongly described as a surrender by some pundits, this accord allowed Nixon to have his cake and to eat it: he got a platform better able to win over Democratic voters in the Northeast and conservatives blamed Rockefeller not him for the changes. As one aide commented, 'That guy is taking high ground for us we could never have taken on our own.'[63]

Nevertheless, Nixon could not inhabit the political center unless he shed the bad-guy image that made him such a divisive figure. Personal considerations reinforced political need. The fury of Democratic counter-attacks in 1954 combined with Herblock's cartoon portrayals of him as 'a sewer-dwelling denizen' (Nixon's own words) had got under his skin. Worried too about the effect on his children, he began to wonder 'where party loyalty left off and masochism began'.[64] Eisenhower's heart attack in September 1955 provided the opportunity for the launch of a 'new' Nixon, who deputized for the sick president in a responsible manner that bespoke no hunger for the power that he would inherit if his boss did not survive. In the 1956 presidential election campaign, Nixon was far more moderate in his rhetoric than in 1952 and 1954, reflecting awareness of being judged as someone just a heartbeat away from being president if Ike's health failed again. Perhaps his sole aberration was to denounce Adlai Stevenson's proposal for a unilateral nuclear test ban as 'treasonable nonsense', but otherwise he was at pains to acknowledge the loyalty of the Democratic Party. Caught off-guard, Stevenson continued to campaign against the old Nixon, hoping to goad him into rhetorical excess but this only undermined his own dignity and emphasized the poverty of his issue-agenda.

The red-baiting bogeyman did make a final appearance two years later when Republicans experienced their worst midterm defeat in a generation in the wake of the recession and the Sputnik crisis. Charged once more with fronting the campaign, Nixon was desperate to limit GOP losses for fear that his credibility to head the 1960 ticket was on the line. He fell back on old charges of Democratic 'retreat and appeasement' causing the loss of China and the outbreak of war in Korea. This earned him rebuke from Eisenhower, who feared that such rhetoric could undermine the congressional Democrats' bipartisan support for administration foreign policy. A chastened Nixon moved to defuse the issue and remove foreign policy from the campaign: 'There is no party of surrender in the United States,' he now declared. '. . . There is only one party of treason in the United States – the Communist party.'[65] These words brought down the curtain on the issue on which he had built his early career and with which he was most associated in the public mind.

By and large Nixon was able to rein in his pit-bull tendencies, at least in public, in his later campaigns. Of course, Democrats neither forgave nor forgot his past conduct and did all they could to keep alive memories of the 'old' Nixon, aided by occasional outbursts of traditional Nixonspeak. Nevertheless, many Nixon supporters felt that he had moved too far in the other direction. 'You're not coming across', Bryce Harlow complained near the end of the 1960 election, '. . . you're making convincing stump speeches but where's Dick Nixon? You're not in 'em. There's no vibrance, no emotion. People don't feel you in the campaign.'[66] Whatever people felt about the 'old' Nixon, everyone had known where he stood, but the 'new' Nixon appeared to lack sincerity. In 1958 journalist William S. White described him as the 'perfect model of the political leader who finds his inspiration and ultimate mode from the public'.[67] Two years later CBS News correspondent Eric Sevareid contended that Nixon and Kennedy came from the same mold: to him they represented a 'managerial revolution' in politics – two 'tidy, buttoned-down men', devoid of any conviction other than their own ambition, and packaged for selling on television like a consumer product.[68]

Nixon's embrace of the substance and style of the middle way failed to endear him to Eisenhower. The President and Vice-President were not personally close. Eisenhower resisted joining the Nixon club of older male patrons. He never forgot how the slush-fund crisis had nearly cost him the 1952 election. 'Immature' was the word that Ike used most often in private about Nixon, whose extreme partisanship he disdained. This attitude was hypocritical, since it was Eisenhower who sent Nixon to do the dirty work so that he could keep his own hands and mouth clean. Despite Nixon's widely praised performance during his illness, the President increasingly viewed his Vice-President as a liability now that he faced a Democratic Congress. As a result Eisenhower tried to dump him from the Republican ticket in 1956. Ike hoped to run with a conservative Democrat to chart a bipartisan middle way in the second term, but none of his preferred choices was willing to serve. Meanwhile there was no Republican alternative of Nixon's stature who was so broadly acceptable within the party. In the end, a reluctant Eisenhower recognized that he was stuck with him.

In 1952 Nixon had blamed Eisenhower's backers, not the politically inexperienced General, for trying to dump him from the ticket. In his memoirs, he laid bare his anger about being deserted by 'my former Republican friends', who had 'panicked when the first shots were fired'.[69] In 1956 he had to suffer Ike's machinations in silence because he still hoped to be anointed the chosen heir in 1960. It was a humiliating experience but there was more to come. The best way that Eisenhower could have helped Nixon was to give him more credit for his role in the administration. This would have legitimized the claim of experience in government that would be his strongest card against any Democratic rival. In reality Nixon had established himself as the most effective vice-president to date in American history. He was well briefed on foreign policy, knowledgeable about domestic policy and an active party leader. It was Eisenhower who had given him the opportunity to do all this but the President could never bring himself to recognize Nixon's achievement. Just two months before the 1960 election Ike famously remarked in response to a press conference question that he would need a week to name any major policy that derived from a Nixon idea.

Eisenhower had hoped in vain to promote Treasury Secretary Robert Anderson, a Democrat, as the 1960 Republican presidential candidate but could not persuade him to run. This was a curious choice, even for a non-partisan like Eisenhower – Anderson lacked the track record to suggest that he could do the job, had no support within the Republican Party, and was not the man of integrity idealized by Ike (he went to prison for tax fraud in 1987). Eisenhower's infatuation did Nixon and the Republican Party, not to mention himself, a disservice. He let down the man who would have done most to safeguard his legacy and Nixon's eventual defeat in 1960 opened the way for the capture of the GOP by right-wingers sworn to tear down the edifice of Eisenhower Republicanism.

Eisenhower's ambivalent attitude about his suitability to be president was not the only problem he caused Nixon. During his second term, the President became increasingly concerned that rising budget deficits would cause ruinous inflation. He refused to increase spending on programs that Nixon supported. The

Democrats charged – wrongly it transpired, but too late to help Nixon – that Republican parsimony had allowed the Soviets to forge ahead in missile development. More seriously, Eisenhower's insistence on balancing the 1960 budget weakened the economy's recovery from the 1958 recession and did much to precipitate a new downturn shortly before the 1960 election. Tipped off by an economic adviser about the likelihood of new recession, Nixon pleaded in Cabinet for preventive action, but Eisenhower clung to balanced-budget dogma.[70] In a very close election, the economic slowdown was critical to Kennedy's narrow victory. Pocket-book worries solidified Democratic support in the lower half of the income distribution, reversing the promising trend of Republican gains among blue-collar voters in 1952 and 1956. A Kennedy insider, Theodore Sorensen, acknowledged that concern about rising employment was the main reason for the large urban majorities that gave the Democrat his margin of victory.[71]

Kennedy won with 49.7 percent of the popular vote to Nixon's 49.5 percent, making the 1960 presidential election the closest in the period spanning the 1888 and 2000 contests, in both of which the electoral college victor failed to achieve a popular majority. In such a tight race, the loser was inevitably plagued by the thought that he could have won if just one thing had been done differently. One 'what if?' concerned Eisenhower's handling of the economy, but Nixon was personally responsible for most of the other questionable decisions that affected his campaign.

Nixon's selection of Henry Cabot Lodge as his running-mate was ill starred. Far from boosting the ticket's appeal in the Northeast, the patrician Lodge proved a poor campaigner with little working-class appeal. A better choice, urged by some advisers, might have been Secretary of Labor James Mitchell, a Catholic and a proven friend of trade unions. Nixon's refusal to help either through gesture or deed the recently arrested civil rights leader, Martin Luther King, caused a sharp decline in his African-American support late in the campaign. By contrast, John and Robert Kennedy did come to King's aid, prompting the latter's father to urge fellow blacks to back the Democratic candidate, whom he had previously opposed on grounds of his Catholicism. Another 'what if?' concerned Nixon's decision not to take up Eisenhower's offer to barnstorm in key states in the final campaign week. Whatever his ambivalence about Nixon, Ike had no respect for Kennedy and tore into him in the few speeches he was allowed to make. In his memoirs, Nixon claimed that he bowed to Mamie

Eisenhower's confidential request to veto Ike's further involvement for fear his heart would give out. It seems more likely, however, that Nixon was so confident of victory that he wanted to claim full credit for it and emerge finally from Eisenhower's shadow. This was a huge mistake – Kennedy's momentum had peaked by the last week and the Republicans' most popular campaigner might have tipped the balance decisively.

By far the most serious of Nixon's self-inflicted wounds was his agreement to debate Kennedy on national television. The first ever presidential debate on 26 September marked the coming of age of television in American politics. A handsome, cool, poised Kennedy gave a confident performance that established his presidential credentials in front of a record audience estimated at eighty million. By contrast, a tired and unwell Nixon (recently hospitalized with an infected knee) appeared anxious, defensive and lacking in confidence. With no make-up covering his five o'clock shadow and sweating under the studio lights, he looked like a caricature of Tricky Dick. Kennedy's campaign was boosted by the viewing public's sense that he had won the debate, but this was a triumph of style not substance. Significantly the radio audience thought Nixon the winner, an impression that a reading of the debate transcript tends to confirm. Nixon later admitted to making 'a basic mistake. . . . I had concentrated too much on substance and not enough on appearance.'[72]

Arguably, however, his real mistake was to have participated in the debates at all. Eisenhower and others counseled that there was nothing to be gained by giving the comparatively unknown Kennedy national exposure and effective parity with the Vice-President. Nixon brushed these doubts aside, adamant that his long experience as a debater and proven skill as a television performer would ensure victory. But what would 'victory' entail? The political equivalent of a knock-out blow is almost impossible to deliver in a presidential debate and it is the unseen public not any studio judge who gets to decide who won and why. If Kennedy 'won' the first debate, Nixon at least held his own in and may even have 'won' the other three debates, but to no avail. Kennedy's real victory was not to have 'beaten' Nixon but to seize the opportunity presented by Nixon to show himself a credible presidential aspirant. This was a crucial factor in an election where little separated the candidates in terms of substantive policy.

There was a final 'what if?', of particular interest in view of America's experience in the 2000 election. Kennedy's triumph was tainted by allegations of extensive ballot rigging in Illinois and Texas, whose combined electoral college votes ensured his victory. These were more serious charges than the miscounting which prompted Al Gore's challenge to the Florida result in 2000. Pat Nixon, Eisenhower and other Republican leaders urged Nixon to contest the results in both states, but at a meeting with Kennedy at Key Biscayne one week after the election he gave a promise not to do so and stuck to this. It is unlikely that a legal challenge would have reversed the election results. Kennedy's margins in both states were much wider than George Bush's wafer-thin Florida majority in 2000. A partial recount later undertaken in 40 percent of Illinois precincts only trimmed a few hundred votes from Kennedy's 8,800 majority (in Texas, his lead was 46,000 votes). Nevertheless legal procedures, if instituted, and any subsequent recount would have taken an inordinate amount of time – an estimated eighteen months in Illinois, even longer in Texas, which had no legal provision for a recount – and thrown American government into disarray. The orderly transfer of power to a new administration could have been long delayed.

Nixon may have calculated that he would forever be damaged by the image of being a sore loser if he set in motion this train of events. In view of his quick decision not to proceed, however, it is more likely that he instinctively acted out of concern not to widen partisan rifts at a time when the Cold War had taken a dangerous turn that put an onus on national unity. He told journalist Earl Mazo that the country could not afford a constitutional crisis 'and I damn well will not be a party to creating one just to become President or anything else'.[73] Nixon deserves credit for this statesmanlike posture, but inside he was burning with resentment. He told friends shortly afterwards, 'We won but they stole it from us'.[74] Believing himself the victim of electoral theft in 1960, Nixon would have no qualms about doing some thieving of his own when he ran for president again.

The murky question of who *really* won in 1960 may never be satisfactorily answered. What was not in doubt was the immensity of Nixon's achievement in coming so close to victory. Whatever blunders he committed, the real albatross round his neck was the Republican Party. America was still a Democratic country and the popular identification of Republicanism with hard times had been strengthened by the recessions of 1958 and 1960. Nixon garnered some 1.5 million fewer votes than Eisenhower in 1956 but still ran 7 percent ahead of his party in

Congress and outpolled GOP House candidates in 235 of the 359 competitive districts.

Given this strong performance, Nixon looked to have unusually good prospects for a man who had just lost a presidential election. Within two years, however, the pundits were writing Nixon's political obituary. In early 1961 he took his family back to California, went to work as a Los Angeles attorney on an annual salary of $100,000, and wrote a best-selling volume of memoirs, *Six Crises*, that earned him $250,000. Wealth was never previously a driving force for Nixon. Now he was intent on making money to finance an affluent lifestyle and provide for his daughters' education. Pat Nixon hoped in vain that the joys of the new life with its opportunity to spend more time with his family might extinguish Nixon's political ambitions. The pull of battle proved too strong. In 1962 Nixon unwisely decided to run for the California governorship. He had little enthusiasm for the job but was answering the call of his party to take on popular Democratic incumbent Pat Brown. He also thought that victory would spare him from having to make a quixotic run for president against an unbeatable Kennedy in 1964 and give him a good base from which to launch another White House bid in 1968.[75] Instead, Nixon put his political future in jeopardy by losing what was for him a skirmish rather than the big battle.

Both sides engaged in dirty tricks and smears in a hard-fought campaign. The Democrats raked up Nixon's clandestine dealings with eccentric billionaire Howard Hughes, which had been revealed in the last days of the 1960 campaign. In 1956 he had interceded personally to obtain a secret Hughes loan on very favorable terms for his brother Donald, whose restaurant business was in trouble. Two months later, the Inland Revenue Service reversed a previous decision in awarding tax-exempt charity status to the Hughes Medical Institute, though whether this was due to Nixon was never proven.[76] Nixon complained bitterly about unfair press coverage of this and other issues. In truth, accustomed to biased coverage in his favor in previous California campaigns, his gripe was more with the even-handedness of the media. Nixon's real problem was that he was happier focusing on national and international issues, but California voters were more interested in parochial affairs like schools, roads and water projects. In the end, he went down to heavy defeat by 297,000 votes out of some six million cast. The next day, tired, dejected and – by some accounts – hungover, Nixon delivered an impromptu, rambling and bitter critique of the media in what he said would be his last ever press conference. This abject performance prompted some observers, including President Kennedy in private, to question his sanity. There was a widespread feeling that he was finished. In *Time* magazine's judgment, 'Barring a miracle, Richard Nixon can never hope to be elected to any political office again.'[77]

But miracles do happen – and Nixon's resurrection came about because the center ground in American politics became a vacant lot in the mid-1960s. With Nixon sidelined, the right seized control of the Republican Party to nominate Barry Goldwater for president in 1964 after a bitter struggle with Nelson Rockefeller. Goldwater's famous clarion call – 'Extremism in the defense of liberty is no vice! Moderation in the pursuit of justice is no virtue!' – was the political equivalent of the bugle that set off the Charge of the Light Brigade. Nixon deemed it an 'unforgivable folly'.[78] Goldwater's futile crusade for New Deal roll-back ended with the Democrats winning the largest ever popular-vote majority and strengthening their hold on Congress. The victorious Lyndon Johnson's mandate was merely to preserve FDR's legacy but he set about building the new Jersualem. The Great Society, as LBJ's new program became known, took liberalism beyond the existing parameters of consensus in its concern to eliminate poverty and establish racial equality. The consequences for the Democratic Party were immense. Many working-class and lower-middle-class whites in the North as well as the South were uncomfortable with this new agenda and resentful that the party of Roosevelt seemed no longer interested in their concerns. By 1968 these voters were ripe for plucking from the Democratic vine.[79]

In 1964 some analysts had pronounced the Republican Party close to extinction as a serious political force. Four years later the situation was tailor-made for the second coming of Richard Nixon, the centrist Republican with strongest appeal to the 'plain folks' that the Democrats had forsaken. Even in supposed retirement he had never stopped running for president. The fortune he could make as an attorney after becoming senior partner in the Wall Street law firm of Mudge, Stern, Baldwin & Todd in 1963 paled in comparison with the seductiveness of his true love. His strategy, as one historian put it, was to play the role of 'unifier and regular party man . . . staking out the middle ground and leaning slightly to the right'.[80] Nixon kept his name in the political spotlight by delivering addresses, giving interviews and writing articles. No one worked harder to breathe new life into the Republican corpse. He was tireless as a party fund-raiser and campaigned strenuously for other Republicans in the 1966 midterm elections. Everywhere he went he won column inches for the GOP and laid the ground for a presidential run in 1968.

The nation that Nixon still aspired to lead was in turmoil. The anguish of John F. Kennedy's assassination in 1963, the ghetto disorders of 1965 and 1967 and the divisiveness engendered by the Vietnam war had dented America's self-confidence. In these circumstances, one aide observed, Nixon's 'quality of unchanging durability promised that he could navigate a way through the chaos for the rest of us'.[81] His campaign slogan – 'Nixon's the One' – conveyed the message that he was the man for the times. In the primaries he began to develop the theme of a political realignment emerging from the turbulence of the 1960s. In one address, Nixon avowed that he spoke for a new majority embodying 'the silent center, the millions of people in the middle of the American poltical spectrum who do not demonstrate, who do not picket or protest loudly'.[82]

The center was exactly where Nixon positioned himself in the presidential nomination contest with rivals from opposite wings of the party. The liberal Nelson Rockefeller had little appeal outside the Northeast. A more serious threat came from the new darling of the right, Governor Ronald Reagan of California, who could put across the conservative message in far more appealing fashion than Goldwater. In an age when most delegates were handpicked by state parties rather than selected by binding primary vote there was a danger that Southern Republicans could switch to Reagan after the first presidential ballot at the Republican convention. To forestall this danger, Nixon reached a pre-convention agreement with his Southern supporters to go slow on racial integration and spend big on defense, a vital cog in the regional economy.[83] This was the first significant indication of the South's growing power in the GOP, which would reach full bloom in the 1990s.

As well as this nod to the future, Nixon tied himself to the heroic past. Chastened by the 1964 debacle, Eisenhower helped Nixon with a preconvention endorsement that was both early and enthusiastic in comparison with previous prevarications. His principal reason for supporting Nixon, Ike avowed, was 'my admiration of his personal qualities: his intellect, acuity, decisiveness, warmth, and above all, his personal integrity'.[84] This blessing was heavy with sword-passing symbolism, since Eisenhower was now a very sick man with less than a year to live. The two men were also bound together in another way: Ike's grandson David and Nixon's younger daughter Julie had become America's newest celebrity sweethearts and were married in December 1968.

With his triumphant nomination, Nixon's comeback was almost complete. He had been in the forefront of Republican politics for twenty years. Nixon rose because he had unmasked one Communist in government and because he was both effective and unscrupulous in tarring the Democrats with the taint of treason. However, he stayed on top because of his skill in positioning himself in the center ground of American politics. The middle is rarely a heroic place in politics. It is broad and shallow in comparison to the deep and narrow passions of the right and left. Nixon's brand of Republicanism lacked the inspirational quality of Taft's or Goldwater's or Rockefeller's but it was the GOP's only hope of power in the postwar quarter-century. Leadership of the Republican Party was something of a poisoned chalice in this era of internal divisions. More than once a despairing Eisenhower fantasized about creating a new center party. Nixon was not ready to give up on the elephant just yet. Alone among GOP leaders of this period, he was the man acceptable to all factions. This was as true in 1968 as it had been in 1952. Critics might argue that this bore testimony to his political hollowness, but it spoke more to his immense skills in holding the party together. However, the middle ground is a movable feast in American politics. By the end of the 1960s the New Deal order was on the verge of collapse. As president Nixon would have the opportunity to build a new majority on the foundations of a reconfigured center.

|4|

American Disraeli

In 1969, Richard Nixon promised 'to begin a decade of govern-ment reform such as this nation has not witnessed in half a century'.[1] Most pundits paid his words little heed, expecting instead that he would be a do-nothing president in domestic affairs. Two decades later, however, Senator Daniel Patrick Moynihan of New York, a Democrat who served as Nixon's domestic policy adviser, adjudged his administration 'the most progressive' of the postwar era.[2] In similar vein, revisionist histo-rian Joan Hoff contended that Nixon's domestic initiatives were far more successful than his better-known foreign policies and 'went beyond, and in some instances significantly tried to redi-rect', New Deal and Great Society programs.[3] However, Nixon did not identify with either FDR or LBJ. Instead, he saw himself as an American version of Benjamin Disraeli. One of the books that made the deepest impression on him as president was Robert Blake's biography of the Conservative Prime Minister of Victorian Britain, which he had read on Moynihan's advice.[4] There were striking similarities between Nixon and Disraeli: they had risen from humble origins to lead right-wing, elitist parties, they were pragmatists rather than ideologues, and they were advocates of social reform to expand working-class support for their party. In an evident reference to his affinity with Disraeli, Nixon once remarked that it was 'Tory men with liberal policies who have enlarged democracy'.[5]

The impressive list of Nixon administration domestic mea-sures includes extension of the Voting Rights Act, postal reorga-nization, the end of Selective Service, a host of environmental reforms (notably the Clean Air Act of 1970, the Noise Control Act of 1972, the Marine Mammal Protection Act of 1972, the Endangered Species Act of 1973 and signing the international

Ocean Dumping Convention in 1972), establishment of the Environmental Protection Agency (EPA), extension of the vote to 18-year-olds, expansion of the national park system, creation of the Occupational Health and Safety Administration, expansion of social security, expansion of the food stamp program, the Rail Passenger Service Act (establishing Amtrak), the State and Local Fiscal Assistance Act of 1972 (revenue-sharing) and large increases in federal support for the arts. Nixon – not Lyndon Johnson – was the last of the big domestic spenders. In the 1971 budget federal spending on domestic programs exceeded that on defense for the first time since 1950. In his final 1974 budget, Nixon allocated 60 percent more for social spending than LBJ had done in his final budget. In terms of the change in domestic spending as a share of gross national product during each administration, Nixon leads all twentieth-century presidents.

Yet Nixon has received precious little credit from historians for this record. This was partly because his program did not have an overarching theme that provided a sense of its direction. It also lacked a symbolic title: at various times Nixon referred to it as the 'New American Revolution' or the 'New Federalism', but these rather leaden terms did not catch on in the manner of the 'New Deal', 'Fair Deal' and 'Great Society'. Acknowledging the unclear identity of his domestic programs, Nixon commented to aide John Ehrlichman in 1972 that 'we have done an excellent job of conceiving them and a poor job of selling them'.[6] The real problem was Nixon's own lack of philosophical convictions and distrust of ideology. A resolute pragmatist, he once told an aide: 'There is only one thing as bad as a far left liberal and that's a damn right wing conservative'.[7] This attitude made Nixon open to new ideas but did not facilitate development of a coherent program. One scholar has claimed that his domestic measures were based on a 'slapdash agenda', 'political expediency' and 'moral indifference', which produced an 'ad hoc pattern of interesting but essentially unco-ordinated and incoherent policy initiatives (or inaction)'.[8] This opinion reflects the suspicion of many historians that Nixon promoted policies in which he did not really believe. Accordingly, they give the congressional Democrats greater plaudits for the enactment of measures whose pedigree was more traceable to their party's tradition than to the Grand Old Party's (GOP).[9]

According to Joan Hoff – once a skeptic herself but more recently the author of the first significant reassessment of Nixon's domestic policies – historians have tended to believe that Nixon could not 'ever do the right thing except for the wrong reason'.[10] His policies are conventionally regarded as the product of political calculation, specifically the need to ensure his reelection, rather than political values. This viewpoint found cogent expression in Melvin Small's recent assessment of the Nixon administration, which combined a relatively favorable evaluation of its domestic achievements with criticism of its motives. While acknowledging that Nixon could fittingly be labeled 'the last liberal president' and that his domestic measures were similar to what a Democratic administration might have pursued, Small contended that it was 'difficult to imagine' a Democratic president acting 'in such a cynical and completely political fashion'.[11] Yet it is equally difficult to imagine a Democratic president who enacted such a substantial body of reforms receiving such meagre scholarly praise and having his motives scrutinized so unfavorably.

A more generous assessment of Nixon's domestic accomplishments is called for, though revisionism should not go too far in casting him as a liberal hero. Some of his domestic initiatives were inspired by good intentions. Many were nakedly political. White House chief of staff H. R. Haldeman recorded in his diary for 10 June 1971 the President's exhortation that it was essential to relate 'everything we do to the political side, without appearing to do so'. Nixon also avowed, 'It's OK to do a few nice things, but damn few. And even if they don't directly help us politically . . . [but] failure to do it looks political in the act of failing to do it, then we should do it because we have to.'[12] But did it really matter whether Nixon's domestic measures were based on calculation rather than conviction? In the view of biographer Tom Wicker, it did not. 'Presidents', he argued, 'are elected to make such judgments and devise acceptable means of doing the necessary'.[13] This verdict is too sweeping. In some cases, Nixon's self-interest was not a drawback, but in others it had a signal effect on the scope and significance of administration policy. Finally, analysis of Nixon's domestic record should not focus exclusively on his liberal deeds. His desire to build a new electoral majority also led him to appeal to the social conservatism of the white working class. In this regard Nixon's rhetorical demonization of a liberal elite intent on undermining traditional values was instrumental in the eventual downfall of the liberal political order.

Nixon's domestic record cannot be considered in isolation from his political need to secure reelection after his surprisingly narrow victory in the 1968 presidential election. What had once promiseu to be an easy triumph over a divided and disillusioned Democratic Party turned into one of the closest races in American history. Though a comfortable winner in electoral college terms, Nixon took only 43.4 percent of the popular vote, the lowest winning margin since Woodrow Wilson in 1912 (only Bill Clinton with 43 percent in 1992 has since fallen below this). Moreover, Nixon was the first president since 1853 to assume office without his party in control of at least one branch of Congress (and the first since the disputed election of 1876 without it controlling the House of Representatives).

After distancing himself from Johnson's Vietnam policy, specifically in regard to stopping the bombing of Vietnam, Democratic presidential candidate Hubert Humphrey had steadily eroded Nixon's lead in the final month of the campaign. Another blow came from the third-party candidacy of former Alabama Democratic governor George Wallace, who won 13.5 percent of the popular vote with a populist right-wing campaign against the social and cultural changes of the 1960s. Having expected to carry the white South and challenge Humphrey for blue-collar whites in the North, Nixon found Wallace eating into both these constituencies. Nevertheless, the Democratic coalition was unraveling – Humphrey won only 42.7 percent of the popular vote just four years after LBJ had won the largest ever share of 61.1 percent. Nixon now had the opportunity to effect a significant electoral realignment if he could bring the Wallace vote into his column in 1972. As two analysts famously put it, this meant appealing to those Americans who were 'unyoung, unpoor, and unblack . . . middle-aged, middle-class, and middle-minded', in other words those who were uncomfortable with the social changes promoted by 1960s liberalism.[14]

In spite of Nixon's political needs, not all his domestic programs were driven by the pursuit of votes. If he did not bleed for the poor in the manner of Lyndon Johnson or Hubert Humphrey, nor was he flinty-hearted toward society's disadvantaged. In particular, Nixon's Native American program was more progressive than anything envisaged by the New Deal and Great Society. It reflected a genuine desire to alleviate the plight of Indians.

Influenced by a group of White House advisers, including John Ehrlichman and Leonard Garment, he declared in a special message to Congress in August 1970 that federal policy should abandon the integrationist approach pursued since World War II in favor of restoring Native American self-determination based on tribal government.

With support from Congress, Nixon increased the Bureau of Indian Affairs (BIA) budget by over 200 percent during his presidency, promoted the Indian Education Act of 1972 to finance new school programs and strengthened tribal land claims. He returned the sacred Blue Lake to the Taos Pueblo of New Mexico in 1970, despite strong opposition from Democratic Senators Clinton Anderson of New Mexico and Henry Jackson of Washington, and settled the Alaska Native Claims in 1971 far more generously than proposed by the Johnson administration. The Nixon administration also responded patiently and constructively to new Indian militancy, such as the occupations of Alcatraz Island in 1969 and Wounded Knee in 1973 and the trashing of the BIA headquarters in 1972. Its initiatives made only a small dent in the poverty and isolation afflicting many Native Americans but they represented an important change for the better in official policy. Nixon could therefore bask in warm praise from groups like the National Congress of American Indians, while Navajo tribal head Peter MacDonald declared that he should 'be viewed as the Abraham Lincoln of the Indian people'.[15]

Nixon's idealistic side was also evident in his health initiatives. His memoirs made much of his own background to explain his activism in this field.[16] Despite Nixon's tendency to be self-serving in his writings, there is no reason to doubt his sincerity on this score. The deaths of his two brothers and the financial burdens from Harold's long illness made a lasting impression. Though Nixon firmly opposed a compulsory or nationalized system of health insurance and delivery, he had long supported a greater federal role in health care. As a new congressman in 1947, he surprised conservative Republicans by supporting a liberal plan to this end, and during his brief Senate tenure he advocated a voluntary system of national health insurance.

Nixon's proposal in 1971 for a National Health Insurance Partnership was consistent with his past record. It called for private employment-related health insurance, a government-sponsored plan for low-income families and health maintenance organizations for better delivery of service. This was the most comprehensive national program proposed by any president between Harry Truman's 1949 initiative and Bill Clinton's 1994 measure, but like them it went down to defeat. Conservatives led by the American Medical Association deemed the plan too radical, while liberal Democrats felt it did not go far enough. Nixon made a final effort to sell the program in a public address in February 1974 that played heavily on his family background, but by now Watergate had severely diminished his influence. He gained some consolation from having obtained federal funding for a 'war' on cancer in 1971, though his hopes that a cure could be found within five years proved grossly optimistic. Less altruistic was his insistence that the initiative be titled the 'President's Cancer Program' in order to reap the public relations benefits.[17]

Even bolder than Nixon's health insurance initiative was his welfare reform proposal, the Family Assistance Plan (FAP), but it too was never enacted. By the late 1960s America's welfare system was widely perceived as being a mess. Between 1959 and 1968 poverty had declined by 41 percent, yet numbers receiving welfare had risen by 36 percent. Like many Americans, Nixon felt that the mushrooming of welfare services in the 1960s had 'encouraged a feeling of dependence and discouraged the kind of self-reliance that is needed to get people on their feet'. In his view, the billions poured into services like Medicaid, food stamps and free school lunches, for which the poor qualified if they could prove their income was below a certain level, absolved them of 'responsibility for spending carefully and looking after themselves'.[18]

On the other hand, Nixon realized that the income-transfer approach of the Aid for Families with Dependent Children (AFDC), created by the New Deal and expanded by the Great Society, was neither efficient nor equitable. Because of requirements for state matching contributions, there were startling variations in payments to equivalent families across the nation. Most states also made higher payments to fatherless families, which many analysts blamed for the increase in absentee fathers and illegitimacy in welfare families. Moreover, revelations of corruption in the New York City welfare department bred concern that a system with a multitude of regulations and huge sums of cash was vulnerable to graft. The FAP was intended to replace the welfare patchwork by a system of direct payments with uniform standards in all states and for which the 'working poor' as well as families with no breadwinner would be eligible. In essence,

Nixon – not FDR nor LBJ – was the first president to propose a guaranteed annual income, from which all poor families would benefit on equal terms regardless of where they lived and whether or not the father worked or resided in the household. Writing in the *New Republic*, the voice of American liberalism, one analyst adjudged the FAP 'the most substantial welfare reform proposal in the nation's history'.[19]

Nixon acted out of belief that the welfare system was in crisis and needed thorough overhaul rather than incremental improvement. A study of the FAP, published as his presidency ended in disgrace, had the title *Nixon's Good Deed*, implying of course that it was his only one![20] While Moynihan, John Ehrlichman and other aides were responsible for developing the proposal, it was typically Nixonian in its boldness and its blend of liberal and conservative principles. The President also supported the FAP for reasons of compassion, which he outlined in a memorandum to speechwriter Ray Price. It helped the working poor, it provided cash to uplift the poor and it encouraged welfare fathers to stay with their families. It eliminated 'the degradation of social workers snooping around' to make sure that fathers were absent and the poor qualified for welfare. Most importantly, it allowed the children of welfare families 'to stand proud with dignity' instead of having to rely on services that marked them out as a class apart. Nixon's views on this score had been reinforced by his daughter Julie's anguish about the segregation of free-lunch recipients from other pupils in the canteen of the predominantly black school in Washington DC where she was doing teaching practice.[21]

On the other hand, the FAP – whose original title of Family Security System was changed on grounds of sounding too 'New Dealish' – departed from the liberal tradition in several ways. The family allowance idea traced its lineage to the negative income tax proposed by conservative economist Milton Friedman to provide a safety net for low-income workers with unstable earnings and replace other forms of welfare. Another element of its agenda was the scaling-down of the federal bureaucracy. Asked by Nixon whether the FAP would 'get rid of social workers', Moynihan played to his prejudices in replying, 'It will wipe them out.'[22] Finally, it embodied conservative notions that the poor had to take some responsibility for self-improvement. Nixon insisted that the Moynihan plan be amended to include conservative presidential counselor Arthur Burns's demand for a work–welfare provision requiring able-bodied heads of family to accept work or training or lose the parent's share of the allowance (the children's portion was unconditional). In this way the President hoped eventually to transform the adult poor from welfare recipients to wage-earners.

Unveiled in August 1969, the FAP proposed a national income floor for a family of four of $1,600 plus a food stamp allotment, but states were allowed to offer supplements beyond the minimum. Right-wing Republicans, headed by California governor Ronald Reagan and supported by the US Chamber of Commerce, complained that the measure would triple welfare rolls and double welfare costs, while conservative Southern Democrats feared that the income floor would diminish the supply of cheap labor that attracted new business into their region. Even Milton Friedman disowned the proposal because it was not tied to tax reduction and roll-back of welfare services.

What surprised the administration, however, was the chorus of complaints from the program's putative allies. The President saw the FAP as the means of helping the disproportionately large number of African-American poor. 'The *whole* problem is the blacks', he told Haldeman and Ehrlichman. 'The key is to devise a system that recognizes this while not appearing to.'[23] Nixon hoped that the inclusion of the mostly white working poor would safeguard the program politically from identification as a racial minority program. It was estimated that the measure would have tripled the gross income of impoverished Southerners, many of them black. However, the National Welfare Rights Organization, which represented poor Northern blacks, objected to the FAP on grounds that the income floor should be raised to $5,500 to support a minimum urban standard of living, the work–welfare requirements would force the unemployed into low-paid and demeaning jobs, and the needs of childless adults (20 percent of the poor) were ignored. Its stand divided liberal Democrats, some of whom supported the FAP as the only politically feasible welfare reform, while others opposed it as inadequate. As a result, though the plan won approval from the House, it was held up by an unholy alliance of conservatives and liberals in the Senate Finance Committee.[24]

An angry Moynihan blamed this failure on a refusal by Democrats to allow their sworn enemy credit for modernizing FDR's legacy. 'You know the libs will never forgive Richard Nixon for this . . .', he fulminated. 'Because he's done what they wouldn't do, what they wouldn't *dare* do. And they can't stand that'.[25] After this setback, Nixon appeared to lose interest in the program. Though the plan was submitted to Congress twice more, and with an income ceiling raised to $2,500, he did not fight hard to save it. On 13 July 1970 Haldeman recorded in his diary that Nixon 'wants to be sure it's killed by Democrats and that we make big play for it, but don't let it pass, can't afford it'.[26] Some scholars seize on this as evidence of his shallow commitment. By contrast, Moynihan was adamant that Nixon 'did not think that society was operating under a perfectly equitable arrangement, and he was prepared to use government where appropriate to make this arrangement more equitable'.[27]

Nixon's cooling on FAP was probably due above all to the realization that it was a lost cause. He later referred to it not inaccurately as 'an idea ahead of its time'.[28] Nevertheless the FAP represented a lost opportunity. While not a miracle cure for poverty, it would have extended federal aid to an additional thirteen million Americans, many of them children, redressed some of the failings of the existing welfare system, and effected a substantial reduction in the number of poor – by three-fifths, at the most optimistic estimate. A later generation of liberals, forced to swallow conservative welfare reform in the shape of the Personal Responsibility and Work Opportunity Act of 1996, would have cause to lament the shortsightedness of their 1970s forebears.[29]

In contrast to his experience with the FAP, Nixon presided over the most significant advances in environmental protection in American history. He is not remembered as a green president because he was a reluctant convert to the cause rather than a true believer. It was political calculation that drove him to respond to growing public concern about the environment, but this does not lessen the importance of what he did.[30] Best-selling jeremiads like Rachel Carson's *Silent Spring* (1962) and Paul Ehrlich's *The Population Bomb* (1968), rising levels of air and water pollution and headline-hitting oil spills combined to raise environmental concerns from an esoteric issue to a mainstream matter during the second half of the 1960s. Nothing symbolized this more than the first Earth Day, held on 22 April 1970, the largest single nationwide demonstration in American history, when possibly as many as three million people engaged in environmental awareness activities. While Congress adjourned to permit its members to participate in well-publicized teach-ins and moratoriums, Nixon took no part in these proceedings. This reflected his personal ambivalence that environmentalism was overrated, elitist and a threat to blue-collar jobs in smokestack industries. Nevertheless, he could not ignore public concern, particularly as the putative front-runner for the 1972 Democratic presidential nomination, Senator Edmund Muskie of Maine, had a fine environmental record. Anxious not to lose votes, Nixon told John Ehrlichman, 'Just keep me out of trouble on environmental issues.'[31] Accordingly the administration promoted middle-way policies that compelled private enterprise to mend some of its ways but fell short of what greens wanted.

Nixon's 1970 State of the Union address was the most comprehensive environmental statement any president had yet made. It contained no less than thirty-six proposals, most of them devised by a White House task force established by John Ehrlichman, assistant to the president for domestic affairs and a former Seattle land-use lawyer with a personal interest in environmental matters. Nixon's principal initiative was the creation of the EPA to centralize federal responsibility for environmental protection, hitherto fragmented among forty-four agencies within nine departments. In the interests of the broader economy, however, he insisted that its policies should be subject to cost-benefit analysis by the Office of Management and Budget (OMB). Ably led by William Ruckelshaus and then Russell Train, the new agency pursued a more forceful agenda than the White House had expected. Required to mediate in its many disputes with the OMB, Nixon tried to make the EPA more conscious of the need to consider the adverse effect of tougher environmental standards on the competitiveness of American industry, but with only partial success. 'I don't believe Train's analyses', the President angrily wrote Ehrlichman in 1971, 'get me an *honest* report (*not* by an environmentalist)'.[32]

Creating the EPA and putting the OMB on its tail typified Nixon's environmental balancing act. In like vein, he cooperated in enacting a significant corpus of environmental laws that required concessions to and from congressional Democrats. The Clean Air Act of 1970, still the most controversial and far-reaching effort to control air pollution, established automobile emission standards that horrified Detroit but were softer than Muskie wanted. Nixon personally thought it went too far and used the 1974 energy crisis to justify a relaxation of the timetable for auto emission reductions. Similarly, the Coastal Zone Management Act of 1972, which protected estuaries, was less sweeping than

Henry Jackson's original bill. The Clean Water Act of 1972 marked the only major breakdown in the administration's strategy of legislative cooperation over the environment. Nixon was prepared to support a $6 billion allocation, vastly more than he originally intended, but he vetoed a bill carrying a $24 billion tag, knowing that he would be overridden. Politics was at work in this instance – and on both sides. With good reason, Nixon suspected that Democrats were trying to draw a veto to embarrass him in the forthcoming election. Rejecting Ehrlichman's counsel that he approve the measure to avoid this trap, he decided on a veto so that he could blame his opponents for any increase in taxes to pay for the measure. Fearful that a partisan vendetta over taxes would blight Nixon's second term, Ehrlichman persuaded him instead to impound the excess funding approved by Congress, a constitutionally dubious action that the legislature found unpalatable.[33]

Environmental activists decried Nixon's tendency to place short-term economic concerns above the nation's long-term interest in protecting the environment. The President once remarked to a speechwriter, 'In a flat choice between smoke and jobs, we're for jobs'.[34] The sole aspect of the environmental cause that truly engaged Nixon's enthusiasm was the expansion of the national park system, which played well with blue-collar voters and drew on his youthful memory of the prohibitive cost of long trips to Yosemite and Yellowstone. As president, he often remarked, 'We have to bring the parks to the people.' To this end his administration transferred over 80,000 acres of federal land to the states, enabling them to develop 642 new parks, many near cities.[35] Otherwise, Nixon's personal sympathies were with private enterprise rather than the green crusade. In an Oval Office conversation with automobile executives Henry Ford II and Lee Iaccoca on 27 April 1971, he declared that environmental activists were intent on '*destroying the system.* They're the enemies of the system . . . *I am for the system'.*[36] When revealed, his words caused outrage, but it was hardly remarkable that a Republican president (or, indeed, a Democratic one) should identify with the capitalist system as the engine of prosperity and jobs.

In the final reckoning, Nixon's environmental record offers support for those who prefer to praise his policies rather than question his motives. Whatever his own beliefs, he saw the need for action and did not prevaricate on protecting the environment.

This contrasted with Ronald Reagan's later policy of inaction on acid rain. A more committed president might have gone further on some issues, but Nixon was not the first leader to pursue moderate aims in the hope of preempting more radical measures. Many of FDR's New Deal initiatives had this very goal. Whoever was president in the early 1970s would have made concessions to business interests on environmental policy, worried about the impact of increased regulation on jobs and tried to control the fiscal costs of environmental action. Nixon's record on the environment was superior to any of his successors. Of course, he had the advantage of being in office when the first environmental initiatives tackled the worst abuses, while later presidents were restricted to fine-tuning measures or incremental improvement, but this does not diminish the significance of his achievement.

Politics was also the principal driver of Nixon's management of the economy, but the outcome was less benign. Though instrumental in ensuring his reelection, economic policy was the most signal failure of his broadly successful domestic agenda. Nixon took office as America's quarter-century-long postwar boom was drawing to an end. The nation soon found itself in the grip of stagflation, an unprecedented combination of inflation and stagnation. The former was the result of funding the Vietnam war and the Great Society through budget deficits rather than tax increases that would have doused demand in a full-employment economy. The latter was the product of America's declining competitiveness in the face of the renewed trade challenge of Western Europe and Japan. Nixon did not cause these problems, but he made them worse. On the economy, he was like a ship's captain who put to sea blind to the turning weather, lacked a reliable chart to plot his course, and sailed to and fro into a variety of ports in the storm, none of which offered safe harbor.

Nixon's gambit as the manager of prosperity was a typically balanced policy of modest restraint aimed at curbing the relatively high inflation inherited from Johnson but without harm to jobs. However, the Federal Reserve trod too hard on the monetary brakes, which plunged the economy into the first recession in a decade and caused the steepest drop in the stock market since the 1930s. Democrats were not slow to draw comparisons between the GOP's Hooverite past and what they called 'Nixonomics'. Under the new administration, Democratic National Committee Chairman Larry O'Brien proclaimed, 'all the things that should go up – the stock market, corporate profits, real spendable income, productivity – go down, and all the things that should go down – unemployment, prices, interest rates – go up'.[37] Having learned the hard way in 1960 that prosperity was the key to electoral success, Nixon changed tack to combat unemployment by unveiling plans in early 1971 for a compensatory budget with a large deficit. 'I am now a Keynesian in economics', he told ABC correspondent Howard K. Smith, who saw this as a damascene conversion akin to 'a Christian crusader saying, "All things considered, I think Mohammed was right"'.[38] It was nothing of the kind. Nixon had been a 'Keynesian' – in the sense that he supported countercyclical measures to combat recession – since the 1950s.

More radical was the so-called New Economic Policy (NEP) of August 1971, a response to the effective breakdown of the Bretton Woods system of fixed gold convertibility that relied on an overvalued dollar as the linchpin of the postwar international economy. It mandated, among other things, the first peacetime wage-price freeze and the suspension of the dollar's convertibility into gold. Keynesianism and controls were palliatives that could serve Nixon's reelection needs but not cure the economy's deep-rooted problems. In his second term Nixon returned like a prodigal to what Council of Economic Advisers Chairman Herbert Stein called the 'old-time religion' of a reduced public sector in the forlorn belief that market economics would work where government had failed.[39]

Nixon's economic record was worse than that of any other postwar president with the exception of Jimmy Carter. A more patient policy of gradual expansion in response to the 1969–70 recession would almost certainly have achieved recovery in time for 1972 without such harmful consequences. Instead, Nixon responded in overexuberant fashion to stoke up a pre-election boom. While the administration went on a spending spree, Nixon ally Arthur Burns obligingly put the money presses into overdrive as the Federal Reserve's new chairman. The NEP wage-price controls masked the inflationary effects of this expansion, so creating a false sense of security. Their imposition represented a U-turn of mammoth proportions for Nixon, whose wartime experience in the Office of Price Administration made him skeptical of controls, so he was anxious for their swift removal. Unfortunately, abandoning them in early 1973 was a masterpiece of mistiming. It released pent-up demand pressures into the economy that converged with cost-push pressures from rising food, commodity and oil prices to send inflation skyrocketing into double-digit figures. The Great Inflation contained within it the roots of the worst recession to hit the United States since the 1930s. The combination of spiraling prices and consequent tightening of monetary policy rapidly doused demand, which was further depressed by the fiscal drag from the administration's new concern to control the budget deficit. Nixon's only consolation was that he was no longer in office when the downturn occurred in late 1974.[40]

In this catalog of failure, probably Nixon's only significant economic achievement was to have taken the United States off the outdated gold standard. However, the brutal manner in which he did so threw the international monetary order into chaos. In early 1973, after efforts to rebuild Bretton Woods on the basis of a devalued dollar had broken down, America forced the rest of the world to accept floating exchange rates, but currency stability remained elusive because of the 1973–4 oil crisis. Though a sophisticated thinker in geopolitics, Nixon was too much a crude nationalist with regard to the international economy. He paid little heed to the problems of America's allies and trading partners. The Oval Office tapes offered trenchant proof of this when they recorded on 21 June 1972 Nixon's response to reports of speculation against the Italian currency: 'I don't give a shit about the lira.'[41]

Nevertheless, it is too simple to blame Nixon's economic errors wholly on political maneuvering. Significantly he was no more successful in economic management when acting out of principle in his second term than he had been when acting out of electoral calculation in his first term. His failure was in large part a reflection of the sorry state of economic knowledge in the face of stagflation. Keynesianism no longer provided the formula for inflation-free prosperity, while the shortcomings of rival monetarist doctrines were revealed by the recessions of 1969–70 and 1974–5. Though Nixon acted out of self-interest in going for expansion and imposing controls in 1971, his actions were consistent with the counsel of economic advisers like Stein and Burns who had the good of the economy at heart. Had the Democrats been in power, the most insightful analysis of the Nixon economy by historian Allen Matusow has concluded that they would hardly have done better and might have subjected the country to an even bumpier ride by pursuing more exuberant policies in 1971–2.[42] In reality no one had the cure for stagflation. There was a final irony in Nixon's search for one. In prioritizing a cure for unemployment in his first term, he acted in accordance with the tenets of the postwar Keynesian consensus, but the inflationary consequences of his program hastened the downfall of the liberal political economy. The conservative policies that he briefly pursued in his second term foreshadowed the triumph under Ronald Reagan in the 1980s of a new economic orthodoxy that regarded interventionist government as the cause of rather than the cure for the nation's economic problems.

Even more political but far more successful than Nixon's management of the economy was his handling of civil rights. He showed his good and bad sides more glaringly on race than on any other issue. Before becoming president, Nixon had forged a relatively good record in this area. Awoken to the nature of Southern racism during his student days at Duke, he had become an honorary member of a California chapter of the National Association for the Advancement of Colored People (NAACP) in 1950. On meeting Martin Luther King at Ghana's independence celebrations in 1957, he invited him back to the White House to discuss civil rights matters. Nixon's strong support for enactment of the 1957 Civil Rights Act convinced King that he would have done more than Eisenhower to help Southern blacks had he been president.[43] Later, as a very public private citizen, Nixon had given unswerving support for enactment of the Civil Rights Acts of 1964 and 1965 (in contrast to another private citizen and future Republican president – George Bush Sr). In recognition of his record, 32 percent of African-American ballots were cast for Nixon in 1960, a figure far beyond current Republican aspirations (George Bush Jr carried only 9 percent in 2000).

As president himself, however, Nixon did not appoint any African Americans to his Cabinet, shunned black congressmen and encouraged the Inland Revenue Service to audit a number of organizations and individuals involved in promoting civil rights. In conversation with aides, he referred to blacks as being 'just down out of the trees' and 'genetically inferior'.[44] Despite this, Joan Hoff contends that his civil rights record 'far outweighed' those of his Democratic predecessors, while Melvin Small adjudges it 'surprisingly progressive'.[45] On the other hand, Nixon's courting of both the white South and Northern blue-collar whites prevented him from taking more committed positions on some racial issues. As such, race offers the litmus test of the cynical Nixon's capacity to do good.

Nixon's greatest achievement was the desegregation of Southern public schools: by 1974, only 8 percent of African-American children in the South attended all-black schools compared with 68 percent in 1969. This was not something that he was wont to boast about. 'Our people have got to quit bragging about school desegregation', he told Ehrlichman. 'We do what the law requires – nothing more.'[46] In fact, Nixon initially tried to do less. To appease Senator John Stennis of Mississippi, whose support it needed for defense-related issues, the administration looked to delay implementation of the desegregation schedule set for thirty-three school districts in the Magnolia State by the outgoing Johnson administration. In doing so, Nixon became the first president to send attorneys into court arguing for the postponement of desegregation already ordered, but the judiciary was not on his side.

In response to a NAACP suit, the Supreme Court ruled in *Alexander* v. *Holmes County Board of Education* (1969) that school desegregation had to be implemeted at once. This closed the loophole in the original *Brown* v. *Topeka Board of Education* judgments of 1954–5, which had only required the South to act with 'all deliberate speed'. Nevertheless, Nixon did change the Johnson administration's policy of cutting off federal funds to non-complying schools. Instead, he approved a plan whereby the Justice Department would bring suit against such schools through the courts. In this way Nixon sought to pull off what the administration's chief Southern strategist, Harry Dent, termed the 'miracle of this age' by achieving 'total desegregation' of Southern schools in such a way that the white South would hold the judiciary responsible.[47]

It is fair to say that Nixon desegregated Southern schools not because it was right but because he had no choice. On the other hand, the record is unambiguous that the Nixon administration did more than any of its predecessors in this field. Once action was unavoidable, Nixon grasped the bull firmly by the horns. According to Dent, the success of the administration's efforts was largely due to 'the personal attention and direction given by the president himself'.[48] One of the more critical of his former associates, John Ehrlichman, also praised Nixon for giving a greater degree of leadership on school desegregation than on any other issue outside foreign policy.[49] The President met frequently with key aides and departmental heads to monitor progress on the matter. He also went into the heart of the South to give an

address in New Orleans in 1970 in support of school desegregation. 'It will be politically harmful', he griped, 'but it will help the
schools, so we'll do it'.[50]

The Nixon administration desegregated Southern schools
without provoking the kind of massive resistance that had swept
the region in the 1950s and early 1960s. Many white Southerners
recognized that such opposition was futile in the wake of the civil
rights revolution, but Nixon also deserves credit for an approach
that emphasized persuasion rather than coercion. Beginning with
the most racist state, Mississippi, the Cabinet Committee on
Education under the leadership of Secretary of Labor George
Shultz set up nonpartisan state advisory commissions to promote
integration. In most cases these bodies brought together for the
first time Southern white and black leaders in the common cause
of building a better future for all the region's children.

By contrast Nixon deserves no plaudits for his handling of
another aspect of school integration. If the law no longer supported segregation, demography still did – and throughout the
whole nation, not just in the South. While African Americans
remained economically trapped in the inner cities, the nation's
growing suburbs were 95 percent white by 1970. More than half
of black schoolchildren in the North attended schools that were
over 95 percent black by 1974. In 1971, the Supreme Court
unanimously ruled in *Swann* v. *Charlotte-Mecklenberg Board of
Education* that the busing of pupils outside their local school districts could be ordered by lower courts as a means of balancing
the racial composition of schools if other methods failed. Busing
proved deeply unpopular with the vast majority of Americans,
who wanted their children educated in their own neighborhoods.
Nixon's own opposition was sincere, and a defensible position if
reasonably articulated, but instead he exacerbated tensions over
the issue for political gain. George Wallace's vow to stop busing
made him the early front-runner for the 1972 Democratic presidential nomination. Determined not to be outbid, Nixon advocated a moratorium on all new busing rulings to allow Congress
time for devising uniform national standards for desegregation
that would utilize busing only as a last resort. He also called for
an appropriation of $2.5 billion to help make the nation's poor-
est schools better places for learning. When Congress rejected
this proposal, the President threatened to seek a constitutional
amendment against busing. This was a wholly cynical ploy. 'I
know it's not a good idea', Nixon confided to aides, 'but it'll

make those [Democratic] bastards take a stand and it's a political plus for us'.[51]

Nixon's Supreme Court nominations further manifested his tendency to play politics over civil rights. In 1968 he had promised Southern leaders that he would select new justices who would slow the pace of racial change. In 1969 he seized the opportunity to nominate South Carolina's Clement F. Haynsworth in place of the liberal Justice Abe Fortas. But concern over Haynsworth's civil rights conservatism combined with conflict-of-interest allegations in his past resulted in him becoming the first Supreme Court nominee since 1930 to experience Senate rejection. Seventeen Republicans, including minority leader Hugh Scott of Pennsylvania, joined thirty-eight Democrats to vote against him. Determined to nominate a son of Dixie, the President angrily instructed Harry Dent to find a suitable candidate 'further south and further to the right' of Haynsworth.[52] A onetime advocate of segregation and white supremacy, Florida's G. Harrold Carswell, got the nod, but the choice was ill-advised because his judicial record was mediocre – his circuit court judgments had experienced double the average reversal rate by higher courts. His defenders only made things worse: Republican Senator Roman Hruska of Nebraska famously avowed that even mediocre people deserved 'a little representation . . . and a little chance'.[53] As had been the case with Haynsworth, presidential use of strong-arm tactics against wavering Republicans also backfired. Following Carswell's rejection, Nixon told journalists that he had 'reluctantly concluded' he could not appoint to the Supreme Court a Southerner 'who believes as I do in the strict construction of the Constitution'. Praising the two rejects, he avowed that the real issue was their 'misfortune of being born in the South'.[54]

Nixon's nomination and defense of the two Southerners earned him huge political credit. In Dent's opinion, 'No action by the president did more to cement the sinews of the southern strategy'.[55] White Southerners now saw that they had an ally in the White House. As further proof of this, Nixon eventually succeeded in changing the tenor of the Supreme Court from liberal to moderate conservative through his opportunity to make four new appointments to this body. Paradoxically, these included a Southerner – Virginia's Lewis Powell – who grew increasingly liberal as time passed. Perhaps Nixon's most significant appointment was Arizona's William Rehnquist, who would later be promoted to Chief Justice by Ronald Reagan in 1986. This cerebral conservative's belief in states' rights had made him an opponent of the 1964 Civil Rights Act and a fan of the Supreme Court's 1896 *Plessy* v. *Ferguson* judgment that employed the 'separate but equal' doctrine to approve state-mandated segregation. As Rehnquist's appointment indicated, Nixon's legacy was a Supreme Court that was no longer in the vanguard of the twentieth-century struggle to expand black rights. Proof of this came shortly before he quit office. The *Milliken* v. *Bradley* ruling of 1974, which effectively invalidated cross-district busing, marked the first occasion since 1954 that the Court had not approved a desegregation remedy advocated by the NAACP.

Nixon had always believed that jobs and prosperity would do more to uplift blacks than enforced desegregation. To this end he built substantially on the Johnson administration's modest initiatives to assist African Americans in the economic arena. Nixon established the Office of Minority Business Enterprise, whose remit was to channel federal loans and grants to minority-owned businesses and to set aside fixed percentages of federal contracts for them. 'Politically, I don't think there are many votes in it for us', Nixon told Commerce Secretary Maurice Stans, 'but we'll do it because it's right'.[56]

More controversial was the administration's initiative to guarantee minority access to decently paid blue-collar jobs in construction and other industries that had a history of racial exclusion. Known as the Philadelphia Plan, after the city where the first agreement was made, the program established federal authority to require firms with federal contracts to set goals and timetables for minority hiring.[57] Unions immediately denounced this as a racial quota system that practiced reverse discrimination against whites, while some black organizations and their Democratic allies called for even more sweeping affirmative action targets. Before long the two sides were locked in combat over this emotive issue, while the Nixon administration, in Ehrlichman's words, 'was located in the sweet and reasonable middle'.[58] Nixon was not blind to the political advantages of this position with regard to winning blue-collar support. While his administration continued to implement the most significant program of affirmative action to date, he began to speak out against racial-preference policies as unfair. 'When young people apply for jobs . . .', Nixon declared in 1972, 'and find the door closed because they don't fit into some numerical quota, despite their ability, and they object, I do not think it is right to condemn those young people as insensitive or even racist'.[59]

Statements such as this were typical of Nixon's first-term rhetoric on racial issues. They stood in marked contrast to the words of John Kennedy and Lyndon Johnson, both of whom had used the presidential bully-pulpit to identify their office both symbolically and substantively with the civil rights cause. In defence of his boss, speechwriter Pat Buchanan claimed: 'Though Mr Nixon's government shorted the civil rights movement on rhetoric, it was not short on delivery'.[60] Similarly, Attorney General John Mitchell told black leaders in 1969, 'You would be better advised to watch what we do, rather than what we say.'[61] Blacks had long claimed that white liberals fobbed them off with fine words in place of action on civil rights, but they had cause to miss such rhetoric in the Nixon presidency.

Nixon developed a message that straddled support for the abstract principle of racial equality with skepticisim about government enforcement of this ideal. This entailed abandonment of the liberal paradigm of social responsibility in favor of the conservative paradigm of legitimate self-interest. Nixons offered comfort to those working-class and middle-class whites who believed that denial of legal and political rights to African Americans was wrong but balked at having themselves to bear the cost for socio-economic equality. The New Deal had made the Democrats the party of the working man. Through his rhetoric on race, Nixon helped to make the Republicans the party of the average white American. According to political analysts Thomas and Mary Edsall, he pointed the way to a new 'non-economic polarization of the electorate . . . isolating a liberal, activist, culturally-permissive, rights-oriented and pro-black Democratic Party against those unwilling to pay the financial and social costs of this reconfigured social order'.[62]

There is no easy answer to the question of whether African Americans were better or worse off as a result of Nixon's policies. In the plus column could be counted the desegregation of Southern public schools, aid to black business and the attempt to increase black employment in firms with government contracts. In the opposite column were his Supreme Court appointments and the disassociation of the rhetorical presidency from the cause of equality. At first sight the balance sheet appears to weigh heavily in favor of the positives. However, Nixon did lay the foundations for the political and judicial counter-attack that would constrain progress toward racial equality and in some instances reverse it from the late 1970s down to the present day.

Nixon's handling of race fitted into the political strategy outlined by campaign aide Kevin Phillips in *The Emerging Republican Majority*, which became something of a bible for the new administration.[63] Boldly (if not always accurately) reinterpreting the past, Phillips claimed that ethnic, racial and regional antagonisms had been the bedrock of party supremacy in every electoral cycle from 1800 to 1968. The party that aligned with the hardworking, culturally mainstream masses against the Northeastern establishment gained national dominance for a generation or more. In the 1930s, the Democrats had won the hearts of the working class through New Deal programs that taxed the wealthy few for the benefit of the many, but thirty years later the Great Society fractured this alignment by taxing the many on behalf of the impoverished few. In addition, Phillips argued, liberalism had offended the social conservatism of ordinary Americans through its association with unpatriotic dissent against the Vietnam war, judicial and bureaucratic efforts to impose social equality between the races, the cultural progressivism of the 1960s (sexual freedom, women's rights, gay rights, the youth rebellion), and the mollycoddling of law-breakers through Supreme Court judgments that seemingly prioritized the rights of the accused over those of the victim (most notably the *Miranda* ruling of 1966).

According to Phillips, the formerly conservative Northeastern establishment had now recast itself in liberal mold. The opportunity therefore beckoned for the once elitist Republicans to redefine themselves as the party of populist conservatism. In this way, they could gain the support of the Sunbelt states of the South and West, the suburbs, and the socially conservative blue collars – especially Catholic ones. The Democrats would be left with upper-income liberals, blacks and Latinos as their only reliable voting blocs. This was a blueprint perfectly suited to the talents of Richard Nixon. As *Fortune* editor James Reichley observed, Phillips's advice to his boss was akin to Machiavelli counseling Cesare Borgia, 'describing in naked words what his hero had all along been doing by instinct'.[64]

Measures with a liberal pedigree had their place in the new conservative strategy. The groups targeted for realignment into the Republican majority were still beneficiaries of Roosevelt's legacy. Accordingly, Nixon happily expanded the New Deal state in pursuit of blue-collar votes. The most obvious examples were the creation of the Occupational Safety and Health Administration, which made the workplace safer for labor, and the 20 percent increase in social security benefits enacted in 1972. In essence, Nixon's populist conservatism was socio-cultural rather than socio-economic in character.

Some first-term initiatives sought roll-back of the social legacy of the 1960s. These included a raft of law-and-order initiatives: the District of Columbia Crime Control Act of 1970, which featured tougher bail and search procedures; prosecution of the Chicago Eight group of radicals, who had been indicted for traveling across state lines to foment anti-war riots (their 1970 convictions were later overturned); and support for the Federal Bureau of Investigation campaign, which resulted in the imprisonment of over a thousand Black Panthers and effectively destroyed their organization. Though Nixon supported measures outlawing gender discrimination in the workplace, his stand on other women's issues outraged feminists and gratified traditionalists. In particular, he vetoed the Child Development Act of 1971, which would have provided free child care for the poor, on grounds partly of cost and partly because its communal approaches to child-rearing would 'Sovietize' the American family.[65] The veto reinforced two traditional attitudes, firstly that the nuclear family was natural and private, and secondly that child-rearing was primarily the mother's responsibility. Nixon also expressed opposition to abortion and restricted its use in military hospitals. His actions caused Democratic Representative Bella Abzug of New York to label him 'the nation's chief resident male chauvinist' at a National Women's Political Caucus meeting in 1973.[66] The Nixon administration also ran down Great Society anti-poverty initiatives, like the Job Corps and the Youth Program, which were widely perceived as boondogglings that ate up the tax dollars of hard-working families.

Nevertheless Nixon's reputation as a conservative rests more on his words than his deeds. As one historian noted, 'Brilliant opportunist that he was, the president talked like a grassroots conservative while often governing like a liberal'.[67] A British commentator recently adjudged Nixon 'the most influential 20th century conservative' because his strategy of vilifying liberalism as the preserve of an educated elite intent on destroying traditional values was adapted by Ronald Reagan and Margaret Thatcher to

legimimize their economic policies.[68] Such a judgment underesti-
mates the significance of the anti-statist ideology of two leaders
who gave their names to variants of conservatism. In contrast to
them, Nixon made no serious attempt to conceptualize a new
conservative ideology in place of the existing liberal vision.
However, Nixonian rhetoric played a crucial role in the disintegration of the electoral coalition on which liberalism depended.
The Republican base had always been white middle-class voters.
Now that postwar affluence had made many ordinary Americans
into home-owners and consumers, Nixon seized the chance to
expand the GOP's appeal across income and occupation lines by
making it the party of middle-class *values* of hard work, family
and community.

In 1969, the administration set up a Middle American
Committee to plot the creation of the new majority. 'Middle
America' was a term coined by the media to describe the non-cos-
mopolitan, non-rich but non-poor, law-abiding, patriotic mainstream. In 1970 *Time* magazine made Middle Americans its
'Man and Woman of the Year' and called Nixon 'the embodiment of Middle America'.[69] It was not a term the President
warmed to because he did not 'think people like to be known as
such'.[70] Accordingly, 'Middle America' was soon replaced in the
administration's lexicon by 'Silent Center' and 'Silent Majority'.
Though Nixon's most famous evocation of this group was his
nationally televised speech of November 1969 urging 'the great
silent majority of my fellow Americans' to support his Vietnam
policies, he had aimed his words at them long before this. In
many respects the quintessential 'silent majority' speech (though
it did not employ this term) was his 1968 nomination acceptance
address, which struck many of the notes that would form a con-
tinuous refrain over the next four years. With the nation beset by
protests, riots and lawlessness, Nixon called for another voice to
be heeded: 'It is the voice of the great majority of Americans, the
forgotten Americans, the non-shouters, the non-demonstrators.
They're good people, they're decent people. They work and they
save and they pay their taxes and they care. They work in
American factories, they run American businesses, they serve in
government. They provide most of the soldiers who die to keep it
free. They give drive to the spirit of America.'[71]

Nixon's rhetoric not only delineated 'the silent majority' but
also defined its enemy in the shape of liberal elites. He had always
been at his most effective when practising the politics of division.

For the erstwhile red-baiter who had associated liberals with treason some twenty years earlier, it was virtually a case of business-as-usual to portray them now as threats to mainstream values. Judges and bureaucrats who tried to enforce busing came in for particular condemnation. The school bus, Nixon declared in 1972, had become 'a symbol of social engineering on the basis of abstractions' and was 'wrenching . . . children away from their families and from the schools their families may have moved to be near'.[72] Radical anti-war protesters and the professors and politicians in the liberal establishment who supported them were another favorite target. Responding to hecklers (including future biographer Stephen Ambrose) at Kansas State University in 1970, he denounced 'those who would choose violence and intimidation to get what they wanted. Their existence is not new. What is new is their numbers, and the extent of the passive acquiescence, or even fawning approval, that in some fashionable circles has become the mark of being "with it".'[73] Above all, Nixon portrayed himself as the defender of hard-working Americans against the anti-meritocratic, redistributionist bent of liberals. In a 1972 radio address, he avowed there were 'a great many people in politics . . . who believe that the people just do not know what's good for them. Putting it bluntly, they have more faith in government than they have in people. . . . To them, the will of the people is the "prejudice of the masses".'[74]

In the 1970 midterm campaign White House efforts to focus voter resentment against socio-cultural liberalism had not played well because recession had elevated pocketbook concerns over social issues. For his reelection, however, Nixon had stoked up an economic boom and was close to ending American involvement in Vietnam. His position was further strengthened because he no longer had to worry about being outflanked in the South by George Wallace, whose bid to become the Democratic nominee was terminated by an attempted assassination that left him permanently disabled. Mainly as a result of new party rules governing presidential selection but also (see pp. 179–80) partly because of dirty tricks by the Nixon campaign organization, the Democrats had ended up choosing the most left-wing candidate in their circle of contenders, Senator George McGovern of South Dakota.

Though an outspoken critic of American intervention in Vietnam, McGovern was by no means a radical, but television images of strident feminists, militant blacks and long-haired anti-war protesters at the Democratic convention saddled him with the reputation of being one. Republicans gleefully depicted McGovern as 'the candidate of the 3 A's: acid, abortion and amnesty'.[75] While rarely deigning to mention him by name, the Nixon organization brought the social-issue strategy fully into play against the hapless Democrat. It was a supreme irony that this father of five, Methodist lay preacher, former World War II bomber pilot and son of the prairie heartland could be depicted as the candidate of cosmopolitan liberal elites. Nevertheless, in the words of a secret Nixon campaign memo, he was to be portrayed 'as the Establishment's fairhaired boy and RN postured as the Candidate of the Common Man, the working man'.[76]

Nixon was reelected with 60.7 percent of the popular vote compared with McGovern's 37.5 percent, the largest ever Republican majority. He carried every state except Massachusetts and the District of Columbia, a GOP winning margin in the electoral college only bettered by Ronald Reagan in 1984. He was the first Republican presidential candidate ever to carry a majority of the Catholic vote. The hawkishly anti-Communist American Federation of Labor-Congress of Industrial Organizations sat out the campaign in protest at McGovern's opposition to Vietnam and big defense spending. This helped Nixon carry 52 percent of the blue-collar vote compared with just 38 percent in 1968. In the South, a number of Democratic governors, led by Jimmy Carter of Georgia, refused to endorse the national ticket because of McGovern's unpopularity in their region. It was small wonder, therefore, that the President's support from white Southerners rose to 72 percent from 38 percent in 1968.

Nixon had created his new majority, but whether it was a new Republican majority was more dubious. Polls indicated that only 23 percent of the electorate were Republican identifers, 1 percent fewer than in 1968. The GOP gained only twelve seats in the House of Representatives and actually lost two in the Senate. Nixon had achieved an unwanted first in becoming the only president ever to win two terms without his party once having a majority in either chamber of Congress. Despairing of his party, the President had fought a personal campaign that extolled his record in office. The word 'Republican' hardly ever passed from his lips during the election. With the campaign over, Nixon turned his attention to developing a new party based on the new majority during his second term.[77]

Nixon had previously toyed with calling a convention to create a new center-right party to fight the 1972 election. This reflected his view, expressed to Haldeman on 17 January 1972, that 'both parties have had it'.[78] Nixon was almost as disenchanted with his own party as with the Democrats. Increasingly he found himself fed up with the GOP congressional leadership that complained about lack of consultation and refused to be cheer-leaders for his legislation. Liberal Republicans who attacked his Vietnam policies irked him even more. Above all he resented having to carry the Republican elephant on his shoulders rather than being able to ride on its back. The new party idea was no pipe dream. In the four months after the 1972 election the administration was engaged in serious discussions with at least forty Democratic congressmen to entice them to switch parties.[79] Many of these were Southerners who felt wholly out of step with the McGovernization of their own party. Such a mass defection would have given the GOP control of the House of Representatives.

A fusion of Republicans and Southern Democrats could have been the first step to the creation of a new party. The next would have been the anointing of Nixon's chosen heir. Most assuredly he did not want this to be Vice-President Spiro T. Agnew. Formerly Maryland governor, Agnew owed his 1968 nomination to Nixon's need for a running-mate who could help him with Southern voters, but this son of poor Greek immigrants proved more useful as a conduit to the broader constituency of the silent majority. Agnew's hard-hitting attacks on so-called Radiclibs in the 1970 midterm campaign convinced Nixon to keep him on the ticket for 1972.[80] On other issues the Vice-President was something of an embarrassment. He neither understood nor sympathised with détente and angered the White House by giving off-the-record press briefings critical of the China initiative.[81] Nor did he comprehend the essentially non-partisan approach to building the new majority at home. In the 1972 campaign he tore into the Democrats in violation of express orders not to use party labels when attacking liberals. A frustrated Nixon wryly commented to Haldeman that 'he seems to have taken our counsel about 50%!'[82] By contrast, the President's preferred successor, John Connally, was politically astute, had shown a keen appreciation of power when serving as Treasury Secretary in 1971–2, and was on-message regarding détente. This former Texas Governor had the added advantages of being a Democrat and a

Southerner. In short, Connally appeared perfect in Nixon's eyes to nurture the development of the new party that he intended to build.[83]

The escalation of the Watergate scandal in the spring of 1973 killed off whatever prospects there were for Democratic congressional defections and new party development. Nixon's downfall was also instrumental in the rightward shift of the GOP that he had spent a political lifetime battling against. Notwithstanding a token conservative challenge from Ohio's John Ashbrook in the 1972 presidential primaries, conservative Republicans had been muted in their criticisms of Nixon's deviations from their faith. His conservative image and anti-liberal rhetoric shielded him from the kind of attacks that Eisenhower had experienced for much milder transgressions in the 1950s. However, Nixon's personal disgrace cast a shadow over the policies with which he was associated. For the Republican right it became open season to attack him for the loss of Vietnam, détente with Communism, huge budget deficits and the growth of government. In the conservatives' reinterpretation of the past, the 1972 victory was tranformed into an endorsement of their agenda rather than of Nixon's presidency. In 1976 Ronald Reagan nearly wrested leadership of the party from the moderate Gerald Ford with the claim 'The mandate of 1972 still exists.'[84] Four years later conservatives would insist that Reagan's thumping election as president, far from being a negative comment on Jimmy Carter's failures, was the landslide endorsement of their values that 1972 had foreshadowed and Watergate had postponed.[85]

However much he was disdained by conservatives and liberals, Nixon's domestic record as president was undeniably significant for both its conservative and its liberal aspects. His place in American political history was that of a transitional leader whose period of office coincided with the decline of a liberal order and the emergence of a more conservative one. The most liberal Republican president in US history, Nixon did not breathe new life into a liberalism that was in the throes of decline during his tenure in office. With the exception of his environmental initiatives, his domestic agenda was primarily a refinement of the New Deal–Great Society state and was soon overtaken by the Reagan Revolution. Nixon's conservative significance was similarly transitional. This judgment may well have required amendment had he survived longer in office to pursue the conservative economic and social policies of his abbreviated second term. As things were, however, Nixon only showed the right how to gain power, not what to do with it in government, so his status as a conservative leader is overshadowed by Ronald Reagan's.

This is not to downplay his domestic achievement. In a 1978 conversation Robert Blake told Nixon that Disraeli had been there 'to govern and deal with events as they came along'. The former president responded that 'this was really just about all that a politician could do'.[86] In fact Nixon himself had done a great deal more than this. He had provided strong leadership in a period of change and uncertainty. The fact that he can legitimately be seen as both the last liberal president and the first in a new cycle of conservative presidents is testimony to his significance in shaping American politics in a time of transition.

|5|

Cold Warrior

For much of his political career, Richard Nixon was, in Stephen Ambrose's words, 'the world's best-known anti-Communist'.[1] This was a thoroughly deserved reputation. Among American leaders in the 1950s and 1960s, Nixon had no equal as a hard-line Cold Warrior. Yet his career as an anti-Communist was complex and multi-faceted. Initially he made his name as a hunter of domestic subversives. In the early 1950s the Korean war and elevation to the vice-presidency shifted his focus to the international threat of Communism. For almost twenty years Nixon led the calls for no accommodation, no compromise, only victory in America's dealings with the Soviet Union and its allies. As president, however, he was the architect of a new era of détente with the Communist world. Nixon's previous Cold War militancy permitted him to effect this change free from charges of being soft on Communism that would have hamstrung anyone else. In spite of this, he could not break free from the Cold War because of unfinished business in Vietnam. He promised 'peace with honor' in Southeast Asia but ended up with neither.

Nixon was, as Tom Wicker observes, 'a creature of the Cold War'.[2] His investigation of Alger Hiss just as this conflict was beginning was the making of his career. His hard-hitting attacks on Democratic foreign policy failures in Asia promoted his rise through Republican ranks. His hopes of succeeding to the presidency in 1960 rested on his reputation as a tough Cold Warrior. Pursuing post-resignation rehabilitation, he portrayed himself as a foreign policy sage who knew how to deal with the Soviets in an era of renewed Cold War. With the collapse of the Soviet Union, he became active in his final years in seeking to protect the legacy of Cold War victory. On 25 February 1992, Nixon sent President George Bush a memorandum criticizing his failure to provide aid and loans to build up democracy in the new Russia. A similar memorandum, sent to fifty American leaders and opinion-makers, was entitled 'How the West Lost the Cold War'.[3]

As a Cold Warrior, Nixon embodied the complex relationship between power and principle in America's struggle against Communism. A cynic about so many things, he believed whole-heartedly that Communism was a terrible evil and had designs of world domination. The United States could have combated Communism by making itself a moral force for good in the world. It could have aligned with the aspirations of colonial peoples for political and economic independence, it could have used its influence to strengthen democracy and human rights in the third world, and it could have used its vast wealth to alleviate poverty in developing nations. Instead the United States chose to contain Communism through building up its military power and engaging in a global struggle for hegemony with the Soviet Union. Moral idealism sometimes shaped Nixon's words and deeds as a Cold Warrior. He fought hard for foreign aid, which many congressmen resented as a giveaway program, and he tried to educate the public about America's responsibilities in the world. In this regard, Stephen Ambrose concludes, 'he did good service for his country and mankind'.[4] Usually, however, Nixon acted on the belief that Communists only respected superior force and the threat of its use.

As a Cold Warrior, Nixon tended to merge the personal and the political. Three of the six crises that formed the subject of his first memoir – the Hiss case, his confrontation with angry demonstrators in Caracas in 1958 and his debate with Nikita Khrushchev in Moscow in 1959 – were Cold War episodes. In two other crises – Eisenhower's 1955 heart attack and the 1960 presidential election – Nixon came close to inheriting the office charged with ensuring the nation's security against the Communist threat.[5] Even the remaining crisis – the slush-fund affair – had a Cold War dimension for Nixon, who saw it as the revenge of the Eastern Establishment for the Hiss investigation. Toward the end of the Checkers speech, he avowed that, regardless of whether or not he stayed on the Republican ticket, he would 'campaign up and down America until we drive the crooks and Communists and those that defend them out of Washington'.[6]

Nixon the Cold Warrior pursued power for himself, his party and his country. He could identify his interests as America's interests, his enemies as freedom's enemies and his Democratic critics as advocates of appeasement. Those scholars who interpret Nixon primarily from a personality perspective lay great stress on his dichotomous attitude toward strength and weakness. In their view his determination to avoid appearing weak drove him to appear exceptionally strong. Whether or not this is an accurate assessment of Nixon's psyche, it is certainly applicable to his Cold War stance. Nixon believed that the Soviets would take advantage unless he and his country appeared strong. As Henry Kissinger observed, 'There was nothing he feared more than to be thought weak'.[7] Nixon also believed that knowledge was power. Accordingly, he set out in the 1950s to make himself one of the best-informed people in American government about global affairs, a goal that served his personal ambitions to become president and his country's need for knowledgeable Cold War leadership.

What Nixon was never able to do as a Cold Warrior was unite the country behind him. Historians acknowledge the existence of a Cold War consensus from the late 1940s to the late 1960s. There was a high degree of domestic agreement about the threat of Communism until Vietnam bred disunity. However, Nixon continually tested the limits of consensus in demanding that the United States confront Communism by whatever means were necessary and denigrating the Democrats as the party of retreat and surrender.

Nixon's status as a divisive Cold Warrior grew out of the Hiss affair. In his view, the case 'proved beyond any reasonable doubt the existence of Soviet-directed Communist subversion at the highest levels of American government'.[8] Whether it actually did so is a matter of dispute. The controversy that the case can still generate makes understandable the passions it aroused a half-century ago. Hiss and his liberal supporters always maintained he was the innocent victim of Cold War hysteria. A well-researched scholarly study by historian Allen Weinstein, *Perjury*, published in 1978, seemingly demonstrated Hiss's guilt, but critics accused it of distorting evidence.[9] The opening of the former Soviet Union's archives in the 1990s further muddied the waters. In 1992 General Dimitri Volkogonov, chairman of the Russian commission on the KGB and military intelligence records, stated that there was no documentary proof that Hiss was a Soviet spy. An overjoyed 90-year-old Alger Hiss claimed vindication. An infuriated nearly 80-year-old Richard Nixon raged: 'Hiss was a goddamned spy, and they still don't want to admit that I was right.'[10]

Fresh evidence was then unearthed, first in the Hungarian

archives and then by Weinstein's new research in hitherto
unopened Soviet archives, that pointed once more to Hiss's guilt.
This was apparently corroborated by the release in 1996 of US
National Security Agency files of American intercepts of Soviet
messages suggesting Hiss was a spy codenamed ALES. In 1998,
some four years after Nixon's death, a *New York Times* editorial
concluded with near finality but still not without some equivoca-
tion: 'Alger Hiss was most likely a Soviet agent.'[11] This was
assuredly not the last word on the affair. While supporters of the
now dead Nixon claimed that their hero had been right all along,
rebuttals from the champions of the also deceased Hiss kept the
issue alive.

After the Hiss case, Nixon did not become directly involved in
any other investigation of suspected Communists. The enemy
without rather than within became his main concern. In his memoirs, Nixon declared that Winston Churchill's Iron Curtain
speech, delivered at Fulton, Missouri, in March 1946, had first
alerted him to the Soviet threat.[12] As a result, he readily supported the Truman administration's 1947 program of aid to
Greece and Turkey that inaugurated the strategy of containing
Communism. In contrast, many conservative Republicans,
headed by Senator Robert Taft of Ohio, opposed this on grounds
of cost and were reluctant to sanction new intervention in
Europe. Nixon also backed Marshall Plan aid to rebuild the war-
torn economies of Western Europe as a bulwark against
Communism, a program that many of his constituents considered an expensive foreign giveaway.

Nixon's researches as a Whittier student debater some fifteen
years previously had persuaded him of the virtues of international economic aid.[13] His education on the matter was completed by service on the bipartisan congressional select committee
delegated to visit Europe under the leadership of Representative
Christian Herter in 1947 and report on the need for the foreign
aid plan advocated by Secretary of State George Marshall. In six
weeks of travels throughout non-Communist Europe Nixon
came to appreciate at first hand the need for humanitarian assistance to prevent starvation and aid to reconstruct industry.
Unless the United States provided this on a long-term basis, he
concluded, 'Europe would be plunged into anarchy, revolution,
and, ultimately, communism'.[14] On his return home he worked
hard to convince his constituents that Marshall aid was a matter
not only of conscience but also of national self-interest, because

the fall of Europe would leave the United States to face the Communist threat alone. It was an impressive performance for a freshman congressman previously unversed in foreign affairs but who now revealed an intelligent and undogmatic understanding of Europe's situation.

Nevertheless, Nixon became a critic of the Truman administration's policies in Asia. In essence America's Cold War strategy, as outlined in the Truman Doctrine of 1947, aimed to prevent the further expansion of Communism. It rested on the assumption that containment would lead ultimately either to the disintegration of Communism through its internal contradictions or to its accommodation with the West in order to gain access to trade and investment. Containment had been pursued successfully through political and economic means in Europe, but this form of assistance had not saved Chiang Kai-shek's Nationalist government in China. From the Truman administration's perspective, stated in its China White Paper of 1949, nothing that the United States could have done within reasonable limits of its capabilities could have changed this outcome because Chiang's unpopular, inefficient and venal regime had squandered $3 billion of aid. Republicans, by contrast, avowed with varying degrees of vehemence that Chiang had been betrayed. Nixon joined in the attack but did not go as far as Joseph McCarthy in claiming that China was lost to Communism because of traitors in the State Department. Nor did he go along with the demands of the China Lobby, a loosely organized conservative group, for an Asia-first policy against Communism. However, he did blame the loss of China on Truman's failure to combat Communism in Asia with the same vigor as in Europe. 'Communism', he declared in 1950, 'requires a worldwide resistance'.[15]

The Korean war marked Nixon's emergence as one of the foremost advocates of Cold War victory in Asia. Truman initially committed the US to lead a United Nations intervention in defense of South Korea against invasion by Communist North Korea. As Burton Kaufman has observed, 'after the Communist victory in China, Korea became the only symbol left of America's willingness to contain Communist expansion in Asia'.[16] Early military success prompted the President to pursue the unification of Korea free of Communism, but this provoked China to intervene in the conflict and a long stalemate ensued. The last thing the Truman administration with its Europe-first outlook wanted was a major war in Asia, so it reverted to fighting a limited war for the limited goal of preserving South Korea. In April 1951 the President fired General Douglas MacArthur as military commander in Korea for insubordination in publicly calling for all-out war against China. This provoked another heated debate between the administration and critics of its Asia policy. Though a freshman senator, Nixon was delegated by Robert Taft to spearhead Senate Republicans' demands for MacArthur's reinstatement. This was a reward for his recent demolition of Helen Douglas and his relative moderation in comparison to wilder Republican anti-Communists.

In a press statement, Nixon avowed that 'the choice is not between a little war or a big war . . . [but] between continuing the Korean war with no real hope of ending it or of adopting a new policy which will allow our Commanders in the field to end the war with a military victory'.[17] In the Senate Nixon echoed MacArthur's call for Chiang's forces, currently ensconced in Taiwan, to be unleashed for a diversionary attack on China that would compel redeployment of Communist troops from Korea. He also advocated strategic bombing of targets inside China and a naval blockade to cut off China's trade with European countries, especially Britain. The Democrats countered that this would alienate America's United Nations allies and could bring the Soviets into the war in support of China. Was Nixon playing politics with the issue? He assuredly was – there was no chance that the Truman administration or the American people would support such a venture, so he was out to score partisan points. Did he believe in his words? Just as assuredly he did – and would continue to believe in the possibility of military victory over Communism in Asia until Vietnam compelled a reassessment.

Nixon's focus on Asia did not cause him to neglect the crusade against Communism elsewhere. He still supported generous aid to reconstruct Europe and big appropriations for the fledgling North Atlantic Treaty Organization. His ability to bridge the Republicans' Europe-first Eastern internationalist camp and their Asia-first camp helped earn him the vice-presidential nomination in 1952. However, Nixon soon found that Eisenhower's foreign policy views were much closer to the Truman–Acheson line than to his own. In 1950 the Truman administration's National Security Council memorandum 68 (NSC-68) heralded the globalization and militarization of containment. Eisenhower broadly upheld this strategy but scaled back the grandiose defense estimates inherited from Truman. As president he wanted a more cost-effective military containment based on air-atomic superiority over the Soviets. Peace in Korea and the avoidance of other land wars in Asia were essential to this end. In May 1953 Eisenhower secretly warned Beijing that all limits on weapons and targets would be removed unless a ceasefire was agreed. This was a thinly veiled threat of atomic warfare against Red forces, perhaps even against China itself. It broke the deadlock in the peace talks, but the resultant armistice required no major concessions from the Communists and maintained the partition of Korea. It was the kind of settlement that Nixon would have damned Truman for negotiating, but as Ike's vice-president he had to go along with it. So began a period of eight years when he would loyally support Cold War policies that he did not always believe in.

Eisenhower sent Nixon to Asia in the fall of 1953 to reinforce the message to America's more belligerent allies that the Korean war was truly over. In essence he had to affirm the continuation of containment strategy that he privately regarded as tantamount to appeasement of Communism. One of his tasks was to tell Chiang Kai-shek, who still harbored hopes of retaking the Chinese mainland, that the United States 'would not be committed to support any invasion he might launch'.[18] More significantly, he had to extract a promise from Syngman Rhee not to invade North Korea, a threat that the South Korean leader was wont to make in public. After two tough meetings, Rhee acknowledged, 'In my heart I know that Korea cannot possibly act alone.'[19]

Nixon's Asia trip also took in Vietnam, where the French were engaged in a war to preserve their colonial regime from a Communist uprising. Seeing the French treat the Vietnamese with arrogance and contempt, he concluded that they had failed to build popular support to resist the anti-colonialist appeals of the Communists. Vietnam's own soldiers were largely untrained, had no confidence in themselves and lacked both a leader and a cause to inspire them to fight. Accordingly he decided that 'the United States would have to do everything possible to find a way to keep the French in Vietnam until the Communists had been defeated'.[20] Though Nixon did not appreciate it at the time nor acknowledge it twenty-five years later in his memoirs, the situation exemplified a critical problem concerning America's Cold War policy outside Europe. In Vietnam and elsewhere in the third world, the United States would time and again tie itself to an authoritarian, undemocratic and unpopular regime in the cause of leading the free world against Communism.

The weakness of France's position in Vietnam quickly became apparent. In April 1954 the French appealed for US military aid to save their beleaguered garrison at Dienbienphu. The only elected politician of stature to support this option was Nixon. Thirty years later he avowed that, by not intervening to save the French, the United States 'lost its last chance to stop the expansion of Communism in Southeast Asia at little cost to itself'.[21] On 17 April at an off-the-record talk with newspaper editors, Nixon avowed that, if France stopped fighting in Indo-China 'and the situation demanded it, the United States would have to send troops to fight the Communists in that area'.[22] This statement made sensational headlines when leaked but is best seen as an effort both to keep the Communists guessing about US intentions and to alert public opinion about the seriousness of the Southeast Asia crisis. Nixon remained hopeful that US preparedness would suffice to deter the Communists and save the French from defeat. As he put it later, 'We all hoped that by being prepared to fight we would never actually have to do any fighting.'[23]

If the United States did have to fight, Nixon believed that air power would save Dienbienphu but was willing to use nuclear strikes if necessary. Meeting with Eisenhower on 30 April, he and National Security Adviser Robert Cutler advocated readiness to use small atomic bombs. Years later, Eisenhower told one biographer that he had responded, 'You boys must be crazy. We can't use those awful things against Asians for the second time in less than ten years. My God!'[24] In Nixon's recollection, by contrast, Eisenhower had been willing 'to do whatever was necessary' to stop the Communists but he himself 'was probably prepared to stand up at an earlier point' than his boss.[25] The truth lies somewhere in between. Eisenhower had certainly contemplated using atomic weapons against Korea and China in 1953, so his protestations of moral concern for Asians were disingenuous. What held him back were amoral calculations about the negative reaction of public opinion at home and abroad, the reservations of America's allies, logistical and strategic doubts and the Soviet response. Nixon's willingness to use atomic weapons in Vietnam manifested his risk-taking proclivity and his absolute certainty that they would deter the Communists from further aggression in Vietnam. In this case Eisenhower's judgment was certainly wiser. America's strategic interests in Vietnam hardly justified the risks

involved. The Cold War would also have been dangerously escalated. Once atomic weapons were used in such circumstances, a
precedent was established for their further use and their deterrent
quality was diminished. The likelihood of eventual nuclear war
between the superpowers themselves would have been significantly increased.

Eisenhower eventually rejected military intervention of any
kind: Dienbienphu fell before two preconditions he had set for
US involvement could be met – congressional approval and the
support of the Western alliance. The surrender of the fortress on
7 May effectively signaled the end of the French regime.
Nevertheless US diplomatic maneuvers and threats of intervention swayed the Soviets and Chinese into pressurizing their local
allies to accept less than their victory warranted. The Geneva
peace accords partitioned independent Vietnam between the
Communist North and the non-Communist South. To Nixon's
satisfaction, the US withheld its signature from this agreement so
as not to be a party to any surrender of Asian territory to
Communism. Now began Nixon's and America's twenty-year
struggle to save South Vietnam.

Since Eisenhower did not consider South Vietnam important
enough to merit US military involvement, he adopted an indirect
strategy to preserve it through creation of a Southeast Asian
regional alliance to counter subversion, development of indigenous military strength and provision of economic aid. As one historian noted, this program was open-ended: 'it could – and
would – lead the nation into the quagmire of real war'.[26] Nixon
realized this from the start and was readier to bring it on than
anyone else. He wanted no further negotiations that surrendered
ground to Communism in Asia. If it became necessary to prevent
South Vietnam falling, he advocated air-strikes, a naval blockade
of Communist-held territory, and – as a last resort – a quick
injection of American troops. He also wanted to keep the
Communists guessing as to whether the United States would use
nuclear weapons to preserve its client regime.[27] His was a military
solution to what was essentially a political problem. The
Vietnamese people would never be partners in the struggle until
they had good reason to believe in it. Their hearts and minds
might have been won through land redistribution and political
reform, but the new native leaders of South Vietnam were as
authoritarian and unpopular as their French predecessors.

From his Asian tour onward, the threat of international

Communism became Nixon's primary area of interest as vice-president. He set out to educate himself thoroughly about the Cold War. The ideas and positions he developed shaped his later conduct of foreign policy as president. He undertook intensive study of international affairs through his own reading and regular briefings and was not shy about displaying his knowledge. 'He sure does his homework', one intelligence official remarked, 'and if you don't know the real answer when he asks a question, it's a lot better to say so'.[28] He learned from regular attendance at NSC meetings. His Cold War education also owed much to Secretary of State John Foster Dulles.

Nixon had more respect for Dulles than any other person he met in public life excepting Eisenhower, and both men enjoyed each other's company, which was not true of the Nixon–Eisenhower relationship. Nixon kept Dulles abreast of political affairs at home in return for tuition in global affairs. Eisenhower was never aware of the closeness of their relationship. The two would meet regularly over cocktails and dinner in Dulles's home to talk their way around the world. As Nixon later acknowledged, 'It was an incomparable opportunity for me to learn from one of the great diplomats of our time'.[29] Sometimes they disagreed, as when Dulles was more cautious than Nixon over Vietnam in 1954 and critical of his efforts to make the Quemoy-Matsu crisis into an election issue in 1958. They were more often in agreement, since both believed in the liberation of Communist-dominated peoples. Soviet leader Nikita Khrushchev hated them with equal passion. In his memoirs he called Dulles 'that vicious cur' and Nixon 'an unprincipled puppet' of Joseph McCarthy and a 'son-of-a-bitch'.[30] Shortly before Dulles's painful death from throat cancer in 1959, his last words to Nixon were to stand firm against Communism. Fittingly, Nixon wrote his eulogy in *Life* magazine, completely redrafting the ghosted version that publisher Henry Luce wanted him to put his name to. Referring to criticisms of Dulles's commitment to liberation, he asked, 'What other tenable position can self-respecting free peoples take?'[31]

The most important source of Nixon's Cold War education was foreign travel. The Herter Committee was the first step in a globe-trotting career that made him the most traveled American leader of all time. As vice-president he toured extensively in Asia, Africa, the Middle East, South and Central America (Chile would be the only country he never got to) and Europe. He got behind the Iron Curtain, becoming the first American leader to visit Poland and Russia itself since the onset of the Cold War. All this made Nixon the most visible vice-president in history. He continued his travels as a private citizen in the 1960s, often using his law firm's representation of the Pepsi Cola company's global interests as the ostensible purpose of his foreign trips. Finally, he became the first American president to visit China. As a result, Nixon developed an unrivaled network of contacts with foreign leaders and an unmatched fund of knowledge about the affairs of a host of countries.

What Nixon learned from his travels informed his thinking on the Cold War for the rest of his life. Based on his experience with the Herter Committee, he made it his practice to meet ordinary people in walkabouts rather than confine himself to the embassy circuit. Over the years he filled myriad notebooks with jottings about comments made to him by workers, housewives and small businessmen. In this way he learned something about their views of the United States and their hopes for material improvement that he always regarded as the greatest safeguard against Communism.[32]

While serving on the Herter Committee, Nixon also insisted on meeting Western European Communist Party leaders in order to understand better their thinking. All impressed him as tough, intelligent and vigorous, none more so than Italian trade unionist Giuseppe Di Vittorio. After this experience he would never underestimate the ability of Communist leaders anywhere, but he also came away believing that the only thing they 'would respect – and deal with seriously – was power at least equal to theirs and backed up by a willingness to use it'.[33] He made a penciled note in Italy in 1947 that guided his outlook for the remainder of his career: 'One basic rule with Russians – never bluff unless you are prepared to carry through, because they will test you every time.'[34] Nixon also drew another conclusion from his meetings with European Communists. He was struck by the identical party line, even down to the same phrases, articulated by British, French and Italian Communists. To him this was proof 'that the Communists throughout the world owe their loyalty not to the countries in which they live but to Russia'.[35] This view of Communism as a monlithic, Soviet-controlled world movement blinkered Nixon to the divisions that existed from the mid-1950s onward between Russia and China, until serious border fighting in the late 1960s opened his eyes to their split. It also underestimated the importance of the nationalist dimension in third world Communism, which he always regarded as a mere front for Soviet or Chinese expansionism.

Almost as important in developing Nixon's international perspective was his 1953 trip to nineteen countries in Asia. He came home a strong devotee to the domino theory that the loss of Vietnam would soon be followed by the spread of Communism throughout Southeast Asia, the Malay penninsula and Indonesia, eventually putting Japan and even Australia at risk. The trip also confirmed his conviction that the rot had started with the loss of China, whose Communist leaders had gone on to sponsor war in Korea, Vietnam and Malaya. In a report to the American people, he was implicitly critical not only of the Truman administration but also of Eisenhower's. 'We should recognize that the time is past when we should try to reach agreement with the Communists at the conference table by surrendering to them', he declared. 'We are paying the price in Asia for that kind of diplomacy right now.'[36]

Other seeds of Nixon's future thinking were planted on the Asia trip. He had the opportunity to compare a successful and unsuccessful effort by a colonial power to defeat a Communist insurgency. In contrast to the French in Vietnam, the British in Malaya enlisted the support of native leaders and trained native troops to fight a Communist insurgency. Their strategy aimed to persuade Malayans that it was their war, fought for the prize of independence, nationhood and the right to determine whether their country stayed in or left the British Commonwealth.[37] In essence this became the model for the Vietnamization policy that Nixon would pursue as president to build up South Vietnam's forces in order that they could assume responsibility from the Americans for fighting their war.

Syngman Rhee's counsel that the Communists should never be allowed to think 'that America wants peace so badly that you will do anything to get it' also made a deep impression on Nixon. The South Korean leader claimed his public statements about invading North Korea were a positive asset to the free world because his unpredictability worried the Communists and tied down enemy troops. Nixon gave much thought to this insight, commenting in his memoirs that, as time passed, 'the more I appreciated how wise the old man had been'.[38] As president, the use of unpredictability and apparent irrationality – what Tom Wicker called 'the uncertainty principle' – became a trademark of his foreign policy.[39] When trying to extricate America from Vietnam, he ordered tactical escalations of the war on several occasions in order to convince the enemy that he did not seek peace at any price. Top aide H. R. Haldeman also recounts conversations with Nixon in the summer of 1968 in which he toyed with implementing what he called the 'madman theory' if elected president. This entailed exploiting his reputation as a hard liner to frighten North Vietnam that he would launch a nuclear attack if it did not make peace.[40]

As well as educating him, Nixon's travels made him an on-the-ground participant in the Cold War. Wherever Nixon went, he made the Communist threat the main issue of attention. He took every opportunity to observe Communists at close quarters and never shied away from confrontation with them, an in-your-face attitude that sometimes put him in physical danger. Perhaps it was a case of needing to prove his courage, perhaps it was an extension of his political tendency to go on the attack, or perhaps he saw himself as a symbol of America's determination to stand up to the Communists. Whatever the reason, his experience as a front-line combatant in the struggle against Communism was a unique dimension to his role as a Cold Warrior and made him distinct from every other American leader of the Cold War era.

Talks with Communists leaders were not his only brush with the enemy during his Herter Committee travels in 1947. In Trieste Nixon was caught up in a street battle between Communists and anti-Communists, in which he witnessed killings and bloodshed. Shortly afterwards he took a nerve-wracking flight in a doorless C-47 plane into the Greek mountains to visit communities that were under regular attack from Communists.[41] During the Asia trip of 1953, he faced down Communist demonstrators who confronted him as he walked with Pat to a Buddhist shrine in the Burmese town of Pegu. Nixon had been advised to cancel the visit by his local hosts, but insisted that Communists should not be allowed to interfere with the itinerary of the United States Vice-President. In his memoirs Nixon recounted how he had gotten the better of an exchange with the demonstration leader, whose followers then dispersed in disappointment at his loss of face. This experience, he avowed, 'bolstered my instinctive belief that the only way to deal with Communists is to stand up to them'.[42]

On the Vietnam stage of the journey, Nixon donned military fatigues to visit the front line of fighting in jungle fifty miles from the Chinese border. Later, in April 1964, according to a new study, the Green Berets took Nixon back into the Vietnam jungle close to the Cambodian border on a secret mission to arrange with the Viet-Cong an exchange of five American prisoners in return for gold. Though Nixon always denied the authenticity of this much-rumored story, he was in Vietnam at this time, ostensibly on a business trip for Pepsi Cola but actually for a fact-finding tour, which almost certainly extended to talking with Communist fighters.[43]

Nixon's most dangerous encounter with Communists took place on his eight-nation goodwill tour of South America in May 1958. On a continent where a number of military dictators had recently been overthrown, Nixon was a personal symbol of America's willingness to cosy up to authoritarian regimes who were tough on Communism. Having been photographed in friendly commune with hated despots like Rafael Trujillo of the Dominican Republic, Anastasio Somoza of Nicaragua and Fulgencio Batista of Cuba, he became a ready target for leftist demonstrations. After a quiet start to the tour, the trouble began in Peru at Lima's University of San Marcos, where student demonstrators threw stones and spat on Nixon and his entourage when he got out of his limousine to talk with them. In response he berated them, 'Cowards! You are cowards! You are afraid of the truth!' During the fracas, Nixon later admitted, he felt 'the excitement of battle', and an aide noted that even his assailants acknowledged his courage, quoting one of them as saying '*el gringo tiene cojones*' (the yankee has balls).[44] On returning to his hotel, Nixon encountered another group of demonstrators, one of whom caught him full in the face with a wad of tobacco spittle and got a hard kick on the shin in return from the Vice-President. In Nixon's eyes, these minor confrontations assumed epic proportions as veritable Cold War battles. When US Foreign Service officials expressed reservations that his conduct contravened the goodwill purposes of the tour, he exploded: 'The Communists are out to win the world. . . .We are doomed to defeat in the world struggle unless we are willing to risk as much to defend freedom as the Communists are willing to risk to destroy it.'[45]

If Nixon had sought confrontation in Lima, he was blameless in the case of the life-threatening situation he experienced in Caracas. When the official motorcade that ferried him from the airport entered the city, his limousine was cut off from its inept police guard and attacked by a mob wielding rocks, clubs and pipes. Although the crowd was baying '*muera* Nixon' and two fellow passengers were injured by spraying glass, he ordered his secret service guard not to fire and behaved with great composure during the twelve-minute attack.[46] Venezuelan troops eventually rescued him and imposed order, but a communications breakdown prevented word that the situation was under control from reaching Washington. A worried Eisenhower ordered that a military rescue mission, codenamed Operation Poor Richard, be readied as a precautionary measure. Fortunately, it was not needed and Nixon flew home to a hero's welcome. One of the first to greet him was Democratic Senate leader Lyndon Johnson, who had previously referred to Nixon as 'chicken shit'. When reminded of this by a reporter, LBJ replied, 'Son, in politics you've got to learn that overnight chicken shit can turn into chicken salad.'[47] Nixon's conduct merited praise, but whether he learned the right lesson from the episode is another matter. Though he briefed the Cabinet that America had to pay more heed to the voice of the common people of Latin America, he failed to appreciate the roots of their anger. In *Six Crises*, published four year later, he openly praised the military regimes of this continent as 'a great and stabilizing force' against Communism.[48]

Nixon's most famous confrontation with a Communist was not in the least life-threatening and made him a racing certainty for the 1960 Republican presidential nomination. In July 1959, 'keyed up and ready for battle', he flew to Moscow to meet Nikita Khrushchev, an encounter he had prepared for by reading countless briefing papers and getting appraisals of the Soviet supremo from foreign leaders and Americans who had met him.[49] While ostensibly on a goodwill visit to open the first ever United States Exhibition in the Soviet Union, Nixon saw the opportunity to demonstrate his anti-Communism. He told military aide Major Robert Cushman that his speechwriters were not to use the phrase 'peaceful coexistence'. 'This is the Acheson line in the State Department and I will not put it out!!!!!!', he warned. '. . . whoever does [use] it will be shipped [out] on the next plane'. The term Nixon wanted used instead was 'peaceful competition.'[50]

The highlight of the visit occurred in the model American kitchen in the Exhibition, where Nixon and Khrushchev held an impromptu debate, by turn jocular and intense, about the superiority of each side's consumer products, technology and weaponry. Helped by a dramatic photograph of him jabbing his finger at his adversary's chest for emphasis, Nixon won world-wide headlines for holding his own against the tough Soviet leader. He built on this success by making two addresses to the Russian people, the first American leader to be allowed to do so. His official address opening the Exhibition, which was published in the Soviet press, held up the American way of life as the epit-ome of prosperity and freedom. Then, in a half-hour televised address, he criticized the Soviet leadership's aggression, rejection of America's peace overtures and distortion of Western motives. His words made a good impression back home but not in Russia. From their private conversations, Nixon knew that he had not gotten through to Khrushchev and left Moscow in depressed spirit.[51] After this experience, he never again argued with Communist leaders about the merits of the two systems.

Nixon believed that his record as a tough anti-Communist would win him the White House in 1960, but in one of history's little ironies he found himself outbid by a tyro challenger whose *curriculum vitae* as a Cold Warrior could not hold a candle to his. John Kennedy's banner promise to 'get the country moving again' was a wake-up call to reassert America's power and lead-ership in the Cold War after recent setbacks like sputnik, the mis-sile gap and new Communist insurgencies in Laos and South Vietnam. Nevertheless, Kennedy's private polls showed that Nixon's reputation stood him in good stead when foreign policy issues were defined in tough-on-Communism terms. To weaken his adversary's standing, the Democrat began to urge support for anti-Castro elements seeking to overthrow Communism in Cuba, safe in the knowledge that Nixon could not respond in kind.[52]

Nixon was unsure what to make of Fidel Castro when he came to power in January 1959. After a private meeting with the Cuban leader in April, he formed the impression that Castro was not a Communist and recommended to Eisenhower that the US should try to 'orient him in the right direction'.[53] Within a year, however, Castro was counted amongst the enemy because he appeared to align Cuba with the Soviet Union and confiscated American and other foreign investments in his country. In April 1960 Eisenhower approved a Central Intelligence Agency (CIA) plan, codenamed Operation Pluto, to build up anti-Castro oppo-sition to overthrow the Cuban regime. Impatient for Pluto's implementation before the presidential election, Nixon was so zealous in monitoring its progress that CIA officials regarded him as the administration's point man on the project. The investigations of journalist Anthony Summers also indicate Nixon's complicity in CIA plans to assassinate Castro.[54] Fifteen years later, in written testimony to the Senate Intelligence Committee investigation of CIA plots to murder foreign leaders, Nixon avowed that assassination was 'an act I never had cause to consider'.[55] Nevertheless, as president he had an obsession about getting hold of the CIA's voluminous records on the anti-Castro operation to see if they contained damaging revelations about him.[56]

By the time of the election Operation Pluto had evolved into a planned invasion of Cuba by anti-Castro exiles, details of which were secretly leaked to Kennedy.[57] In the fourth and final televised debate, Nixon found himself in the unusual position of having to rebut his opponent's call for US assistance to Cuban exiles as a breach of international law because he could not confirm the existence of the secret CIA plan. As he recalled, 'I was in the position of a fighter with one hand tied behind my back.'[58] Those whom Nixon normally counted amongst his critics in the press corps praised his words as responsible and statesmanlike, but he did not want their plaudits. As he acknowledged in his memoirs, 'Kennedy conveyed the image – to 60 million people – that he was tougher on Castro and communism than I was.'[59] Nixon was firmly convinced that this was the real reason he lost the close-fought election, though more dispassionate analysis pointed to other factors – notably the state of the economy – as being more significant. He vowed, 'I would never again enter an election at a disadvantage by being vulnerable to them [the Kennedys] – or anyone – on the level of political tactics.'[60] It was a lesson he drew on with regard to Vietnam in 1968.

Vietnam is sometimes referred to as Lyndon Johnson's war, but it could equally be called Richard Nixon's. He had been the first major American politician to urge military intervention to save Vietnam from Communism. After Johnson Americanized the war in 1965, Nixon repeatedly urged the adoption of ever more hawkish measures to bring about military victory. At a White House meeting in April 1966 Johnson personally thanked Nixon for supporting the US commitment in Vietnam, which was coming under attack from many in his own party. In October, however, the President called Nixon a 'chronic campaigner' because of his critique of the Manila Communiqué offering an American military withdrawal within six months if North Vietnam ceased all support for the Viet-Cong Communist uprising in South

Vietnam. Among other things, Nixon warned that American withdrawal would open the way for a Communist victory and asked whether it was better to escalate the war in order to shorten it. This was hardly a responsible position because his intelligence about the Vietnamese Communists was woefully inadequate and he could not guarantee that escalation would bring victory at an acceptable cost, if at all. Nevertheless Johnson's riposte put him at center stage in the Vietnam debate to the benefit of his presidential nomination prospects. LBJ's aides later told William Safire that he had deliberately boosted Nixon in the belief that his candidacy would drive anti-war voters back into the Democratic fold.[61]

The war destroyed Johnson's presidency before he could lock horns with Nixon. In March 1968 he announced that he would seek to negotiate peace, a tacit admission that the war could not be won through continued escalation, and would not be a candidate for reelection. In the second half of October hopes of a negotiated settlement were seemingly boosted when North Vietnam finally agreed to allow South Vietnam's government to participate in peace talks in Paris if Johnson called a bombing halt. Over the years, the story grew that Nixon sabotaged this promising development just to win the presidential election. The allegation centers on his role in secretly encouraging Colonel Nguyen Van Thieu, South Vietnam's leader, not to participate in the talks. Speaking in 2000, Richard Holbrooke, then a senior diplomat and in 1968 a junior member of the Vietnam negotiating team, deemed the Nixon intrigue a massive and inexcusable interference in 'one of the most important negotiations in American diplomatic history'.[62] While this judgment rightly condemns Nixon's conduct, it implicitly exaggerates the effect of his maneuvers. Former foreign policy official William Bundy was more accurate in his assessment that 'probably no great chance (of peace) was lost'.[63]

There is compelling evidence from Federal Bureau of Investigation wiretaps and other sources that senior members of Nixon's campaign team, mainly John Mitchell but also Spiro Agnew, used businesswoman Anna Chennault as an intermediary to transmit messages urging Thieu's non-participation in the talks and promising him stronger support from a Republican administration. Nixon had full knowledge of this and repeatedly lied to Johnson and to reporters about his involvement with Chennault.[64] The evidence is equally compelling, however, that

Nixon's intervention was not the decisive influence on Thieu's stand. With or without this, the South Vietnamese leader would almost certainly have refused to participate in negotiations because his regime had nothing to gain from a peace settlement that might require a power-sharing arrangement with the Communists. Though well aware of Thieu's reservations, Johnson made premature statements about a diplomatic breakthrough, especially in his televised address of 31 October. Three days later the Saigon regime announced that it would not participate in the talks.

Nixon can justifiably be cast as the villain in the affair. His intervention may not have been the decisive factor but it was a breach of the Logan Act that forbade US citizens from conducting private diplomacy with foreign governments. More significantly, if there was any chance for peace, he should have helped it not hindered it. The Vietnam settlement that he himself negotiated four years later was hardly better than what might have been obtained in 1968. Nixon also paid a price for his intrigue. Henceforth he would always worry that the Democrats had evidence of his wrongdoing, a fear that helped to set in train the illegal intelligence operations that eventually destroyed his presidency. Thieu also thought he was owed for helping to elect Nixon and would be reluctant to cooperate with his later efforts to end the war.

Despite his pre-election maneuvers, Nixon had changed his mind about the possibility of military victory in Vietnam. This was a remarkable turnaround, but his new thinking was shaped by a realistic assessment of America's prospects in Southeast Asia and the effect of the war on its global position. In preparation for his presidential bid, he had engaged in intensive study of the international situation and taken four trips abroad in 1967 (to Europe, Asia, Latin America, and the Middle East and Africa). As a result he became concerned that America's global interests had been 'held hostage' by Johnson's obsession with Vietnam.[65] Significantly, Nixon's campaign statements focused on the need for 'honorable peace', not the 'victorious peace' that he had called for up to the end of 1966. Though this distinction received little attention in the heat of the campaign, it signified his intention to de-Americanize the war. Nixon was now determined to end America's involvement in a conflict that had cost the lives of 38,000 servicemen, massive outlays of national treasure and huge divisions amongst its people.

Nixon had fully expected an acceptable, if not totally satisfactory solution within his first six months in office. 'I'm not
going to end up like LBJ', he told Haldeman, 'holed up in the
White House, afraid to show my face on the street. I'm going
to stop that war. Fast'.[66] However, he ended up fighting a sav-
age war of peace that lasted another four years, during which
more than 20,500 Americans, 107,500 South Vietnamese soldiers, over 500,000 Communist troops and more than a million
civilians in the two Vietnams, Laos and Cambodia lost their
lives. This was a heavy price for a 1973 peace settlement whose
terms were little if any better than might have obtained through
negotiation in 1969. 'Because of his faith in mad strategies and
triangular diplomacy', concludes the most definitive study of
Nixon's Vietnam policy, 'he had unnecessarily prolonged the
war, with all of the baleful consequences of death, destruction
and division for Vietnam and America that this brought
about'.[67]

Aside from Watergate, Nixon's handling of Vietnam ranks as
the most controversial aspect of his presidency. According to
Stephen Ambrose, his slow-motion retreat from the war was 'one
of the worst decisions ever made by a Cold War President' and
the 'worst mistake of his presidency'.[68] Nixon's own view was
that he achieved an honorable settlement that preserved
America's regional and global credibility and constituted a solid
foundation for South Vietnam's continued independence. But for
Watergate, he contended, he would have retaliated against North
Vietnamese violations of the settlement to prevent the collapse of
South Vietnam that occurred in 1975. This view is outlined in a
chapter of his book *No More Vietnams* entitled 'How We Won
the War'. Another chapter, 'How We Lost the Peace', claims that
Congress through its refusal to sanction renewed air attacks and
economic military aid to the Saigon regime 'proceeded to snatch
defeat from the jaws of victory'.[69] These were the words not of a
rational analyst but of a man fearful of going down in history as
the president who lost South Vietnam to Communism. In reality,
Nixon was guilty not of losing Vietnam but of trying in pursuit
of the global imperatives of containment to save a regime that
was beyond salvation.

As National Security Adviser Henry Kissinger observed, Nixon
was 'convinced that how we end this war will determine the
future of the U.S. in the world'.[70] In his memoirs Nixon presented
his goal of 'peace with honor' that preserved America's interna-

tional credibility as essential for the achievement of the new for-eign policy of détente. In truth, he approached Vietnam in thrall to the Cold War past that he had helped to shape. In one of his later books, written after the collapse of détente, he explictly linked his determination to preserve South Vietnam from Communism to the policies of Truman, Eisenhower, Kennedy and Johnson. Like them, he avowed, he regarded a Communist victory as a human tragedy for the South Vietnamese people, a threat to the survival of other free nations in Southeast Asia, a blow to America's strategic interests and an incentive for Communist aggression in other parts of the world.[71] 'Peace with honor' meant avoiding defeat in Vietnam, which required the preservation of the Saigon regime, which was little different from the 'victory' that Lyndon Johnson had pursued.[72] In other words, Nixon's Vietnam policy began not as part of a new and far-sighted grand design but as part of the old Cold War orthodoxy.

The trouble was that Nixon had no sure-fire formula for win-ning an honorable peace even though he had pledged in the 1968 campaign that 'new leadership will end the war and win the peace in the Pacific'.[73] According to Jeffrey Kimball, he had no new Vietnam policy on entering office and never really developed one. Instead he and Kissinger relied on *ad hoc* and sometimes contradictory initiatives that reacted to rather than shaped events. Perhaps the closest Nixon came to devising a new policy was the so-called madman theory.[74] Outlining this to Bob Haldeman in 1968, he declared, 'I want the North Vietnamese to believe I've reached the point where I might do *anything* to stop the war. We'll just slip the word to them that "for God's sake, you know Nixon is obsessed about Communism. We can't restrain him when he's angry – and he has his hand on the nuclear button" – and Ho Chi Minh himself will be in Paris in two days begging for peace.'[75]

The policy was certainly implemented, but the results were dis-appointing. On 15 July 1969 Nixon wrote a personal letter to Ho Chi Minh setting a deadline of 1 November for a serious breakthrough in peace negotiations. This was delivered by French businessman Jean Sainteny, who was instructed to convey a verbal warning that without such progress the President would have recourse 'to measures of great consequence and force'. Though the North Vietnamese quickly agreed to hold secret talks in Paris with Kissinger, they had no intention of dancing to Nixon's tune. On 25 August, Ho responded to his ultimatum

with a letter restating North Vietnam's insistence on US withdrawal from the conflict in order to allow the Vietnamese 'to
dispose of themselves'.[76]

An angry Nixon instructed Kissinger to convey to the Soviets
that he was 'out of control' over Vietnam and might start using
nuclear weapons. Kissinger claimed to have said nothing to the
Russians because the order was too dangerous to carry out.[77] Yet
he had already sent this very message indirectly through Nixon
aide Leonard Garment. It was Garment's task on a visit to
Moscow in July to tell the Soviets that Nixon 'is somewhat
"crazy" . . . at moments of stress or personal challenge unpre-
dictable and capable of the bloodiest brutality'.[78] The use of insan-
ity as an instrument of diplomacy is at best a contradiction in
terms and at worst dangerous brinkmanship that could rebound
disastrously in a crisis. Even judged on Nixon's own dictum that
no American leader should try to bluff the Communists unless he
was willing to carry out the threat, the madman strategy was
unsound. He could do nothing in the face of North Vietnam's
refusal to be cowed into making peace. Whatever impression
Nixon tried to create, he was not mad and he knew that a nuclear
strike was not an option now that the Soviets had something they
had not possessed in 1954, namely nuclear parity.

With the 'madman theory' disproven, Nixon fell back on the
strategy of Vietnamization to win peace. This was hardly a novel
idea. Developed and partially implemented by the Johnson
administration in 1968, the Vietnamization policy effectively resurrected the Kennedy administration's plan to enhance South
Vietnam's capacity to defend itself. The only thing new about
Vietnamization was its name, coined by Defense Secretary
Melvyn Laird in place of the more accurate but less positive 'de-
Americanization'. Nixon hoped to build up the self-sufficiency of
South Vietnam's army so that it could bear the brunt of the fighting while American forces staged a phased withdrawal. There
were successful precedents for this policy in Malaya and South
Korea, but it did not work in Vietnam. Despite a massive injection of US money and weaponry and a huge mobilization of its
adult population, South Vietnam was never strong enough to
stand on its own. In part the problem was logistical – South
Vietnam's army was equipped to fight a high-fire-power war that
could not defeat a guerilla enemy. But mainly the problem was
political – rank-and-file troops had no reason to fight and die for
a corrupt and incompetent officer class and a government lacking

any vision of reform or desire to end a war that kept its coffers full. In 1969, Sven Kraemer, a member of Kissinger's staff, wrote a blunt report after visiting South Vietnam that the only hope of improving matters was through 'American *presidential* action, making improved leadership the condition of continued American support'.[79] There is no evidence that Nixon ever got tough with Thieu to this end, or even thought of doing so. Some scholars conclude that he felt a personal debt to Thieu for 1968. Whatever the reason, Nixon's failure to grapple with this thorny problem was one of the most substantial defects in his Vietnamization policy.

Lyndon Johnson created the credibility gap by misleading the American people that the stalemated military situation in Vietnam promised victory. Nixon perpetuated it with his regular avowals that South Vietnam's ineffective army was capable of taking on the Communists despite overwhelming evidence to the contrary. In spring 1970 he relented on using American troops to support the incursion into Cambodia after US military chiefs warned that South Vietnam's army was unready for the operation. In February 1971 a crack division of South Vietnamese marines was routed on a search-and-destroy expedition into Laos. Nixon had insisted that the operation went ahead to prove that Vietnamization was working, even though American commanders estimated the job needed at least four divisions. The President announced that the mission 'had gone according to plan', but television footage of South Vietnamese soldiers fighting among themselves for places on US helicopters sent to evacuate them gave his words a hollow ring. Nixon was still in denial when he evaluated the incursion in his memoirs as 'a military success but a psychological defeat' because of media coverage.[80] In the spring of 1972 Hanoi launched its first conventional offensive since the Tet assault of 1968 in a bid to strengthen its hand in the peace negotiations and pave the way for a coalition government in Saigon. With almost all American combat troops now withdrawn, the Communists easily cut through the South Vietnamese army that Nixon was wont to describe as 'a formidable fighting force'.[81] Only massive tactical air attacks on Communist forces, the bombing of Hanoi and the mining of Hanoi and Haiphong harbors to cut off Soviet war supplies to North Vietnam saved the situation.

Nixon engaged in tactical escalations to buy time for Vietnamization to work and keep the enemy guessing about his intentions. Some proved effective, most notably the escalation of the air war that halted the Communist offensive of 1972. Others did not, most notably those measures that brought the war to South Vietnam's neighbors. To disrupt Communist supply lines that ran through neutral countries, Nixon stepped up air attacks and border raids on Laos initiated by Johnson, culminating in the unsuccessful 1971 incursion by South Vietnamese forces. The spilling-over of the conflict turned a fifth of all Laotians into refugees and resulted, by some estimates, in 350,000 civilian deaths. Cambodia suffered an even worse fate. It was the target in 1969 of covert bombing raids, in 1970 of an overt invasion that did not succeed in its stated aim of capturing the enemy's mobile field headquarters, and in 1973 of renewed bombing against Communist insurgents. Some 600,000 Cambodians lost their lives as a direct result. Their country was also drawn deeper into the regional conflict by the coup that brought an anti-Communist regime to power in 1970. To protect its interests, North Vietnam stepped up support for the Khmer Rouge rebels, who eventually seized power in 1975 and inflicted the horror of the 'killing fields' holocaust that cost the lives of between one and two million Cambodians.

If Nixon inherited the Vietnam war, he did much to create the Cambodian war. Henry Kissinger has borne the brunt of criticism for being the architect of American policy.[82] In reality it was the President himself who made the key decisions on Cambodia, abetted by Alexander Haig.[83] It was a policy that resulted in unmitigated disaster. Had America not intervened, Cambodia would certainly have fallen to Communism eventually but probably without the the bloody consequences of the killing fields. Nor is there any evidence that the loss of Cambodia would have made the defense of Vietnam strategically more difficult. This sideshow was a major deviation from the Vietnamization policy of American withdrawal from Southeast Asia. The United States ended up acquiring another weak client whom it could not preserve from Communism. Of course, Cambodia's neutrality was initially compromised by North Vietnam and no one could have foreseen what America's intervention would eventually lead to. Asked by David Frost in their 1977 interview whether he had the destruction of Cambodia on his conscience 'in a Quaker sense', Nixon replied emphatically in the negative. However, as journalist William Shawcross has argued: 'Statesmen must be judged by the consequences of their actions. Whatever Nixon and Kissinger intended for Cambodia, their efforts created catastrophe.'[84]

Whatever else the tactical escalations achieved, they did not cause North Vietnam to doubt that Nixon was set on withdrawal from the war. This was the real weakness of the American position. The Communists knew that their enemy was leaving, so they had no incentive to make concessions in a negotiated peace. Nixon had signaled his intent early in his presidency. In a national address on 14 May 1969 he declared that he would accept simultaneous withdrawal of US and North Vietnamese troops from South Vietnam (a significant modification of LBJ's 'Manila formula'), an exchange of prisoners-of-war, and the holding of free elections in South Vietnam as the core terms of a peace settlement. Though North Vietnam rejected his overtures, Nixon promptly announced from Midway Island on 4 June that 25,000 troops would be pulled out immediately as part of a phased American withdrawal, the pace of which would depend on South Vietnam's military self-sufficiency, progress in the Paris peace talks and the level of enemy activity. Regular withdrawals of US forces followed over the next three years until the last combat troops left on 23 August 1972, but there was no corresponding progress in meeting the Midway conditions.

On the issue of troop withdrawal, Nixon was never able to achieve the right balance between putting pressure on the North Vietnamese and buying time for Vietnamization, on the one hand, and satisfying the American public, on the other. In reality it was an impossible equation that defied solution. Ultimately, Nixon's policy was weighted heavily toward the domestic dimensions of the problem. By the time he took office, most Americans thought that involvement in Vietnam had been a mistake. Though not in favor of immediate withdrawal, which was tantamount to an admission of defeat, they were opposed to prolonged escalation and expected Nixon to end the war on his watch. In these difficult circumstances Nixon proved very adept in appealing to popular patriotism to keep public support on his side in opposition to the peace movement. According to one historian, his successful campaign for the hearts and minds of the American people on this issue, culminating in his reelection by a landslide in 1972, 'was a more remarkable feat than ending the war itself'.[85]

In his first three years in office, Nixon went on televison seven times to ask the nation's backing for his policy. The most famous occasion was the 'silent majority' address of 3 November 1969, which undercut the second of the nationwide Moratorium anti-war protests. 'North Vietnam cannot humiliate the United States', he avowed. 'Only Americans can do that'. Nixon later claimed that this address, watched by seventy million people, was one of the few speeches that actually influenced the course of history: 'Now, for a time at least, the enemy could no longer count on dissent in America to give them the victory they could not win on the battlefield'.[86] In fact, it changed very little. The President's anxiety to avoid prolonged domestic turmoil still drove his policy of unconditional phased withdrawal of American troops. Although the 'silent majority' speech warned that foreign policy should not be made by a minority demonstrating in the streets, this was in effect what was happening.

On balance Nixon handled the anti-war protests more effectively than Johnson.[87] In contrast to his predecessor, who wanted to be loved and admired, he was used to being vilified and felt less agony about having to endure verbal assaults from peace campaigners. Yet Nixon could not ignore the doves. In late 1969 his decision to abort a plan – codenamed Duck Hook – for escalatory measures in Vietnam, including possible use of tactical nuclear weapons, was based in part on doubts about its military effectiveness and in part on concern about domestic reaction. Anti-war protest intensified after the invasion of Cambodia and bloodshed resulted: four Kent State University students were killed by the Ohio National Guard and two Jackson State University students were shot dead by Mississippi State Police. A massive demonstration gathered in Washington on the weekend of 9–10 May 1970. This was the occasion for a bizarre nocturnal visit by Nixon, accompanied by only his personal valet, to speak with protesters encamped at the Lincoln Monument.

Nixon may well have been indulging in his customary practice of facing up to the opposition in person, just as he had done to Communists in the past, but he had no success in persuading the young demonstrators to see things his way. As the episode is portrayed in Oliver Stone's film, *Nixon*, it is the President who is forced to recognize the truth of a remark by one of the students that he cannot get out of Vietnam because he cannot control 'the system', in other words American militarism and imperialism, which is like a 'wild animal' that cannot be tamed. That exchange never happened in reality. There was no meeting of minds: symbolizing this, as he was being chauffeured away, the President of the United States gave the finger back to a protester who had flipped him![88] Whatever Nixon's feelings of defiance, when he next addressed the American people on 3 June, it was to pledge the removal of all US troops from Cambodia by the end of the month and the withdrawal of a further 150,000 soldiers from Vietnam by the end of April 1971.

The secret peace talks started after Nixon's 1969 ultimatum dragged on with little progress for another three years. Banking on American war weariness, the North Vietnamese held out for unconditional withdrawal of American troops and for a coalition government from which Thieu would be excluded. The growth of anti-war opinion in the Democratic Party also encouraged them. In October 1972, however, there was a breakthrough in the secret talks. Hanoi softened on the issue of Thieu's inclusion in a coalition government. Its change of heart reflected a combination of factors: the effect of the American bombing campaign of mid-1972; pressure to compromise from Russia and China, who were looking to improve relations with the US; and the realization that Nixon was certain to be reelected. Even so, there was a final snag, because Thieu rejected the terms, prompting the North Vietnamese to break off talks. Nixon's response was to order the massive B-52 Christmas bombing campaign, which rained down a greater bomb tonnage on North Vietnam in twelve days than for the whole of the 1969–71 period. The cities of Hanoi and Haiphong were especially hard hit, with civilian casualties exceeding two thousand. As one of Kissinger's aides commented, 'We bombed the North Vietnamese into accepting our concessions'.[89] Nixon's aim, however, was to reassure Thieu that American air power would keep the Communists in check. He also promised his ally that the United States 'will respond with full force' if the settlement was violated, but these were personal pledges that did not bind Congress or his successor.[90]

A peace settlement was eventually agreed by all parties in January 1973. This allowed the North Vietnamese to keep 140,000 troops in South Vietnam, while America effected a complete withdrawal of all its forces. Hitherto Nixon had always insisted on mutual withdrawal. Had he been willing to make this concession in 1969, the North Vietnamese might have compromised on Thieu and peace could have been achieved much earlier with considerable saving of American and Asian lives. Nixon could not do so at the start of his presidency because he was still thinking in traditional Cold War terms about what the loss of South Vietnam would mean. His repeated assertions in retirement that he would have bombed North Vietnam with the full weight of American air power in retaliation for any violation of the peace treaty may have been sincere but they have to be understood within the context of his campaign to reconstruct his reputation at a time of renewed Cold War. In 1973, however, détente was in full bloom with no sign of the winter wilting to come, so the survival of South Vietnam was now less significant for Nixon than in 1969.

Nixon told the American people he had got 'the right kind of peace', but this could be interpreted differently.[91] It is possible that in his heart of hearts he knew that he had bought nothing more than a decent-interval settlement that allowed a face-saving passage of time between US withdrawal and the inevitable collapse of South Vietnam. According to John Ehrlichman, Kissinger privately remarked that letting North Vietnam keep its troops in South Vietnam effectively signed the death warrant of the Saigon regime. 'If they're lucky', he predicted, 'they can hold out for a year and a half'.[92] In fact, Thieu's government survived just over two years before being toppled by the North Vietnamese spring offensive of 1975. Determined not to get drawn back into the conflict, the US Congress refused to give emergency economic military aid to what it regarded as a lost cause. Even had Nixon still been in office and unwounded by Watergate, it is highly unlikely that he could have rallied a war-weary public to put pressure on the legislature to re-escalate the war.

Nixon's role as a Cold Warrior is an essential element in his historical reputation. Once his attention switched from the domestic to the international threat of Communism, he had constantly proclaimed that Cold War victory was possible through the effective application of American power. In Vietnam, Nixon had to face up to the limitations of US militarism. The continued insistence in his post-presidential writings that he had established the basis for South Vietnam's independence is nothing short of preposterous. Even if his contention was correct, he never confronted the question of whether the price in lives and destruction had been worth paying. It is interesting to compare his perspective with the reflections of William Bundy, a senior policymaker in the Democratic administrations that Americanized the war in the 1960s. In the latter's estimate, the war did have a positive outcome – if it failed to save South Vietnam, it bought time to build up confidence and stability in the rest of Southeast Asia, which prevented the domino effect leading to a Communist takeover of the entire region. Nevertheless, Bundy acknowledges that the cost was far too great and that 'on any reading, American policy in Indochina, from the early 1950s right through to 1975, was a disaster'.[93]

Nixon never thought of Vietnam as a disaster. In his version of history the prolongation of the war was a price worth paying to assist in the achievement of his grand vision of global peace and stability. Nixon was confident that the new foreign policy would ensure his place in history and overshadow all the controversial aspects of his career. Yet his claim to greatness would have been unquestioned had he got the United States out of the war by the end of 1969 on the terms that he eventually obtained in 1973. In addition, an early withdrawal from Vietnam would almost certainly have rescued him from the Watergate scandal that destroyed his reputation.

|6|

World statesman

When it came to foreign policy, Richard Nixon was like the school thug who happened to be the smartest kid in class. The man who for twenty years had consistently urged the use of American military power in pursuit of Cold War aims would as president demonstrate a sophisticated grasp of geopolitical diplomacy in bringing about the most significant improvement in America's relations with the Communist world since the containment doctrine was first mooted. In 1966, when planning his return to the political arena, Nixon confided to law partner Leonard Garment that 'his life had to be dedicated to great foreign policy purposes' because of his 'pacifist mother's idealism' and the overriding importance of foreign affairs in the modern world.[1] After his death in 1994, his gravestone bore an inscription that eulogized his presidential legacy as he would have wished: 'The greatest honor that history can bestow is the title of peacemaker'. After his public career ended in disgrace, Nixon took comfort from the belief that he would be seen by history as a great statesman of peace who had extricated America from the Vietnam war, engineered détente with the Soviets and opened a new relationship with Communist China. The evaluation of Nixon's foreign policy is therefore central to an assessment of his reputation. Was he truly the architect of a new era of peace in global politics or was the sum of his achievements less significant than he claimed?

With the exception of Dwight Eisenhower, Nixon came to the presidency better prepared to conduct the nation's foreign affairs than anyone who has ever held the office. Compared to him, Bill Clinton and George Bush Jr were rank novices in this field. It was not just that he had paid greater heed to foreign policy and traveled abroad more before taking office than any other president.

He had also built an extensive network of contacts among foreign leaders who had kept him appraised of world affairs throughout his wilderness years. Two of these – West Germany's Konrad Adenauer and France's Charles de Gaulle – were particularly influential in shaping his ideas about developing a new relationship with Communist China to counterbalance the Soviet threat.[2] Jonathan Aitken, a Nixon biographer who first met his subject as a young aide in Britain's Conservative Party in the mid-1960s, recounts that his bosses, including former prime minister Alec Douglas Home, thought that Nixon possessed 'a first-class brain, a profound understanding of international affairs, and a superb speaking ability . . . [and] would have made a far better President than Kennedy or Johnson.'[3]

As president, Nixon broke existing records by hosting 142 foreign leaders in the White House and continued his globe-trotting ways, meeting 42 foreign heads of state on fifteen trips abroad during his first two years in office. Some analysts have suggested that he often permitted the personal feelings he developed about foreign leaders in face-to-face diplomacy 'to color . . . [his] national security decisions'.[4] The most oft-cited case is his stance favoring Pakistan in its 1971 war with India. Journalist Seymour Hersh claimed that Nixon was engaged in 'a personal vendetta' against Indian leader Indira Ghandi.[5] Without doubt Nixon disliked Ghandi, whom he regarded 'in every way . . . her father's daughter', not a complimentary remark, since Jawaharlal Nehru had called him 'an unprincipled cad' for endorsing economic military aid to Pakistan in 1953.[6] However, his stance toward the India–Pakistan war owed far more to considerations of triangular diplomacy with the Soviets and Chinese than to personality factors.

More generally, the charge that Nixon's policies were overly personal is not convincing. The most obvious example of personal animus shaping American national security policy was John F. Kennedy's vengeful campaign to overthrow and assassinate Fidel Castro in the wake of the 1961 Bay of Pigs fiasco.[7] Nixon did not take his own antipathy toward the Cuban leader to similar extremes. Despite starting his presidency where he had left off in 1960 by ordering the Central Intelligence Agency (CIA) to intensify covert operations against Castro after the lull of the Johnson era, this campaign was small beer and secondary to the pursuit of détente. Another missile crisis loomed in the fall of 1970 when the Soviets began expanding their Cienfuegos naval base in Cuba to harbor nuclear submarines. Instead of exploiting this to win votes in the midterm elections, as Kennedy had done in 1962, Nixon acted in the words of one historian 'with intelligent and admirable restraint'.[8]

Nixon bade Kissinger negotiate secretly with Soviet ambassador Anatoli Dobrynin to obtain a commitment against basing offensive missiles in Cuba in return for written affirmation of Kennedy's personal pledge not to invade Cuba, which had helped defuse the 1962 showdown. Nixon thereby established clear limits on the tolerated level of Soviet naval activities without disrupting the general improvement in relations with the Kremlin. The price he was willing to pay was Castro's continuation in power, because he abided by Kissinger's verbal assurance to Dobrynin that the United States would not use force 'to bring about a change in the political structure of Cuba', a pledge that ruled out coercive subversion as well as invasion. On the downside, Nixon's critics contend that his covert diplomacy gave Castro a free hand to intervene as a Soviet surrogate in the Angolan war in 1975 without fear of direct American retaliation against Cuba.[9]

Moreover, Nixon's personal dislike of some allied leaders did not prevent him from working with them. In general he got on less well with the new leaders of the 1960s, particularly those who wanted to be more independent of the United States, than with the older leadership generation that had undertaken postwar reconstruction with American support. He was especially suspicious of Willy Brandt, whose *ostpolitik* aimed to forge independent détente between West Germany and the Soviet Union. Though he never trusted Brandt, Nixon came to believe that his parallel overtures to East Germany might work to America's advantage by arousing Soviet worries about German reunification. The Kremlin's acceptance of the Quadripartite Agreement on Berlin in 1971 appeared to prove him right. This treaty removed Berlin from the front line of Cold War confrontation by resolving the key issues of control and access that had made it a flashpoint for nearly a quarter-century.[10] Nixon's dislike of Brandt was nothing in comparison to his disdain for Canada's Pierre Trudeau, whom he once described as an 'asshole', partly because of his independence but mainly because of his flamboyant lifestyle that included high-profile girlfriends like singer Barbara Streisand.[11] Nevertheless the two men signed the Great Lakes Water Quality Agreement of 1972 that initiated the environmental recovery of the Great Lakes (especially the very polluted Lake Erie).

In pursuit of diplomatic ends, Nixon was far more willing to forgive foreign critics and adversaries than he was domestic ones. As president he developed good relations with Communist leaders who had denounced him in vituperative terms for years. On his headline-grabbing visit to China in February 1972, Nixon made a point of extending his hand to foreign minister Zhou Enlai, who greeted him at the airport. 'When our hands met', he later avowed, 'one era ended and another begun'.[12] The symbolism was significant: it was known that Zhou had felt personally insulted when John Foster Dulles refused to shake his hand at the Geneva Conference on Indo-China in 1954. Shortly afterwards in May 1972, Nixon visited Moscow for his first summit with Soviet leaders. He patiently sat through a three-hour diatribe against US policy in Vietnam without getting distracted from the agenda of détente that had brought him to Moscow. In contrast to his 1959 confrontation with Nikita Khrushchev, he was no longer interested in scoring debating points with the Communists. As a result he made a good impression on Soviet boss Leonid Brezhnev, who concluded, 'You can do business with Nixon.'[13]

Three years earlier Nixon's diplomatic touch had smoothed over problems with a close ally. The British ambassador-designate to Washington, John Freeman, had described him in a 1962 article for the leftish *New Statesman* journal as 'a man of no principle whatsover' and applauded his defeat in the California gubernatorial election as 'a victory for decency in public life'. Counseled by Eisenhower that the appointment was an insult, Nixon made some bullish remarks in private about refusing to meet with Freeman when he visited London on his forthcoming European tour. A diplomatic incident nearly ensued when an overzealous aide demanded Freeman's removal from the guest list at a reception for the President at 10 Downing Street. Though the Americans relented on this, the party was initially tense until Nixon's gracious toast. 'Some say there's a new Nixon', he declared. 'And they wonder if there's a new Freeman. I would like to think that that's all behind us. After all, he's the new diplomat and I'm the new statesman'. Prime Minister Harold Wilson wrote Nixon an impromptu note of thanks on the back of his dinner menu: 'That was one of the kindest and most generous acts I have known in a quarter of a century of politics'. Freeman proved an effective ambassador and became a considerable admirer of Nixon. At his farewell audience with the President in 1971, he apologized for misjudging him. Nixon's response suggested that perhaps he had not entirely forgiven and forgotten: 'Well, you couldn't have said that before without browning your nose'.[14]

Any assessment of Nixon's foreign policy must take note of the role played by Henry Kissinger, his first-term National Security Adviser and second-term Secretary of State. Nixon and Kissinger formed what one historian has termed the 'odd couple' of Amercian diplomacy, partners so different yet so similar, who did not like each other but who were locked together by mutual need. Nixon summed up their relationship to an aide in 1969: 'I don't trust Henry, but I can use him.'[15] In spite of their different backgrounds – Kissinger was a Jewish refugee from Nazi Germany, Harvard professor of government and member of the Eastern Establishment – the two men were alike in many ways. They were risk-takers contemptuous of the slow-moving foreign policy bureaucracy, they enjoyed secrecy, surprise and power plays, and they harbored a cynical attitude toward democracy. Both had large egos but were insecure and always on the look-out for enemies, real and imagined. Their unorthodox outlooks made them well suited to undertake an innovative foreign policy, but each brought out the worst in the other and they spent more time together than was healthy. Their determination to centralize foreign policy powers in the White House enabled them to pull off some spectacular diplomatic triumphs, but it also insulated them from the moderating influence of individuals and institutions who had a different perspective from theirs and prevented them developing broad and lasting support for their policies.[16]

The question of who was the lead partner in this dynamic duo has long fascinated analysts. When the administration began to notch up international successes, many influential commentators credited the academically prestigious Kissinger as the brains of the operation, but the tide of scholarly opinion now runs in Nixon's favor. Comparison of Kissinger's writings with Nixon's statements and writings in 1967–8 reveals that with regard to their thinking on Russia and China the former was stuck in the old groove while the latter was breaking the mold. It was Nixon who conceived the new foreign policy and whose international credibility opened doors for its implementation. Moreover, Nixon formulated and presented at least two of its key aspects – the Nixon Doctrine and the idea of a pentagonal structure of global power – without consulting Kissinger. Not surprisingly, the President was resentful of his adviser's encouragement of press speculation that he was a 'lone cowboy' in the diplomacy of détente, a term Kissinger used in a 1972 interview that caused him to be banished from the White House inner circle for a month. As Joan Hoff put it, Kissinger actually played Tonto to Nixon's Lone Ranger, that is the faithful sidekick who carried out his boss's plans.[17] Aside from the dubious idea of linkage, he contributed little to the conceptualization of the new foreign policy. What made him important to Nixon was his willingness to use the National Security Council (NSC) as a quasi-State Department within the White House, his skill as a negotiator and his influential status with the media as a foreign policy intellectual. Only when Watergate began to consume Nixon's attention during his final year in office did Kissinger assume greater responsibility for directing foreign policy, but the major achievements of détente were in place by then.

Nixon possessed the two basic requirements that every statesman credited with the development of a new foreign policy has needed: opportunity and vision. In his case opportunity stemmed from changes taking place in the international order. The relative decline of US power was the primary impulse for détente. Vietnam was only one manifestation of this. America had also lost its nuclear lead over the Soviets, prompting the Johnson administration to adopt the strategic doctrine of mutually assured destruction (MAD), premised on the idea that both sides possessed the offensive capability to destroy the other in a nuclear war. Nixon signaled his acceptance of MAD by announcing in his press conference of 27 January 1969 that his administration would seek 'sufficiency not superiority' in nuclear weapons.[18] Gone too was the economic dominance that the United States had enjoyed while other nations rebuilt their war-torn industries. As Nixon informed Americans in 1971, Japan and Western Europe had 'regained their vitality . . . [to] become our strong competitors'.[19]

Changes within the Communist camp also favored innovative diplomacy. Though Willy Brandt's *ostpolitik* raised questions about Western unity, Communist divisions were more spectacular and significant. Nixon stated bluntly in his first annual foreign policy report that 'international Communist unity has been shattered'.[20] Simmering tensions between the Russians and Chinese, the result of territorial disputes and doctrinal splits, erupted in 1969 into border fighting that made the orthodox American belief in the Communist monolith untenable. Moreover, both Communist powers had their own need for a new relationship with the United States. While China wanted America's friendship to counter Soviet hostility, the Kremlin viewed the normalization of relations as a cure for the ailing Russian economy, because it would reduce defense costs, facilitate the purchase of Western technology and allow for the expansion of consumer production.

Opportunity alone was not enough. Nixon also displayed a more sophisticated geopolitical vision than any other US president in recognizing that the changing structure of global power could be turned to America's advantage. 'The only time in the history of the world that we have had any extended period of peace', he observed in a 1972 interview for *Time* magazine, 'is when there has been balance of power'.[21] Nixon envisaged a new global equilibrium based on recognition that both Soviet and American power was limited, that a multipolar world was emerging and that different ideologies could have similar interests. This was not premised on expectation of total reconciliation with the Soviets, nor on American retreat from globalism. Containment would still be pursued, but on a selective basis, by political and economic means rather than military ones and through mutual concessions. Whereas the traditional policy of containment had been a zero-sum game, henceforth the United States would recognize that a loss in one theater of competition, such as Vietnam, could be counterbalanced by a gain elsewhere. What was important was the global balance of power. The aim was to manage superpower competition so as to preserve equilibrium and prevent a suicidal nuclear confrontation.[22]

Another cornerstone of détente was the conviction that the increasingly fragmented nature of power made a multipolar equilibrium possible, even though the national components in this balance were by no means equal in power. Nixon developed a pentagonal concept of global power that recognized the United States and the Soviet Union as the only genuine superpowers but acknowledged Western Europe and Japan as economic powers and China as an ideological power within the international Communist movement. The multipolar system would permit a more stable balance of power, because the primary responsibility for maintaining equilibrium would not rest with any one nation. In Nixon's view it would be 'a safer world' with these five power centers 'each balancing the other, not playing one against the other'.[23]

Nixon understood that the establishment of the new world order required the United States to eliminate ideology as a driving force of its foreign policy. Since the onset of the Cold War, America's interests had been determined by the need to contain the threat of Communism, whose challenge was perceived in generic rather than specific terms. Henceforth, Nixon declared in 1970, 'our interests must shape our commitments, rather than the other way around'.[24] If America's interests now focused on the geopolitics of global equilibrium, ideological differences between the component elements of this balance no longer constituted a threat. 'What brings us together', Nixon told Chinese leader Mao Zedong in 1972, 'is a recognition of a new situation in the world and a recognition on our part that what is important is not a nation's internal political philosophy. What is important is its policy toward the rest of the world and toward us'.[25] Arguably, only someone with Nixon's impeccable anti-Communist credentials could have gotten away with this U-turn without fear of being labeled naive or soft-on-Communism by domestic critics. As he told Mao, 'In America, at least at this time, those on the right can do what those on the left can only talk about.'[26]

The onetime Cold War ideologue had metamorphosed into a geopolitical advocate of systemic stability. As Soviet Foreign Minister Andrei Gromyko observed, Nixon had become 'a pragamatist uninterested in the theoretical aspects of an issue'.[27] According to historian Walter LaFeber, the new Nixon 'most feared not Communism, but disorder – especially revolutionaries who wanted to destroy order'.[28] Nevertheless, this emphasis on order and stability had an implicit ideological dimension. Third world revolutionaries who were regarded as the enemies of order were often Marxist, albeit of the indigenous variety. Their success could not be tolerated for fear that they would naturally align with Moscow and thereby upset the global balance of power. Nixon also reasoned that if the United States did nothing to resist Marxist movements, whether independent or not, the Soviets would interpret this as weakness and grow more adventurous in expanding their influence.

Within this conceptual framework, five interrelated elements made up the foreign policy of détente.[29] The primary concern was to develop a new US–Soviet relationship based on recognition of each superpower's legitimate security interests and mutual restraint where these were were not involved. Related to this was the concept of linkage, a carrot-and-stick policy that tied Soviet gains in one area to their good behavior in another. 'The great issues are fundamentally inter-related . . .', Nixon told his key national security officials at the start of his administration. 'Crisis or confrontation in one place and real cooperation in another cannot be sustained indefinitely.'[30] The third element of détente grew out of linkage. This was the effort to improve relations with the People's Republic of China and form a Sino-American axis to block Soviet ambitions in Asia. Befriending China lessened the number of adversaries facing the United States and paved the way for the fourth element of détente, the phasing-down of America's military commitments, especially in Asia. The Nixon Doctrine, announced at Guam in mid-1969, proclaimed that the United States would honor existing obligations to provide allies with economic assistance and military equipment but would otherwise expect them to be responsible for their own defense. Finally, lest the reduction of American military commitments appeared a sign of weakness, Nixon favored tactical escalations to create doubt in the minds of adversaries by demonstrating that the US still had the will to use its power.

To implement this complex, interlinked strategy, Nixon developed with Kissinger's assistance a new foreign policy process that centralized decision making to an unprecedented degree in the White House. As president he sought freedom to evaluate what was in America's best interests, to take decisive action whenever necessary and to coordinate the application of linkage between different issues. The last thing he wanted was to have his hands tied by what he perceived to be the narrow, short-sighted and unsophisticated perspective of Congress. He knew that a foreign policy that prioritized order over idealism was bound to offend liberal Democrats and conservative Republicans alike and that congressmen would want to please voters by winding down America's commitments in Vietnam irrespective of how this impacted on the diplomacy of détente.

Even worse than Congress in Nixon's eyes was the self-interested, slow-moving, risk-averse State Department. He did not want foreign policy run by what he called 'the striped-pants faggots in Foggy Bottom'.[31] Already contemptuous of bureaucrats as a breed, Nixon saw that State was organized into regional and functional sub-departments that compartmentalized specific issues without reference to the broader picture. True to form, its Soviet specialists would initially oppose rapprochement with China for fear that this would offend the Kremlin, whereas Nixon saw it as a way to make the Russians more pliable. Having such a clear sense of his destiny, the President was inevitably impatient and contemptuous of those who did not share his bold vision. He would have heartily agreed with Kissinger's comment in his memoirs: 'It seems to me no accident that most great statesmen had been locked in permanent struggle with the experts in their foreign offices, for the scope of the statesman's conception challenges the inclination of the expert toward minimum risk.'[32]

Consequently, Nixon bypassed the State Department as much as possible by using the NSC as the forum for decision making. State even found itself out of the loop in its natural metier of negotiation. Instead, Nixon employed the so-called back channel of secret diplomacy conducted by Kissinger, often circumventing parallel public negotiations between foreign policy bureaucrats. Virtually all his international successes – notably the Vietnam peace settlement, the SALT talks, the Berlin treaty and the opening of China – were achieved in this way. This was humiliating for the State Department in general and Secretary of State William Rogers in particular. Nixon later admitted that his treatment of Rogers, one of his oldest political allies and a personal friend, was 'terrible'. Nevertheless, he and Kissinger were agreed that their diplomatic achievements would have 'proved unattainable by conventional procedures'.[33]

The sweep of Nixon's grand design was impressive, but it is important to understand that its conceptual coherence only evolved as his first term progressed. He did not bring to office a definitive game plan that mapped out a clear course of action. Indeed, the evolutionary conceptualization of détente was in large part a rationalization of a series of maneuvers designed to get the United States out of Vietnam, Nixon's immediate foreign policy priority. According to Raymond Garthoff, a professional diplomat and accomplished academic analyst, 'Improvement of relations with the Soviet Union, and a possible parallel rapprochement with China, were . . . seen as much as means to that end as they were ends in themselves.'[34] The same was true of the Nixon Doctrine, which effectively repudiated the rationale for US military intervention in Vietnam and legitimized the new policy of Vietnamization. In the words of one analyst, this transformed Vietnam from 'a strategic contest . . . into a dirty little war that could . . . be lost or settled in a way that would not gravely damage American interests or increase threats'.[35] In time, however, the Nixon Doctrine was internationalized through the application of Vietnamization first to the entire Far East and then to the Persian Gulf.

Many of the tactical escalations that formed the fifth element of détente were in reality actions intended to improve America's position in Vietnam and only subsequently presented as part of a grand design. Some escalations also contradicted other elements in the strategy of détente. For example, Nixon's decision to mine North Vietnamese ports in order to cripple the Communist spring offensive of 1972 put at risk the holding of the Moscow summit. In a revealing moment, Nixon blurted out to aides, 'The summit isn't worth a damn if the price for it is losing in Vietnam.'[36] Similarly, the invasions of Cambodia in 1970 and Laos in 1971 went against the Nixon Doctrine's intent. When this was pointed out, an irate Kissinger responded: 'We wrote the goddam doctrine, we can change it.'[37] To Nixon, peace and global stability depended above all else on the United States showing itself willing to use its military power in pursuit of its goals. 'If, when the chips are down', he told Americans in 1970, 'the world's most powerful nation . . . acts like a pitiful, helpless giant, the forces of totalitarianism and anarchy will threaten free nations and free institutions throughout the world'.[38]

Since Nixon was by inclination always more a fighter than a peacemaker, the tactical escalations did not occasion any presidential hand-wringing. Facing any challenge, his first instinct was to fight back. Restraint did not come naturally to him for fear that it would be seen as weakness. Being one of the first advocates of US military engagement in Asia made it especially hard for him to retreat from this, but he deemed the Nixon Doctrine the only sound basis for a responsible American role on this continent free from risk of other Vietnams. In his memoirs, however, he rued that it was 'misinterpreted by some as signaling a new policy that would lead to total American withdrawal from Asia and from other parts of the world'.[39]

Nixon was more comfortable with his tough, vindictive side than with his reasonable, conciliatory one. Any other leader of a modern democracy would have hated being tagged with a 'mad bomber' image, but he relished it. Significantly, he believed that 'the most serious misjudgment of my Presidency, including Watergate', was not responding with force to North Korea's shooting-down of an unarmed American EC-121 reconnaisance plane with the loss of thirty-one lives in April 1969.[40] Going against his own retaliatory instincts, Nixon heeded cooler counsel that an air strike might instigate a general conflagration on the Korean penninsula and embroil America in another Asian war alongside Vietnam.[41] But he came to believe that his restraint had encouraged North Vietnam's stubbornness over peace terms. 'When we didn't [bomb]', he told aides in 1972, 'everybody figured we were pushovers, and we've been paying for that ever since'.[42] Clearly there was a fundamental tension within Nixon between the statesman and the warrior. Arguably he deserves more credit than he has got from historians for bottling up his pugnacious self as much as he did in pursuit of détente.

In spite of mutual US–Soviet interest in a new relationship, the road to détente was hardly smooth. For much of his first year in office, Nixon was intent on showing Moscow that he would not be constrained by an increasingly dovish legislature and public, particularly over Vietnam but also on other issues. His biggest fight with Congress was over funding for development of an enhanced antiballistic missile (ABM) defense system, which he wanted to use as a bargaining chip in arms limitation talks with the Soviets. But the main stumbling block to détente was Soviet resistance to linkage. Ambassador Dobrynin conveyed a clear message from his masters in secret meetings with Kissinger that all questions 'had to stand on their own feet and be settled accordingly'.[43] In essence, the Kremlin regarded linkage as a form of bribery, an insult to its belief that normalization of relations should represent American acknowledgment of the Soviet Union as a coequal power with full rights to determine its own global interests. This ran counter to Nixon's goal of making progress toward détente dependent on Soviet assistance in getting North Vietnam to agree peace terms. 'If the Soviet Union found it possible to do something in Vietnam, and the Vietnam war ended, then we might do something dramatic to improve our relations', he told Dobrynin in October 1969. 'But let me repeat that we will not hold still for being diddled to death in Vietnam.'[44]

By the time these words were spoken, however, Nixon had already signified his willingness to begin talks on a Strategic Arms Limitation Treaty (SALT), a clear indication that he would pursue détente even in the absence of a Vietnam breakthrough.

Nixon had talked tough to the Ambassador because of his perennial need to ensure that restraint – in this case not following
through on his ultimatum to North Vietnam – was not seen as
weakness.[45] Though he still clung to the illusion that the Soviets
would eventually rein in Hanoi, progressing détente was effectively delinked from Vietnam by the end of 1969 and prized as a
safeguard against the domestic repercussions of failure to end the
war. The Soviets were initially more anxious for arms limitation,
which would legitimize their status as an equal superpower, safeguard their strategic balance with the Americans in the event of
having to divert resources to meet the Chinese threat, and shore
up their prestige with their increasingly disgruntled East
European satellites. SALT became a means to an end for Nixon
too, in his case a political one. It became the vehicle to open up
the 'era of negotiations' that he had promised Americans in his
inaugural address. It also balanced his record, because – in Tom
Wicker's words – 'the Vietnam warmaker could appear to be a
nuclear peacemaker'.[46]

At the Moscow summit of 1972 Nixon and Brezhnev signed an
AntiBallistic Missile Treaty limiting the superpowers to two
ABM sites each and a five-year Interim Agreement on the
Limitations of Strategic Arms. SALT I, as these treaties are col-
lectively known, has immense historical significance as the first
arms control agreement of the nuclear era. It was also a milestone
in the establishment of nuclear parity and sufficiency and com-
mited both nations to acceptance of the MAD balance of terror,
so halting a trend toward reliance on missile defense. However, it
did virtually nothing to halt the arms race in offensive missiles.
Even Kissinger, who was primarily responsible for its negotiation
in secret meetings mainly with Dobrynin, admitted that SALT
'wasn't the best deal but it was better than nothing'.[47] Gerard
Smith, leader of the arms control negotiating team whose patient
labors in Helsinki in 1970 and Vienna in 1971 had been continually undercut by backchannel diplomacy, complained that
Nixon's 'lust for a summit' meant that the prospects for real dis-
armament were subordinated to the political symbolism of signing any deal at the Moscow summit.[48]

In this case the experts *were* willing to be bolder than the
President in pushing for a complete elimination of ABMs and a
ban on the new generation of multi-headed MIRVs (Multiple
Independent Reentry Vehicles), whose development 'represented
a quantum leap in offensive power comparable to the switch

from conventional to nuclear weaponry'.[49] Although SALT I placed a quantitative limit on each side's missile armory, it did not limit the number of warheads each missile carried, which soon became the focus of a new arms race. The technical details of arms limitation was one of the few areas of national security that did not engage the President's interests (according to Kissinger it 'bored him to distraction') and he was inevitably suspicious of specialists who were holdovers from a Democratic administration.[50] His decision not to pursue a workable ban on MIRVs was a response to the Pentagon's insistence that America should exploit its lead in developing the technology of this weaponry, but more informed opinion believed that the existing Soviet lead in heavy missiles would eventually give them the advantage in multiple warheads.

Nixon's decision making on this issue was certainly problematic. Whether a more rational consideration of the options would have yielded substantially better results is a matter of debate. Smith wanted to propose a deal whereby the United States halted production of MIRVs in return for a ban on Soviet flight testing and deployment of these missiles. Even if the Pentagon would have accepted this, which was doubtful, the Kremlin was adamantly opposed to any arrangement that effectively froze the lead presently held by the other side. Nor was it feasible to place limits on MIRV production by both sides because this would have required a greater degree of on-site verification than the Soviets were willing to concede in the early 1970s. As Smith himself acknowledged in his memoirs, 'While there may have been an opportunity missed, it was not a clear one.'[51]

For Nixon SALT I's real importance did not lie in the technical details of arms control but in the broader transformation of American foreign policy from orthodox containment to new détente. Whatever its shortcomings, it was intended to be the first in a series of SALTs that would eventually complete the agenda of superpower arms limitation. A SALT II was eventually signed in 1979 and from 1972 to the mid-1980s SALT talks were 'a barometer of relations' between the Americans and Soviets.[52] Moreover, SALT I was just one element, admittedly the most important one, in the developing Soviet–American rapprochement. At the Moscow summit of 1972, Nixon and Brezhnev concluded agreements on scientific and technological cooperation, including a joint space mission, and a wide range of economic and trade issues. Additionally, the two leaders signed the 'Basic Principles of Relations between the Soviet Union and the United States', which accorded both sides equal superpower status and proclaimed 'there is no alternative to conducting their mutual relations on the basis of peaceful coexistence'.[53] Finally, Nixon approved the calling of a Conference on Security and Cooperation in Europe, which led to the Act of Heksinki of 1975. This agreement improved relations between East and West Europe and recognized the permanency of 1945 boundaries.

There were two further Nixon–Brezhnev summits, one in America in June 1973 and the other in Russia in June 1974. These were useful for consolidating relations but neither resulted in the kind of breakthrough achieved in 1972. Both were overshadowed to an extent by Nixon's problems with Watergate, which the Soviets attributed to US enemies of détente. Without doubt, the growing scandal limited Nixon's freedom to pursue détente. The military chiefs, supported by new Secretary of Defense James Schlesinger, were increasingly critical of how the SALT II talks were progressing. Congressional critics of détente, both liberal and conservative, also grew more assertive. In June 1974, Paul Nitze, who a quarter-century earlier had been the principal author of NSC-68, resigned from the SALT II delegation out of concern that 'Nixon was too preoccupied with surviving and in his effort to get an arms control agreement, he might collapse under Soviet pressure'.[54] In fact Nixon showed no sign of collapse at the third summit, where the two sides agreed to reduce ABMs to one apiece, to cooperate on environmental and energy problems and to complete SALT II by 1979. Nixon also initialed a draft threshold test-ban treaty: the Soviets preferred a comprehensive test ban, but even this limited agreement became a casualty of Watergate and was never submitted for Senate ratification.

Summits were not the only instruments of the new détente. From 1971 through 1973, the Americans and Soviets concluded more than twenty treaties or agreements that improved relations and relaxed tensions. Some of these dealt with weapons issues, such as the 1971 agreement to ban nuclear weapons from the seabed. Others tied up loose ends from World War II such as the Quadripartite Agreement of 1971 over Berlin. Between 1971 and 1974, the two sides also signed more than ten economic agreements. The most important of these was the 1972 trade agreement giving the Soviets most-favored-nation status (subject to congressional approval) and promising them trade credits.

US exports to the Soviet Union rose rapidly from $162 million in 1971 to $1,190 million in 1973, compared to a parallel growth in Soviet exports from $57 million to $220 million. Far from being the success it appeared, this trade bulge was one of the most embarrassing outcomes of détente. It resulted from the Soviets using their trade credits to purchase America's entire wheat reserves at subsidized prices, which enabled them to corner the world grain market in 1972. The consequence of what Kissinger called the 'Great Grain Robbery' was a massive rise in international wheat prices that pushed up inflation in the United States and the rest of the world.[55] Hawkish critics seized on the affair as proof that Nixon's drive for détente made him blind to Soviet cunning. Democratic Senator Henry Jackson of Washington charged that the President had been responsible for 'one of the most notorious foulups in American history'.[56]

As an episode in the great game of diplomacy, Nixon regarded the Soviets' grain coup as small beer compared to the way he had bested them over China. In mid-1969 he had sent clear signals that he wanted a summit in 1970, which would strengthen his hand in the midterm elections, but the Kremlin expressed preference for mid-1971 in the hope of getting a Berlin settlement by then. Nixon got his revenge when he surprised the world by announcing in mid-1971 that he would visit China in the spring of 1972. Since final arrangements for the Moscow summit had not been agreed, it was evident that he would go to Beijing before Moscow. This was both a threatening development to the Soviets and a blow to their self-esteem. According to one Russian diplomat, Foreign Minister Gromyko 'went about for weeks with a black expression' after learning of Nixon's China breakthrough.[57]

Opening up China was *the* big coup of Nixon's foreign policy, indeed of his presidency. Arguably, rapprochement with Russia was more significant in terms of immediate outcomes, but the approach to China represented a fundamental shift in global politics. It was Nixon's most lasting legacy, whose importance grew with the renewal of US–Soviet confrontation in the Reagan years. Asked on NBC's *Meet the Press* in 1988 what he would be most remembered for in the next century, he replied that his administration had made a real difference on this issue. 'If it had not been for the China initiative', he avowed, 'which only I could do at that point, we would be in a terrible situation today with China aligned with the Soviet Union and with the Soviet Union's power'.[58]

For Nixon personally rapprochement with China was an opportunity to measure himself against real giants. Khrushchev and Brezhnev were important leaders but they had not forged a revolution, and their place in history would always be secondary to Lenin and Stalin. Mao and Zhou, by contrast, were the leaders of one of the greatest revolutions in world history. Both men fascinated Nixon, even while he had counted them as enemies. He actually traveled to China in 1972 without a guarantee of seeing the ailing Mao but was granted an audience at very short notice. This brief but significant encounter put the seal of Mao's supreme authority on his country's pursuit of friendship with the United States. It also showed Nixon that his hosts took him seriously as a statesman. Mao jocularly but pointedly commented 'I like rightists', made it evident that he had read Nixon's 1967 *Foreign Affairs* article on Asia and even adjudged that *Six Crises* 'was not a bad book'.[59] Kissinger later surmised that much had depended on how Mao and Zhou assessed 'Nixon's ability to execute, parallel with them, a global policy designed to maintain the balance of power which was the real purpose of their opening to us'.[60]

The *Foreign Affairs* article that engaged Mao's attention was entitled 'Asia after Viet Nam'. Though based on the false assumption of victory in Vietnam, it showed in one historian's estimate that Nixon was 'the first prominent American politician to understand the emergence of modern Asia'.[61] While everyone by 1967 recognized Japan's development as an economic power, Nixon also predicted that Hong Kong, Malaysia, South Korea, Singapore and Thailand would soon reinforce Asia's manufacturing challenge to the West. He foresaw that America's reluctance to fight another war on the continent would necessitate Asian countries having to defend themselves against 'China's ambitions', ideally through formation of a regional alliance. To this end Nixon advocated Japan's rearmament, forbidden under the postwar constitution imposed on it by the United States. But he also recognized that this was not the only way of dealing with China, which had largely been isolated from the international community since the 1949 revolution. 'We simply cannot afford', he declared, 'to leave China forever outside the family of nations, there to nurture its fantasies, cherish its hates and threaten its neighbors.' Sino-American relations had been characterized by

extreme bitterness for twenty years and Nixon was not propos-
ing to deal with the Chinese Communists as they were, but he
insisted that 'the world cannot be safe until China changes. Thus
our aim . . . should be to induce change.'[62]

In his 1967 article Nixon had been thinking of improved relations with China in the longer term, but as president he took the
view that expeditious progress on this front would make the
Soviets more anxious for détente. It was a risky venture. Nixon
was conscious, as Bob Haldeman recorded, 'that we've got to
avoid making too much hay out of China, because they might
pull the rug out from under us and we don't want to get our neck
out that far'.[63] There was a danger that triangular diplomacy
might drive the Communist powers back into each other's arms.
Nixon gambled that the strain in Sino-Soviet relations was too
great to permit rapprochement. Until the second half of 1971, the
Chinese alternated between responding to his overtures and hoping to repair relations with Russia. This was a result of a power
struggle in the Beijing leadership between Zhou's pro-Western
faction and Lin Biao's pro-Soviet group, but the latter's death in
a mysterious plane crash proved decisive. From then on, both the
Chinese and Russians worried so much about each other's relations with the United States that they engaged in competition to
court it. This was precisely what Nixon intended: in April 1971,
he told aides, 'We're using the Chinese thaw to get the Russians
shook.'[64]

Nixon's opening of China is one of the best examples of
'Presidentially-imposed, Presidentially-initiated policy' in the
annals of American diplomacy.[65] Firstly, Nixon ensured that the
American government's conventional anti-Chinese rhetoric was
toned down. His own statements gave the lead in this. In October
1970, he referred in public for the first time to the People's
Republic of China, instead of 'Red China'. Even his rambling
remarks to student demonstrators at the Lincoln Memorial the
previous May had voiced the hope that China would be opened
up so that they could visit 'one of the most remarkable people on
earth'.[66] Nixon also wooed the Chinese with deeds. He ordered
the State Department and other agencies to make the first low-
key gestures of reconciliation, such as relaxing trade and travel
restrictions and calling for a program of cultural and scientific
exchanges. He made confidential overtures to Beijing through
President Nicolae Ceausescu of Romania and President Yahya
Khan of Pakistan. He offered demonstrable proof of the Nixon

Doctrine's benefit to China by removing the Seventh Fleet from permanent patrol of the Taiwan Straits and withdrawing all nuclear weapons from America's Okinawa base.

All this was done in spite of the reservations of the Secretary of State, who remained loyal to America's traditional recognition of Chiang Kai-shek's Nationalist regime as the authentic Chinese government. This attitude ensured that Nixon kept him in the dark about the development of his China policy. More surprisingly Henry Kissinger was a reluctant convert to this aspect of the President's grand design, even though he implicitly claims equal credit in his memoirs by referring to 'our China initiative'.[67] On 14 August 1969, Nixon told an NSC meeting that the Soviet Union was more aggressive than China, a reversal of twenty years of orthodox thinking that Kissinger dubbed a 'revolutionary thesis'.[68] As late as April 1971 Kissinger remained distrustful of Beijing's motives.[69] It was at this juncture that the Chinese expressed their willingness to receive a high-level American envoy to discuss improving relations. Kissinger was delegated to go in conditions of extreme secrecy and under the code name 'Polo'. The success of this visit, during which he set up Nixon's official visit, changed Kissinger into an enthusiast for Sino-US rapproachement. By late 1971, when Kissinger made a public trip to Beijing, Nixon was growing jealous that the press would give him too much credit for the breakthrough.[70]

In the post-Cold War era, meetings of international statesmen have become commonplace and make for routine headlines. It is a challenge to engage, let alone surprise, today's mass audience accustomed to a constant diet of global news on CNN. In 1972, however, Nixon's visit to the hitherto closed but exotic and alluring China was a huge media spectacle. The pictures of him shaking hands with Zhou and of him and Pat on the Great Wall of China rank among the defining images of the 1970s. Nor could journalists spoil the latter moment by widely quoting his apparently trite remark – 'This is a great wall' – but leaving out the rest of his words that made it a more meaningful statement – 'and it had to be built by a great people'.[71] According to a 1971 poll 56 percent of Americans regarded China as the world's most dangerous nation, but television news pictures of a Chinese army band playing 'Oh Susannah' and 'America the Beautiful' at banquets for the presidential entourage offered reassurance that Beijing was no longer an implacable foe. By the end of his visit, 98 percent of Americans knew that Nixon had been to China, a level of popular awareness inconceivable in today's more apathetic times. With his eye on the 1972 election, the President craftily maximized his media exposure by laying over for nine hours in Alaska on the way home so that his plane could land in Washington at the 9 p.m. prime news hour.

The China visit also had diplomatic accomplishments in the form of the Shanghai Communiqué. This sent a clear signal that America and China had formed an entente against Soviet expansionism. The signatories declared that neither would 'seek hegemony in the Asia Pacific region and each is opposed to efforts by any other country or group to establish such hegemony'. With regard to Taiwan, then as now the most contentious issue between them, the United States recognized that the island was 'a part of China' and affirmed that its 'ultimate objective' was to withdraw its military forces and installations from there when the Chinese adversaries resolved their problems peacefully and tensions in the area diminished. What this meant in practice was deliberately unclear. This policy of 'strategic ambiguity' was designed to keep Taiwan and China guessing about the true level of US commitment to Taiwan. It formed a cornerstone of America's Far Eastern policy for the next thirty years until George Bush signaled in 2001 that the United States would do whatever it took to defend Taiwan from Chinese attack. Mao and Zhou had hoped to be given a guarantee that the United States would formally recognize the People's Republic. However, their new friend held back from this for fear of offending Republican and Democratic hawks who were already up in arms over the recent United Nations decision to seat Communist China in place of Taiwan. Nixon in turn was disappointed at his failure to get Beijing to stop supporting the North Vietnamese war effort. Though Mao gave him an elliptic promise that China would not intervene in the conflict, Zhou stated frankly that it would continue to provide Hanoi with military equipment.[72]

Notwithstanding the success of his triangular diplomacy, Nixon had made two fundamental miscalculations with regard to Vietnam in his dealings with the Soviets and Chinese. Firstly, there was no evidence to support his contention that early withdrawal from Vietnam on unfavorable terms would have compromised America's credibility in their eyes and prevented the development of détente. If anything, the continued involvement in Vietnam hindered the development of détente with China, which proved the key to improving relations with the Soviet

Union. It was certainly grist to the mill of the anti-Western faction in the internal power struggle that caused Beijing to blow hot and cold on improving relations with the US until mid-1971. Significantly, in January 1972 Zhou subjected Kissinger aide Alexander Haig to a bitter harangue against US imperialism in the presence of Communist Party officials. This ploy was intended to show the Americans that the internal opposition to détente had not ended with Lin Biao's death.[73] Nixon's second miscalculation was to overestimate not only the willingness but also the ability of Russia and China to control North Vietnam, whom he wrongly regarded as the pawn of the Communist powers. Unable to shake off one of the dominant orthodoxies of the Cold War, he never understood the nationalist dimension that drove Communism in Vietnam and much of the third world.

For Nixon US relations with Russia and China formed the core of world politics. Little else in the international arena mattered to him. He saw himself as a modern-day Metternich, managing global change for the benefit of his country by entering into a series of accommodations with the Communist powers to create a stable, orderly and peaceful world. However, he failed to appreciate that much of the dynamic for change in the late twentieth century emanated from third world nations' aspirations for political and economic independence. In mid-1969, Robert Osgood, a senior NSC staff member, drew up a confidential inventory of the global situation facing the new administration. Insofar as third world countries were concerned, he adjudged that these would 'not prove a decisive arena of great power conflict' because they were 'too heterogeneous, disorganized, and resistant to external control and influence'.[74] These enlightened insights only encouraged Nixon to ignore most of Africa and Asia in the construction of his grand design. In March 1970 the President told aides that he did care about developing nations, 'but what happens in those parts of the world is not, in the final analysis, going to have any significant effect on the success of our foreign policy in the foreseeable future'.[75] If he thought about the third world at all, it was only if change therein threatened the global balance of power between the US, Russia and China.

Typical of this attitude was Nixon's tilt toward Pakistan in its 1971 war with India.[76] The regional issue at stake was the independence of East Pakistan (now Bangladesh). Pakistan's brutal suppression of the autonomy movement in its Eastern zone had resulted in ten million refugees fleeing into India, who eventually intervened to liberate this territory. Pakistan then retaliated by attacking Indian positions in Kashmir and Punjab. This aroused the mistaken fear in Nixon that the militarily superior Indians would gobble up the whole of Pakistan with dire consequences for the global balance of power.

Vexed that India's expansion would benefit the Soviet Union, with whom it had recently concluded a friendship treaty, Nixon used the hotline for the first time in his presidency to warn Moscow to restrain its ally or face cancellation of the 1972 summit. He also wanted to impress China, who knew of the secret 1962 US commitment to help Pakistan against future Indian attack. In the words of one NSC aide, it was essential to show Beijing 'we were a reliable country to deal with'.[77] This triangular great-power perspective was crudely but effectively summarized by a Kissinger statement that Nixon approvingly quoted in his memoirs: 'We can't allow a friend of ours and China's to get screwed in a conflict with a friend of Russia's.'[78]

Nixon's response was to order a naval task force to the Bay of Bengal to overawe the Indians. Fortunately a peace settlement recognizing Bangladesh's independence was agreed before it moved into position. Nixon would claim this outcome as a vindication of linkage but there is no evidence that Moscow restrained India, whose leaders had no intention of territorial conquest. In reality Nixon had come close to breaching America's neutrality in the interests of triangular diplomacy instead of treating a regional issue on regional terms. There was no direct US interest in the issue that remotely justified risking the confrontation with the Soviets that might have ensued if the naval task force had become involved in the conflict. Nixon had also subordinated the humanitarian issues of the refugee crisis and the atrocities committed by Pakistani soldiers – not only killings but also the rape of as many as 50,000 East Pakistani women – to an amoral concern about America's world position.

Nixon's tendency to view the world solely through the lens of superpower relations also planted a seed that would yield a bitter harvest in Iran. He transformed America's steady low-key support for the Shah's regime into a close and intensive relationship in applying the Nixon Doctrine to Southwest Asia. The President returned home from the Moscow summit via Teheran, where he struck a deal that effectively made Iran the protector of US interests in the Persian Gulf. This was a region where the Soviets had gained new friends in the shape of Syria and Iraq. His coffers overflowing with oil revenues, the Shah was anxious to increase his already substantial purchases of US military equipment so that he could face down any state or combination of states in the Gulf. In spite of State Department reservations that the decision would provoke the Soviets into stepping up aid to their surrogates, Nixon informally agreed to allow the Shah access to the whole of America's military inventory, excluding nuclear weapons but including the latest technology – such as the F-15 fighter plane that was not yet in service. The resultant sales, totaling $16.2 billion from 1972 through 1977, was the largest arms transfer in world history.[79]

The embrace of the Shah proved one of the greatest mistakes of Nixon's foreign policy. According to American diplomat Armin Meyer, the arms sales fed the Shah's grandiose ambitions and turned him into a megalomaniac.[80] Weapons became his drug. To feed his habit, he helped to engineer the massive oil-price hike by the Organization of Petroleum Exporting Countries in 1973. He was untrustworthy in other ways. At the Shah's behest, Nixon agreed to join him in funding Kurdish rebels fighting for independence from Soviet ally Iraq. Encouraged by the US, Kurdish forces stepped up their operations, but were abandoned when the Shah resolved his differences with Saddam Hussein in 1975. Even though Kissinger rationalized the ditching of the Kurds with the comment that 'covert action should not be confused with missionary work', it was hardly a good sign of America's reliability and credibility.[81]

Finally, the domestic perception within Iran of the Shah's close ties with the United States had fateful consequences. The enforced modernization of his country brought his regime into conflict with its traditional and largely rural Islamic society, which saw him as the catspaw of American influence. The legion of American technicians, numbering about 25,000, who had to be imported to train Iranian forces in the use of the complex weaponry bought by the Shah strengthened this perception. Consequently the Iranian Revolution of 1979 had an anti-American character, which found expression in the policies of the new Islamic regime and in the humiliating US Embassy hostage crisis of 1979–81. While Nixon cannot be held responsible for these developments, it was the case that his enthusiasm for the Shah was based on ignorance of the conflict between modernity and tradition in Asia. Regarding countries like Iran as pawns on the chessboard of global diplomacy, he did not understand that they possessed their own dynamic, which could set them apart from the gameplan involving the bigger pieces.

Even if he did not understand Asia as well as he thought he did, Nixon at least respected many of its leaders – excessively in the case of Pakistan's Yahya Khan and the Shah. By contrast, he neither understood black Africa nor respected its leaders. Early in his presidency, he told aides that 'there has never in history been an adequate black nation, and they are the only race of which this is true'.[82] On the few occasions Africa came up for high-level White House discussion, Nixon and his men tended to indulge in racist banter. 'Henry, let's leave the niggers to Bill [Rogers]', the President once remarked, 'and we'll take care of the rest of the world'.[83] Unsurprisingly, administration policy toward Africa was suffused with ignorance and prejudice.

National Security Study Memorandum (NSSM) 39, a secret review of Africa policy ordered by Kissinger in 1969, recommended that the United States should prioritize good relationships with white regimes for geopolitical reasons. South Africa's position at the tip of the continent was deemed to have immense strategic and economic significance for America's world interests, and support for Portugal's colonial regimes in Angola, Mozambique and Guinea was dictated by that country's importance to the NATO security apparatus in Europe. Whilst NSSM 39 envisaged that whites would eventually transfer power peacefully to blacks, it saw no prospect of immediate change in South Africa, neighboring Rhodesia and the Portugese colonies and advised against quixotic idealism. It further warned that nationalist movements in these countries had Communist connections.[84]

This made for an African policy that was based not on African considerations but global ones. According to Anthony Lake, who resigned from Kissinger's NSC in disillusion and later served as Bill Clinton's National Security Adviser, the State Department's Africa specialists disparagingly referred to administration policy as the 'Tar Baby option' that would stick the United States to losing causes in Africa.[85] Such gloomy foreboding was borne out shortly after Nixon left office. In 1975 the collapse of the Portuguese empire in Africa saw Marxist regimes take power in Mozambique and Angola, in the latter case with assistance from the Soviets and Cubans. Five years later there was a peaceful transfer of power to a native regime in Rhodesia/Zimbabwe. South Africa resisted the tide for another decade before following suit. The African policy that Nixon adopted in 1969 on the basis of NSSM 39's expectation that 'Whites are here to stay' has therefore shown, in the words of one critic, 'all the prescience of a Marie Antoinette in 1789'.[86]

Despite Nixon's dealings with the notoriously authoritarian Shah of Iran and his support for racist regimes in Africa, it was the overthrow and murder of Salvador Allende by the Chilean military in September 1973 that many on the Left in Western Europe and the Americas regarded as the most odious example of American imperialism during his presidency. He and Kissinger had done their best to destabilize Chile since the Marxist Allende had come to power democratically in 1970, mainly through economic warfare and a CIA-subsidized campaign of disinformation against his government. They were determined not to have another crypto-Communist government on the American continent, even one that had come to power through the ballot box. As Kissinger asserted, 'I don't see why we have to let a country go Marxist just because its people are irresponsible.'[87]

David Phillips, the CIA section chief responsible for Chile, has stated that the agency was fully aware that the coup would entail Allende's murder and there 'was no squeamishness in Richard Nixon on that score'.[88] There is no clearcut evidence as yet that the President and Kissinger were complicit in his death. Nor can it be claimed unequivocably that he would not have been overthrown but for American destabilization activities.[89] Nevertheless Nixon's policy was a throwback to the Cold War past, when America was hostile to leftist regimes in the third world in case they opened the door to Communism. The execution of as many as 10,000 leftists by the military regime did not prevent it receiving American recognition and financial aid. Regardless of whether Nixon was directly involved or not in the coup, his policy toward Chile stands out as one of the most deplorable aspects of his presidency.

One of the hottest trouble spots in the world during Nixon's presidency, as now, was the Middle East, where Arab states were engaged in the War of Attrition to get back territory won by Israel in the Six Day war of 1967.[90] True to form, Nixon and Kissinger viewed this regional problem primarily in terms of its bearing on the Soviet–American global balance. Initially they had included the Middle East among the 'linkage' issues involving the two superpowers and briefly entertained the notion that American concessions regarding Arab issues might induce the Soviets to cooperate over Vietnam. This idea was utterly impractical, not least because events would repeatedly show that neither superpower could control its regional clients. Within a few months of taking office, Nixon's Middle Eastern policy had shifted from strategic cooperation to strategic rivalry with the Soviets. In August 1970 Nixon told Israeli ambassador Yitzhak Rabin, 'The Soviets are the main cause of Middle East tensions, and . . . if they were removed from the situation Israel would be able to handle matters without difficulty'.[91] The Kremlin's arming of Egypt and Syria kept the regional pot boiling. Nixon therefore sought to show the Arab states that the Soviet Union was an ineffective ally and only America could promote an acceptable regional peace.

In 1969–70, the US sent out signals to Arab states about its willingness to act as honest broker. One such gesture was Nixon's support for the Rogers Plan, a ten-point peace proposal put forward in late 1969 by the US Secretary of State, whose requirements for extensive Israeli withdrawal from occupied territories made it wholly unacceptable to Tel Aviv. The same reasoning underlay Nixon's decision to postpone delivery of Phantom jets to Israel in 1970. On the other hand, Nixon was resolute in his determination to spike Soviet efforts to help Arab states change the regional balance. In September 1970 a large Syrian tank force directed by Soviet advisers invaded Jordan in support of a Palestinian guerilla campaign to overthrow the pro-Western regime of King Hussein. Convinced that 'they're testing us', Nixon responded by deploying a naval task force in the eastern Mediterranean, putting 20,000 airborne troops on alert, and getting Hussein's reluctant approval for the Israeli air force to help against the Syrians if needed.[92] In the end, the Jordanians bested their enemies on their own, but Nixon had sent Arab states a clear message that he would not tolerate Soviet-promoted gains.

In mid-1972 Egypt's new leader, Anwar Sadat, sprang a surprise by expelling 15,000 Soviet military advisers from his country. Whether this was a lost opportunity for avoiding a further war is a matter of debate. To some analysts, Sadat was engaged in a machiavellian ploy to build up covertly for another attack on Israel, while others see him as looking for a negotiated peace. Nixon and Kissinger inclined toward the latter view but thought that his action allowed them to put a Middle East settlement on the back-burner until peace was achieved in Vietnam.[93] Their intention was to apply pressure on Tel Aviv to negotiate in Nixon's second term, but the emerging Watergate crisis weakened their hand against the strong pro-Israeli lobby in Congress. Nixon dismissed Sadat's warnings that he would resort to military force without progress on peace talks as a bluff, while the Soviets advised their erstwhile ally against such action. In October 1973, however, Egypt and Syria launched the Yom Kippur offensive that caught Israel and the United States almost completely by surprise.

It was Kissinger who orchestrated America's response to the new war because Nixon was preoccupied with Watergate. Initially he dragged his feet on resupplying Israel in the belief that Egyptian gains would make it easier to bring both sides to the peace table. Tuning erratically in and out of the crisis, Nixon eventually learned about the delay and ordered greater dispatch on the part of the Pentagon, whom Kissinger had convinced him was at fault.[94] The resupplied Israelis then drove back and encircled the Egyptian army. Anxious to head off a total victory that would harden Israeli intransigence, Kissinger went to Moscow to hammer out a ceasefire agreement with Brezhnev, only for the Tel Aviv government to ignore it. Sadat then invited the Americans and Soviets to send troops to supervise the ceasefire, but Kissinger was determined to 'resist by force if necessary' the introduction of Soviet troops into the region under whatever pretext.[95] When the Soviets threatened to act unilaterally, he ordered a worldwide military alert, moving US armed forces from their normal Defensive Condition IV to DefCon III. Consequently, B-52 bombers lined up waiting for the attack signal, nuclear missile silos were put on heightened readiness and nuclear-armed submarines sped to secret positions off the Soviet coast.

Upon hearing of the Soviets' threatened intervention, Nixon reportedly told new chief of staff General Alexander Haig, 'This is the most serious thing since the Cuban Missile Crisis. Words won't do the job. We've got to act.'[96] Perhaps reflecting the loyalty of an Army man for his commander-in-chief, Haig has portrayed Nixon as providing broad instructions for managing the crisis, even if he was not involved in the crisis meetings. Nixon was certainly not present when Kissinger, James Schlesinger, Haig, Admiral Moorer of the Joint Chiefs and CIA chief William Colby decided to order the military alert on the night of 24 October. Though Haig claims to have acted as a go-between who left the room to keep Nixon fully informed of what was happening at every stage of the meeting, almost every other account by the key participants and their aides depicts Nixon as being out of the loop.[97] The probability is that Nixon was in bed asleep, exhausted by the parallel 'Saturday Night Massacre' in the Watergate saga and suffering the effects of a few stiff drinks. In fact, Kissinger's response to the crisis was driven in large part by a concern that the Soviets hoped to establish a stronger presence in the Middle East while Nixon was incapacitated by his domestic travails.[98]

Moscow's consequent inaction seemingly justified America's tough stand, but whether the Soviets intended acting unilaterally is improbable. Their more likely goal was to pressurize the US into restraining Israel. For this reason the October 1973 crisis was far less dangerous than the 1962 Cuban missile crisis, but this is the wisdom of hindsight. If Moscow had decided to hang tough for fear of losing face, the threat of confrontation would have been magnified. Kissinger later described the alert as 'our deliberate over-reaction' to warn not only the Soviets but also the Israelis about the need for restraint.[99] Nevertheless he deserves credit for making a tough call and getting it right. Nixon, by contrast, merits only criticism for his role. As James Schlesinger later observed, it was inconceivable that any other president of modern times would have been absent from a meeting of comparable significance.[100] Not only was Nixon not in charge at a moment of peril for the whole world, but also his weakness was an essential element in the escalation of the crisis. Whether or not the Soviets were looking to exploit his incapacity is unclear, but Kissinger's authorization of the alert was predicated on the assumption that they were.

Out of the crucible of crisis emerged diplomatic success for the United States. Kissinger's alert had warned off the Soviets, persuaded the Israelis not to cause further problems over the cease-fire and shown moderate Arab nations that only America could get things done in the Middle East. Through his famous shuttle diplomacy between Tel Aviv, Cairo and Damascus, Kissinger built separate Israeli peace settlements with Egypt and Syria in 1974. He also laid the foundations for improved US relations with a neutralized Egypt that has provided a cornerstone for America's Middle Eastern policy down to the present. One immediate benefit of this was Sadat's getting Arab nations to lift their six-month embargo of oil imports to the United States imposed in retaliation for its rearming of Israel.

Having inherited a dangerous situation in the Middle East when it took office, the Nixon administration could claim with some justice that it beqeathed to its successors an ongoing peace process that they could carry forward. This was one area of foreign policy – perhaps the only one – where the plaudits belonged to Kissinger not Nixon. It was also the foreign policy issue on which Nixon's performance was most affected by his Watergate problems. Nixon went to the Middle East in June 1974, becoming the first American president to visit Israel and Syria, but by now he was a broken reed. The man of the hour was Kissinger, who was portrayed on the cover of *Newsweek* in a Superman costume bearing a 'Super K' logo.

Just two months after his Middle East visit, a disgraced Nixon quit office and soon afterward started the long task of rebuilding his reputation as a great statesman. In spite of his achievements, there is by no means a scholarly consensus as to whether his foreign policy record was as significant and innovative as claimed. Doubts surround the man-of-peace image that Nixon's gravestone seeks to make indelible for posterity. The prolongation of the Vietnam war for dubious geopolitical reasons detracts from his reputation as a peacemaker. A major question also hangs over the significance of détente, which was never intended to end the Cold War, only to manage it through new means. The Soviets had no illusions on this score. In the opinion of former ambassador Anatoli Dobrynin, Nixon and Kissinger sought 'a more stable and predictable strategic situation' but their primary goal was always to preserve America's military superiority and national interests. To this end, he declared, neither man 'proved able (or wanted) to break out of the orbit of the Cold War, although their attitude was more pragmatic and realistic than other Cold Warriors in the White House'.[101] In his books, *The Real War* (1980), *Real Peace* (1984) and *No More Vietnams* (1985), written against the background of renewed Cold War, Nixon himself presented détente as a form of containment that his successors had been unable to pursue as skilfully as he had.

The durability of Nixon's legacy was also questionable because the two superpowers wanted something different out of détente. If Nixon viewed it as an instrument of containment, Soviet leaders saw its purpose as not to eliminate superpower competition but to prevent this from escalating to dangerous proportions. In the Kremlin's view, détente's recognition of Soviet parity legitimized its position as a global power and gave it the right to pursue its interests in regions that were not vital to the other superpower's security. This was manifest in the Soviet Union's supplantation of US influence in Southeast Asia after Vietnam, Laos and Cambodia fell to Communism and intervention in Angola in 1975. Its activism undermined support for détente in the United States in the second half of the 1970s. Eventually the Soviet invasion of Afghanistan in 1979 provoked a renewal of American militarism under Jimmy Carter and Ronald Reagan. For the next decade détente remained, in Joan Hoff's words, 'like Nixon himself, a ghost from the past, waiting in the wings to be resurrected by changing world and domestic circumstances'.[102]

Nixon's foreign policy in the third world was neither successful nor a model to guide later administrations in the post-Cold War era. Excessively preoccupied with great power diplomacy, he did not understand the significance and the aspirations of developing nations. Driven by considerations of *realpolitik*, he ignored issues of morality and human rights that were important to help the development of Africa, Asia and Latin America. This outlook was a product of his enduring Cold War mentality that regarded leftist movements in the third world as Soviet pawns. As William Bundy points out, this tendency was reinforced by the overcentralization of foreign policy in the White House. Not only did this make it impossible to be attentive to all nations, but it also cut off the channel of local knowledge provided by American diplomats and foreign service officers in embassies throughout the world.[103]

Even as a crisis manager, Nixon's record was at best spotty. In his first book, he had written, 'We live in an age in which individual reaction to crisis may bear on the fate of mankind for centuries to come.'[104] The international crises he handled as president were, of course, vastly more significant than the personal ones he had chronicled in *Six Crises*. He performed very effectively in the case of the 1969 EC-121 incident with North Korea, the 1970 Cuban missile affair and the 1970 Jordan crisis. However, most of the crises that he faced in Vietnam were largely of his own making. He made the India–Pakistan crisis of 1971 more dangerous than it need have been. Most culpably, his Watergate-affected conduct in the 1973 Middle East stand-off with the Soviets was arguably the worst crisis-management performance by a modern American president.

Finally, Nixon's secrecy and deception in the conduct of foreign policy did not build stable domestic foundations for détente. Behaving more like a nineteenth-century European grandee than the leader of a modern democracy, he created a personal foreign policy that was bound to lose political and popular support with his fall from grace. Soviet gains under the cover of détente fueled the resurgence of the Republican right. Reaction against Nixon's *realpolitik* also engendered Jimmy Carter's human rights crusade, which sought to restore morality as a cardinal principle of American foreign policy.

Set against such criticisms, Nixon had real achievements to his credit. He had recognized both the need and the opportunity to develop new relations with the two main Communist powers. His supreme achievement was to open up China and help bring it back into the global community. This huge country could not have remained isolated forever, but it required skill and courage to carry the China initiative through to success in the early 1970s. It is also doubtful whether any other president could match him for the geopolitical vision that informed the new policy of détente. In great power terms, the diplomacy of triangulation with the Soviets and Chinese had worked very well and made the world a safer place. If détente faltered in the late 1970s, it had still shown that America and the Communist world could peacefully coexist. As such, Nixon's initiatives to the Soviet Union and China marked the beginning of the end of the Cold War. The 1970s may seem no more than a truce before the resumption of hostilities in the 1980s, but the eventual Reagan–Gorbachev reconciliation was arguably facilitated by the precedent of the Nixon era.

Whether Nixon was a great world statesman is very much open to doubt. He was a highly effective player with a new game-plan in the old contest of great power politics. But in the modern world a statesman faces a more challenging task than his predecessors in the days of Metternich or, further back, Machiavelli. He must be judged not solely on his performance in *realpolitik* terms, but also on the morality and idealism of his conduct and vision. Nixon was found wanting on the latter score. His foreign policy had the stamp of greatness in parts but must be judged as a whole. The endurance of his Cold War mentality, his failure to understand the third world, his methods and his handling of Vietnam all count against him. History and historians have to counter the overselling by Nixon and his supporters of the wisdom and effectiveness of his management of international affairs.

|7|

Imperial president

'The history books', the President told his Cabinet on 11 November 1971, 'will write Richard Nixon in large letters'.[1] They have indeed done so, though not in the way that he intended. Nixon's tenure in office was marked by the worst abuse of presidential power in US history. It has gone down in history books as the apogee of the imperial presidency. As historian Arthur M. Schlesinger Jr observed, 'With Nixon there came . . . a singular confluence of the job with the man. The Presidency, as enlarged by international delusions and domestic propulsions, found a President whose inner mix of vulnerability and ambition impelled him to push the historical logic to its extremity'.[2]

Nixon held office at a particularly difficult moment in American history, when the postwar consensus on domestic and foreign policy was breaking down. He had the opportunity to lead his country in new directions but he also faced considerable obstacles to the exercise of presidential governance. He lacked a clearcut mandate because of the narrowness of his 1968 election, he was the first incoming president since 1848 to face a Congress in which neither house was controlled by his party and he had to deal with growing opposition to the Vietnam war.

In a democracy great leadership is marked by success in the politics of persuasion and consent. However, Nixon's tendency to view politics in terms of conflict and crisis made him prone to engage in secrecy and surprise and to violate constitutional norms. Ever focused on victory in the arena, he was impatient with democratic restraints and scornful of the presidency's obligation to respect the Constitution and the American people. In Nixon's view, getting things done by whatever means necessary was the sole mark of presidential greatness. Goodness and morality only got in the way of this. As he remarked in one of his post-presidential books, 'virtue is not what lifts great leaders above others'.[3]

Nixon inherited an office that had been straining the constitutional limits of its power for over twenty years. The presidency had steadily expanded its control over the development and execution of national security policy in the cause of prosecuting the Cold War. Two presidents – Harry Truman and Lyndon Johnson – had committed the United States to fight foreign conflicts without a formal declaration of war by Congress. Every president from Truman through Johnson had sent US troops abroad without consulting Congress. In 1951 Nixon had voted for the Senate's resolution that no troops in addition to the four divisions already earmarked could be sent to Europe as part of America's NATO commitment without its specific consent, but the Truman administration had dismissed this as being without legal force.[4] Moreover, secret executive agreements with foreign governments were routinely used to extend America's Cold War commitments in Europe, Asia and Africa without the impediment of congressional authorization or scrutiny. Increasingly Congress grew to accept its relative impotence in foreign policy as part of the natural order in a dangerous world that necessitated rapid deployment of American power. As Arthur Schlesinger commented, 'The image of the President acting by himself in foreign affairs, imposing his own sense of reality and necessity on a waiting government and people, became the new orthodoxy.'[5]

One clue to understanding Nixon's approach to presidential governance is to examine which other leaders he admired. Among American presidents his heroes were Theodore Roosevelt and Woodrow Wilson, yet neither was a role model for him. Though Nixon was fond of quoting TR's exhortations to be bold in the political arena, Roosevelt had not governed in times when America was a world leader and his period in office was not marked by the challenge of national crisis. Wilson's internationalism was close to Nixon's heart, his moralism was not. Significantly, it was foreign leaders who provided Nixon's inspiration, particularly those who had risen from the ashes of defeat like Mao Zedong, Winston Churchill and – above all – Charles de Gaulle.

In his book *Leaders*, Nixon wrote of de Gaulle, 'He acted a part, playing a role he himself created that fit only one actor. Even more he fashioned *himself* so that he could play it. He created de Gaulle the public person, to play the role of de Gaulle, personification of France'. Nixon also quoted de Gaulle approvingly that 'a leader must choose between prominence and happiness . . . must endure strict self-discipline, constant risk-taking and perpetual inner struggle'.[6] As Stephen Ambrose notes, his remarks about de Gaulle are an 'excellent self-portrait' of Nixon himself.[7] Equally important, Nixon's admiration for a man who had always been unwilling to share power since his days as wartime leader of the Free French offered insight into his own style of leadership.

There was great similarity between the situations into which de Gaulle and Nixon were thrust as national leaders. Both became president after a period in the political wilderness and at a time when their country was in turmoil. Both had to extricate their nation from unpopular overseas wars. Both regarded the entrenched power of parties, interest groups and bureaucracies as obstacles to the achievement of their vision. However, de Gaulle assumed leadership of a nation with a tradition of revolution rather than political stability. Whereas the United States had been governed under the same Constitution since 1787, France had experienced fifteen different constitutional regimes over this period.

With France's IVth Republic on the verge of collapse in 1958, de Gaulle could act in accordance with his country's revolutionary traditions to establish a new regime. In the Vth Republic, whose constitutional arrangements largely followed his personal blueprint, de Gaulle was able to create a new presidency, reshape the bureaucracy and develop a strong party of government that gave him control of the legislature. Nixon, by contrast, operated in a political system where separate institutions of government shared power in order to prevent any one of them being too powerful. The American president could never become what de Gaulle sought to create in France – a plebiscitary president, the personification of the national majority whose votes put him in office and gave him a personal mandate that the other branches of government could not oppose. However, the idea that the American president was empowered by a special relationship with the American people lay at the heart of Nixon's concept of leadership.

In a radio address in September 1968, Nixon declared that the next president 'must articulate the nation's values, define its goals and marshal its will'.[8] The trouble was that this concept of presidential leadership as the embodiment of the nation also entailed an implicit belief that opposition to the president was anti-democratic and the preserve of an unrepresentative elite. In his memoirs, Nixon referred to the Democrats holding 'all four aces in Washington – the Congress, the bureaucracy, the majority of the media, and the formidable group of lawyers and power-brokers who operate behind the scenes in the city'.[9] This spoke volumes about his mindset that his opponents were the entrenched interests of the nation's capital while he as president – significantly not counted one of the 'Washington aces' – represented the real people in the country beyond. Opinion polls that showed a generally high approval rating of his performance as president and correspondingly low public esteem for Congress reinforced such thinking.[10]

To Nixon, his opponents were the enemies of not only himself but also the popular will, so his intention was to defeat them not debate with them. In essence, he regarded himself as president not of all the people but only of those who would follow him. Top aides were of the same mindset. Bob Haldeman liked to speak of the 'four great power blocs in Washington' (he included the intelligence community in place of lawyers) and assured his boss in September 1972 that 'the American people would shout right-on' if he reorganized the executive branch of government to diminish their influence.[11] A chastened Charles Colson later acknowledged that such thinking produced a 'siege mentality' in the White House. 'It was "us" against "them"', he recalled. 'Gradually, as we drew the circle closer round us, the ranks of them began to swell.'[12]

Encircled in his Pennsylvania Avenue citadel by perceived enemies, Nixon reached out to his supporters in the heartland through television. The medium was arguably more important to him than to any other president of the television age. As Godfrey Hodgson noted, 'the key to Nixon's use of television was the idea of control.'[13] Obsessed with image, he surrounded himself with aides who had worked in advertising or television. He developed the White House's first full-fledged public-relations unit, staffed by recruits from the J. Walter Thompson advertising agency where Bob Haldeman had been an executive. Another Nixon first was the creation in January 1971 of the White House Television Office served by a full-time producer.

To get more prime-time exposure, Nixon moved his press conferences from the traditional daytime slot to the evening, but held fewer than any modern president. In early 1970 he decided to

limit them to five or six a year – Kennedy had averaged 22 –
because they took too much time to prepare for and exposed him
to critical questions. Nixon impressed on the briefing team who
prepared his answers that 'what we're actually trying to do here
is make a statement to the television viewer at home'. A press
conference, he avowed, 'is a TV operation' rather than 'directed
at the writing press'.[14] Unsurprisingly his favorite form of televi-
sual communication was the set-piece presidential peroration to
the nation. In all, Nixon made 32 of these, whereas Johnson had
made only fifteen and Kennedy ten. In one such address in
February 1970 he explained why he was rejecting a Health,
Education and Welfare appropriation, so becoming the first president to veto a bill on prime-time television. His most effective
address was the 'silent majority' speech seen by over 70 million
people, but the White House took care to ensure a positive
response by getting friendly organizations like the American
Legion and individual supporters like Ross Perot to produce a
truckload of mail endorsements.[15]

In 1970 Nixon declared, 'I think the American people are entitled to see the President and to hear his views directly and not to
see him only through the press.'[16] Try as he might, however, he
could never control the media. While he wanted journalists to act
as neutral conduits of the president's message to the people, they
saw themselves as guardians of the public interest with an obligation to ask awkward questions of the nation's leader. Instead of
establishing a dialogue with the press, Nixon tended to dismiss
his critics within it as a biased, unrepresentative, liberal elite, out
of touch with the real America that supported him. This was a
dangerous credo that built the media into an enemy to be fought
by fair means or foul. While no modern president has loved the
press, none has made war on it like Nixon did. Neither he nor his
aides ever considered that their actions threatened the constitutional freedom of the press. As Charles Colson remarked in self-
justification, the aim was not to make the media pro-Nixon but
only 'to offset their anti-Nixon bias'.[17]

At a meeting of the administration-elect in December 1968,
Nixon told Cabinet officials to expect a rough ride from print
journalists but to 'let the criticism roll of your back'.[18] He did
not heed his own advice. *New York Times* and *Washington Post*
journalists whose criticisms angered the President found themselves excluded from the White House press pool or Air Force
One. Journalists suspected of receiving information via

unauthorized government leaks, like Joseph Kraft and Henry Brandon, had their phones tapped. Orders were given for income tax audits of owners of unfriendly newspapers, such as Otis Chandler of the *Los Angeles Times*. The administration's most open attack on press freedom was its attempt to get a restraining order against the publication of the leaked Pentagon Papers by the *New York Times* and *Washington Post*. This proved a serious misjudgment. The Supreme Court's ruling in favor of publication endowed these newspapers with a new confidence and sense of legitimacy to investigate any wrongdoing by the Nixon administration.

Nixon's aspiration to be a television president also set him on a collision course with the broadcast media. The usually critical 'Instant Analysis' of televised presidential addresses by network news commentators enraged the White House. A speech requiring hours of preparation, Haldeman complained, would be 'jeered at as soon as it ended'.[19] Shortly after the 'silent majority' speech, Nixon unleashed Vice-President Spiro T. Agnew to assail the unaccountable power of a cabal of 'no more than a dozen anchormen, commentators and executive producers' who decided on how news should be presented.[20] In June 1971, Nixon himself – in Haldeman's words – 'really whapped the NBC top management . . . [that] their newscasters are all completely biased and anti-Administration'.[21] The administration had more than harsh words in its armory. The Justice Department brought anti-trust suits against the three national networks for monopolizing prime time and fostering unfair competition. Wielding various licensing threats, Charles Colson bullied CBS boss William Paley to rein in White House correspondent Dan Rather. Another CBS newsman, Daniel Schorr, became the subject of an FBI field audit for daring to criticize Nixon.

Whenever he took on his putative enemies, Nixon took comfort from the belief that the common people were on his side. In conversation with aides in mid-1971, recounted by Haldeman, he spoke of 'my country, the plain folks out in the middle of America', and 'Henry's country' (Kissinger), namely the intellectual and social elites.[22] But whether Nixon respected 'the plain folks' is another matter. He wanted to speak to and for them rather than with them. Significantly Nixon's most famous depiction of ordinary Americans was as the 'silent majority', a term that hardly suggested any interest in a two-way dialogue with his constituency. 'The American people', he told Haldeman in June

1972, 'are like helpless children yearning for leadership, someone to tell them what to do, and therefore you have to keep doing something in order to satisfy this yearning'.[23] This attitude allowed him to rationalize his penchant for springing policy surprises without consultation or warning. It was entirely out of step with Thomas Jefferson's avowal that the primary duty of leadership in a democracy was 'to inform the minds of the people, and to follow their will'.[24]

As president, Nixon all too often associated dissent against his policies, especially his handling of Vietnam, with a decadent and unpatriotic establishment. In one diatribe, he told close aides in July 1971 that the nation's leadership class had 'absolutely no character or guts'. When the administration faced tough problems, 'we can only turn for support to the noneducated people . . . the uneducated are the ones that are with us'.[25] By 'uneducated' Nixon evidently meant those lacking a college education, an insulting perspective in itself. Moreover, a leader of a modern democracy who encounters the opposition of the 'educated' classes should have cause to question if he is on the right track, but Nixon only treated their criticism with contempt.

Nixon's attitude toward the youth of his country is also revealing about his leadership. Whoever was president in the late 1960s and early 1970s would have had difficulty dealing with the contemporary youth rebellion that shaped the historical character of the era. A decade later the nation's oldest ever president, Ronald Reagan, would enjoy massive support from younger voters who identified with his vision of economic opportunity based on low taxes and small government. Nixon, by contrast, occupied the White House at a time when many young Americans challenged traditional values. It was a mark of his shortcomings as a leader that he never fully understood what moved them. In this he had something in common with de Gaulle, whose regime was severely weakened by the French student protests of May 1968.

Perhaps Nixon's youthful struggles made it inevitable that he would regard student protest and the associated 1960s youth culture of sex, drugs and rock music as the preserve of a hedonistic, cosseted elite who had never had to struggle to enjoy the good life. Moreover, he had some cause to resent the intrusiveness of the youth rebellion. His inauguration as president was the first in American history to be marred by protest and violence. In April 1970 only a journalist's tip-off saved Tricia Nixon's White House

tea for fellow Finch College alumni from the scheme hatched by
one of the guests, Grace Slick of the Jefferson Airplane acid-rock
group, to lace the party punch with LSD hidden under her fin-
gernails. Two months later the Nixons' decision not to attend
their other daughter's Smith College graduation for fear that it
would be disrupted by protest did not save her from being subjected to 'Fuck Julie' chants at the ceremony.

In these trying circumstances Nixon did sometimes try to reach
out to his youthful critics, as in his impromptu midnight visit to
Cambodian invasion protesters at the Lincoln Memorial, but his
heart was not in it. Significantly, there was no presidential effort
to lead the nation in remorse over the killing of student protesters at Kent State and Jackson State. Even in his memoirs, Nixon
still hung tough on these tragic events, citing in implicit justification of his attitude a *Newsweek* poll of May 1970 in which 58
percent of respondents held demonstrating students 'primarily
responsible' for the Kent State deaths.[26]

Confrontation, both symbolic and real, came more naturally
than reconciliation to Nixon. In May 1970 New York City construction workers broke up a peaceful protest against the
Cambodian invasion. Implictly condoning their action, Nixon
invited leaders of their union to the White House and had himself
photographed in a hard hat they presented him bearing the
inscription 'Commander-in-Chief'. Later, Nixon himself took on
anti-war protesters in the 1970 midterm campaign. At San Jose,
California, he experienced what speechwriter Bill Safire described
as a 'mob attack on a U.S. President – unique in our history'.[27]
While Nixon addressed a rally of five thousand supporters, two
thousand protesters demonstrated noisily outside the auditorium.
On leaving, he responded to obscene chants by jumping on the
hood of the presidential limousine to flash his v-for-victory sign,
a gesture that produced a hail of stones, vegetables and eggs in
riposte, with one missile just missing his head. In fact, as Bob
Haldeman's diaries recount, Nixon had 'wanted some confrontation' and had stalled his departure from the hall to let the hecklers 'zero in' on him outside, but things got out of hand.[28]

Whatever he felt about protesters, Nixon did a lot as president
for America's youth. Most notably, he established a lottery system that clarified the likelihood of being drafted (only those with
low numbers would go), ran down troop commitments in
Vietnam and finally abolished the draft system altogether in 1973
to create an all-volunteer army. Meanwhile he signed into law a

1969 bill lowering the voting age from 21 to 18, a proposal he had long favored even though he worried that it violated the Constitution's decree that voting qualifications should be decided by the states. However, Nixon could not build bridges to youth on these solid foundations because he lacked empathy with them.

While Nixon's confrontations with anti-war youth declined with the scaling-down of America's involvement in Vietnam, there was no let-up in his struggles with the US Congress. Scholars conventionally rank Nixon's handling of Congress the least successful of any modern president. Stanley Kutler, for example, characterized his relationship with the legislature as one of 'mutual animosity'.[29] Nixon held office at a historic moment of transition from single-party government that had prevailed for most of the twentieth century. The impressive harvest of legislation produced in 1969–70 suggested that divided-party government could work, but thereafter Nixon's relations with Congress declined dramatically.

At issue was not the kind of ideological division that fueled battles between the Clinton administration and Newt Gingrich's congressional Republicans a generation later. To Gerald Ford, among others, Nixon's difficulties with Congress stemmed from his lack of interest in domestic policy and consequent willingness to delegate management of legislative liaison to an evil cabal of White House advisers who lacked experience in the ways of Washington.[30] However, all the insider accounts of the administration dispel the notion that Nixon was a hands-off president in any sphere of policy. The real problem was Nixon's unwillingness to engage in the give-and-take of presidential–congressional relations that are necessary to make the American system of government operate to good effect.

If Congress had surrendered power to the imperial presidency in foreign policy, it had not done so in domestic policy. Periods of presidential dominance on home affairs, such as the Hundred Days of 1933, were brief and rare. On domestic matters the two branches of government were partners in 'a constitutional marriage of presumed equals'.[31] To enact their legislative proposals, presidents normally had to consult with congressmen, persuade them of the virtues of a proposal, negotiate with them over amendments to smooth the passage of legislation, logroll on their bills, channel patronage towards them, invite them to the White House for photo-opportunities that would impress their constituents and generally stroke their egos.

Insofar as domestic policy was concerned, leadership in the American system of government was a transactional process involving mutual payoffs between the President and Congress.[32] Yet in the view of congressional liaison aide Bill Timmons, Nixon 'felt it was somehow demeaning for the president to ask a member for his vote. It was not in his personality to do it'. According to John Ehrlichman, he 'simply didn't want to spend the kind of time that was required to cultivate these folks'.[33] Nixon may have shown himself a consummate politician in his rise to the presidency, but he neglected some of the political arts in office. Former Republican chairman Len Hall, who had worked closely with Nixon in the nitty-gritty exchanges of party politics in the 1950s, detected a change in his demeanor as president. He had become 'regal, kinglike. . . . He loved power, power to sit in that Oval Office and just issue orders'.[34] However, as any political scientist could have told Nixon, the most effective presidents tended to be those who were the most accomplished political operators because presidential power is more dependent on persuasion than command.

Nixon had no truck with what can be called the Neustadtian model of the presidency.[35] Leadership and command are not synonymous terms in politics. Nixon's preference for the latter over the former caused him to regard those who obeyed as loyal and those who did not as enemies. Persuasion was not a tool that he readily employed. Ideologically rootless and semi-detached from his party, Nixon was motivated less by the socialized concept of power relating to a shared entity than by the personalized power of self-achievement. As one student of leadership observed, 'achievement is a one-man game that need never involve other people'.[36] To Nixon, Congress was not a partner in the process of government but an obstacle to his exercise of presidential power, one that he would increasingly seek to overcome through bullying and deceit.

Things turned sour in Nixon's first year in office over the hard-fought battle to secure Senate approval of the AntiBallistic Missile program. He instructed Haldeman to put maximum pressure on the upper house: 'This is war – have to get it organized.'[37] However, White House aides were so heavy-handed in lobbying senators that they lost several votes previously pledged to the measure. Meanwhile, the White House did not consult with Congress in advance of announcing the Family Assistance Plan, the main item in its 1969 domestic agenda. The struggle over the

Supreme Court nominations of Clement Haynsworth and Harrold Carswell and the controversial invasion of Cambodia further widened the rift between the President and Capitol Hill. The lesson that Nixon drew from these confrontations was not to be more conciliatory but to be even tougher on Congress. As he admitted in his memoirs, the ABM vote had 'confirmed my resolve to pour every possible resource of money and manpower into the congressional elections of 1970 to shore up our position in Congress'.[38]

Nixon had no doubt that Congress rather than himself was at fault for the breakdown of their relationship. At the start of the 1970 campaign he declared that the legislature's antagonism to his programs had produced a deadlock that threatened 'the good repute of American government'.[39] His election speeches continued this theme of holding an obstructionist Congress up to public blame. No president had conducted such a midterm campaign against the legislature since Andrew Johnson in 1866. Predictably, the Democrats retained their huge majorities in both houses and presidential–congressional relations became entrenched in hostility. From 1971 onward, one scholar suggests, Nixon and Congress were not simply political adversaries; they were 'blood enemies'.[40]

Unable to dominate Congress, Nixon began to look for ways to bypass it. He had been doing so with regard to foreign policy since the outset of his presidency. In 1969, he authorized secret bombing raids against Communist sanctuaries in neutral Cambodia. It was his practice not to consult with Congress in advance of any major initiative in the war, whether the invasion of Cambodia, the incursion into Laos, the 1972 Christmas bombing of Hanoi or his pledge to the South Vietnamese leadership that the US would resume air strikes if the Communists violated the 1973 peace settlement. Meanwhile, the diplomacy of détente was pursued through channels that wholly circumvented Congress.

Under Nixon, the imperial presidency also entered the domestic domain. His use of end-of-session pocket-veto tactics to thwart enactment of veto-proof legislation that he disliked and his installation of acting directors in some government agencies without recourse to the legislature's confirmation impelled Congress to go to court to halt such practices. The longstanding but limited doctrine of executive privilege about the president's right to confidentiality on certain matters had been expanded by

President Eisenhower to include all internal deliberative processes within the entire executive branch. While Kennedy and Johnson had put this particular genie back in its bottle, Nixon let it out again with a vengeance. His administration formally invoked the doctrine on 27 occasions – compared with LBJ's two – and effectively exercised it in many more instances through delay and evasion in response to congressional requests for information about executive branch operations. As Congress began to investigate Watergate in the spring of 1973, Nixon went further that any of his predecessors in claiming that a president had discretion to withhold any information in the executive's possession if he believed disclosure would impair the exercise of his constitutional powers. Emboldened by reelection, Nixon also put into effect the basic features of an executive reorganization plan that Congress had previously rejected.

Nixon's greatest challenge to Congress was the impoundment of money it had appropriated to spend on various programs. Presidents from Thomas Jefferson onward had occasionally refused to spend funds on authorized projects, mainly in the realm of national security. However, in the opinion of constitutional expert Louis Fisher, Nixon's impoundments were of 'an entirely different order . . . in terms of magnitude, severity, and belligerence.'[41] They amounted to approximately one-fifth of total controllable expenditures during his first term and affected over 100 domestic programs. In 1973 Nixon claimed that the president's 'right (of impoundment) is absolutely clear' when the expenditure would widen the deficit, which would lead to inflation or the corrective of higher taxes.[42] This statement was an exercise in dissemblance. He was not standing firm against a free-spending Congress. Their dispute centred on political priorities not balanced-budget rectitude. Congress had scaled back some $20 billion from administration spending requests in Nixon's first term, roughly the amount that he had impounded from programs that had received higher appropriations than the administration wanted. The single most significant impoundment affected the Clean Water Act of 1972 – Nixon was only willing to spend a quarter of the appropriation approved by Congress. In other cases – notably the refusal to provide a budget for the Office of Economic Opportunity and its community anti-poverty initiatives – the intention was effectively to terminate the program.

In Arthur Schlesinger's opinion, Nixon's policy-driven impoundment was 'an essential instrumentality of the imperial Presidency' because it threatened to abolish the congressional power of the purse and make spending a matter of executive decree.[43] In 1974 the House Judiciary Committee considered including impoundment in the impeachment charges against him, but its lawyers advised that the President's position was supported by his constitutional and statutory powers. This is one area where post-Watergate history has been on Nixon's side. As the budget deficit went skyrocketing in the 1980s, Nixon's justification of impoundment as a means of expenditure control gained new credence with both the courts and economists. Under the new title of 'deferrals of money', the practice became a valid instrument to repair the nation's finances in the hands of Nixon's successors.[44] In the 1970s, however, the heated controversy over impoundment was symptomatic of the poisoned atmosphere between the President and Congress.

Even without Watergate, Nixon's second term would have been very difficult because Congress was determined to resist further encroachments on its prerogative. In January 1973, House Speaker Carl Albert charged that Nixon was 'creating a crisis that goes to the very heart of our Constitutional system'. Senate Majority Leader Mike Mansfield similarly avowed, 'The people have not chosen to be governed by one branch of government alone.'[45] Thanks to Watergate, the congressional challenge grew bolder and broader, reaching into the foreign policy domain that the presidency had dominated for thirty years. In June 1973, Congress approved an amendment requiring the immediate cessation of the bombing of Cambodia, which Nixon had continued not only to aid the pro-Western government against the Khmer Rouge but also to warn North Vietnam that American air power could still be deployed against it. Although the House sustained his veto of this bill, Nixon found it expedient to agree to terminate all bombing on 15 August, thereby ending finally American military involvement in Southeast Asia.

The President's failure to involve the legislature in the making of détente also rebounded on him. In 1973 a coalition of hawks, liberal supporters of human rights and congressmen with large Jewish constituencies united to enact the Jackson–Vanik amendment that made the granting of most-favored-nation status to the Soviets conditional upon their liberalization of Russian Jewry's emigration rights. These groups allied again in 1974 to put strict limits on trade credits available to the Soviets. Nixon's efforts to insulate the sticks-and-carrots of linkage from congressional interference lay in ruins. These measures now made détente dependent on Soviet good behavior at home as well as abroad.[46]

Meanwhile, Congress moved to clip the wings of the imperial presidency through the imposition of formal restraints. It enacted over Nixon's veto the War Powers Resolution of 1973, which placed limits on the president's power to use troops abroad without congressional approval, and followed this with the Budget and Impoundment Control Act of 1974, which restricted the president's capacity to impound funds arbitrarily. In his post-presidential writings, Nixon railed against these measures as 'clearly unconstitutional' and 'congressional power grabs' that denied the presidency the necessary flexibility to manage foreign policy and economic policy.[47] Such a judgment is self-serving. Congress was seeking not to deny the President his legitimate powers in these fields but to restore its own proper, coequal place in the constitutional order. The decline of the presidency that undoubtedly did occur in the 1970s was due more to the popular mistrust of the office engendered by Watergate than to formal congressional restrictions.

Nixon had even less respect for the federal bureaucracy than he did for Congress. In 1973 he told John Ehrlichman, 'We have no discipline in this bureaucracy! We never fire anybody. We never demote anybody. We always promote the sons-of-bitches who kick us in the ass!'[48] Every modern president has encountered difficulty in what Arthur Schlesinger called the task of 'making the permanent government responsive to the presidential government'.[49] For Nixon it was an article of faith, buttressed by his experience in the wartime Office of Price Administration, that a liberal, pro-Democrat federal bureaucracy was out to sabotage him. In June 1971, Bob Haldeman recounted how Nixon told the Cabinet that many civil servants 'are out to get us. This is true of all administrations but it's worse now. . . . 96% of the bureaucracy are against us; they're bastards who are here to screw us.'[50]

The notion that Nixon faced a Democratic bureaucracy was something of an illusion, but there was just enough truth to sustain it. In 1969, administration efforts to delay the implementation of the Mississippi school desegregation plan provoked 65 line lawyers in the Justice Department's Civil Rights Division to protest to the Attorney General and then go public with their complaint when they received no response. A 1970 interview-survey by two political scientists found that 126 top civil servants, particularly in social welfare departments, were ideologically hostile to the President, though there was no evidence that they systematically sabotaged his policies.[51] If there was liberal bias, it had not benefited Kennedy and Johnson, whose aides frequently experienced frustration in their efforts to get bureaucrats to support presidential policies. Moreover, Nixon himself encountered as much obstruction from what could be termed the conservative elements of the federal bureaucracy, such as the Federal Bureau of Investigation (FBI) and the Central Intelligence Agency (CIA), as he did from the supposedly liberal domestic agencies. In reality, innovating presidents, whether liberals like LBJ, conservatives like Reagan or pragmatists like Nixon, have always found the bureaucracy slow-moving and skeptical with regard to change.

The conduct of civil servants in Nixon's presidency was a case of bureaucratic politics as usual. The main rule was 'where you stand depends on where you sit'. In other words, bureaucrats fought for position and power, and were willing to accept mutually satisfactory trade-offs to safeguard their interests and those of their agency. Moreover, the bureaucracy was locked into a cozy relationship with lobbying organizations and powerful legislators on the congressional committees that approved their funding and oversaw their operations. Together they formed an iron triangle resistant to White House influence. Other presidents might have put up with this, but Nixon expected everyone in his administration to be loyal. Bureaucrats consequently joined the long list of those he counted as enemies.

Nixon's frustration in dealing with the bureaucracy was paralleled by his disappointment in his Cabinet. Originally he expected to delegate considerable independence to departmental heads to get on with running their programs while he concentrated on foreign policy.[52] Nixon announced his entire Cabinet on 11 December 1968 in contrast to the piecemeal selection process of other presidents. A serious effort was made to appoint an African American, but no one of appropriate seniority was willing to serve in a Republican administration. The selection process ignored women. It was a Cabinet of prosperous, white, middle-aged men representing the broad spectrum of views within the Republican Party. They had been chosen for their competence rather than flamboyance and for their expected loyalty to Nixon. Within six months, however, Nixon was seriously disillusioned that Cabinet government could work.

As was usual, departmental heads appointed to serve the President ended up serving their department and the permanent bureaucracy they relied on to run their agencies. William Rogers, a close friend of Nixon, was appointed Secretary of State with a brief to 'manage the recalcitrant bureaucracy of his department', but in a rant to aides in 1973 the President complained that he had been 'totally captured' by his civil servants.[53] Another friend, Robert Finch, who was appointed Secretary of Health, Education and Welfare, came into almost immediate conflict with the White House because of his department's enthusiasm for promoting school desegregation. Like Secretary of Housing and Urban Development George Romney, he caused further friction by appointing under-secretaries who were more liberal on racial issues than the administration wanted. Perhaps the most independent member of the Cabinet was Secretary of Defense Melvin Laird, a former Wisconsin congressman who made full use of his contacts on Capitol Hill to defend his department against competing agencies, especially the National Security Council (NSC). In tandem with Rogers, he was a consistent critic of Nixon's Vietnam esacalations and had no qualms about communicating his views to the media. According to Henry Kissinger, he was the 'master of the inspired leak', praise indeed from another maestro of the unattributed briefing.[54]

Even the expected strong man of the Nixon administration, Attorney General John Mitchell, turned out to be a disappointment. It had been anticipated that this friend and former law partner of the President would act as his confidant on political affairs and foreign policy. However, in a 1970 evaluation of Cabinet personnel Nixon adjudged Mitchell as 'not the compleat [sic] AG' and later complained that he was overly concerned about whether administration actions were 'technically correct'.[55] Mitchell's sin was to be too solicitous of Justice Department bureaucrats who wanted stronger affirmation of civil rights and anti-trust programs than the President. His exclusion from the formation of the Huston Plan, a controversial intelligence project of questionable legality, showed that Nixon no longer trusted him to keep his department on message.

By the time Mitchell resigned office to head up Nixon's reelection campaign, he had long been supplanted in the President's esteem by John Connally, who became Treasury Secretary in 1970. This flamboyant Texan proved himself willing to serve Nixon's interests rather than his department's, as demonstrated in the highly secret manner in which the New Economic Policy was devised. He also provided valued advice on foreign affairs and politics. 'Only three men in America understand the use of power', Nixon once confided to Arthur Burns. 'I do. John [Connally] does. And I guess Nelson [Rockefeller] does'.[56] Like a jealous courtier, Kissinger commented that 'Connally's swaggering self-assurance was Nixon's Walter Mitty image of himself'.[57] Such a man was destined in Nixon's view to captain a much bigger ship than the Treasury. It was his hope to promote Connally as his presidential successor. This ambition had little prospect of realization even before Watergate, but it underlined Connally's one-off status in a Cabinet that lacked the confidence of its chief.

Nixon's response to the inadequacy of Cabinet government was to shift policy formulation and implementation as much as possible to presidential aides, who effectively became an alternative Cabinet less subject to congressional scrutiny than the real one. This made for tense relationships between department heads and White House staff. William Rogers was understandably frustrated about being out of the foreign policy loop. On the other hand, the egotistical Kissinger threatened to resign on several occasions because he felt that Nixon was not doing enough to support him against Rogers. Even Connally threatened to quit because of what he considered lack of consultation by the White House staff. After one Rogers–Kissinger flap, a frustrated Nixon told Haldeman that 'it would be goddamn easy to run this office if you didn't have to deal with people'.[58]

The President's White House bureaucracy grew from four agencies employing 570 people in 1969 to 20 agencies and more than 6,000 employees in 1972. The challenge facing Nixon was to manage this leviathan in a way that enhanced his power without demanding his time. According to Joan Hoff, the unprecedented progress he made toward creating a corporate government was 'one of his most lasting achievements'.[59] To help in this task, Nixon formed the President's Advisory Council on Executive Reorganization, headed by businessman Roy Ash. The Ash Council, as it became known, is one of the most important of the myriad presidential reorganization committees set up since the emergence of the modern presidency. On the basis of its recommendations, Nixon in 1970 adopted a corporate model of presidential reorganization that arranged positions by functional and horizontal lines rather than the traditional vertical ones. This was the first of several reorganizations that would bring him ever closer to a corporate ideal before Watergate intervened.[60]

Irrespective of the Ash Council, Nixon entered office determined to eliminate bureaucratic wrangling between the various departments involved in national security by centralizing decision-making in the White House. To achieve this, Kissinger abolished the National Security Council's (NSC) Senior Interdepartmental Group and created a series of assistant-secretary level interdepartmental groups whose recommendations had to go through a review group of NSC staffers under his chairmanship before being submitted to the entire NSC. In contrast, domestic policy structures were initially much looser, but ideological wrangling between two top advisers – the liberal Daniel Patrick Moynihan and the conservative Arthur Burns – held up the development of the administration's program. To remedy this Nixon set up the Domestic Council under John Ehrlichman in line with Ash Council recommendations. As with the NSC, the real work of this body was undertaken by eight committees staffed mostly by White House aides, who quickly evolved from being mere coordinators to powerful formulators of domestic policy. In parallel with this, Nixon transformed the Bureau of the Budget into the Office of Management and Budget (OMB). This agency's enhanced powers to police the budget process gave the White House greater control over all executive operations. In many respects OMB was Nixon's most 'imperial' reorganization because it created the most powerful managerial unit in government.

In March 1972 Nixon promised 'the most comprehensive and carefully planned . . . reorganization since the executive was first constituted in George Washington's administration 183 years ago'.[61] True to his word, on the morning after his landslide reelection he unveiled plans for an administrative presidency more radical than anything envisaged before or since. Labeled 'the plot that failed' by Richard Nathan, the aim was to create a 'supercabinet' that facilitated presidential control of a streamlined and rationalized executive branch.[62] The plan called for the creation of four 'supersecretaries' with offices in the White House to supervise activities in the functional areas of their own departments and associated independent agencies. The heads of Agriculture, HEW, HUD and the Treasury were to have responsibility for natural resources, human resources, community development and economic affairs, respectively. Otherwise only State, Defense and Justice were retained as conventional departments. In addition, a second tier of sub-Cabinet officials was appointed from the ranks of current or former White House aides to assist in the capture of the bureaucracy.

The government reorganization project showed the best and worst of Nixon. It was a bold solution to the perennial problem of how presidents control the executive branch. It may look through the post-Watergate lens like part of Nixon's grand scheme for presidential tyranny, yet his successors have quietly utilized most of its ideas in their own quest for presidential government. However, the attempted reorganization was handled in a brutal and insensitive manner. Nixon launched it by asking for the resignations of every non-career member of the executive branch, including the Cabinet and White House staff. Even he later admitted that this was a mistake because of its 'chilling effect' on the morale of friend and foe alike.[63] Moreover, while not technically a breach of the Constitution, Nixon's decision to implement this reorganization without congressional authorization poisoned the atmosphere in Washington at the start of his second term.

Alongside executive reorganization, Nixon intended the most significant overhaul of American federalism since the New Deal. The New Federalism, as it became known, was to be the core of Nixon's New American Revolution. The functional ideals of corporate management again informed his actions in this sphere. The President and his advisers sought to devolve more power to the states over programs that entailed service provison, like education, training and public health, while retaining national control over programs involving cash transfers, like welfare, energy and the environment. They envisioned New Federalism as what William Safire termed 'national localism', a framework that accommodated both national goals and local diversity.[64] Its centerpiece was the State and Local Fiscal Assistance Act of 1972, Nixon's most important legislative achievement in the second half of his first term. Enacted after a prolonged battle with Congress, it initiated a shift from federal categorical grants-in-aid to the states to revenue-sharing that gave the states discretion over expenditure of block-grant funds in broad program areas.

Nixon anticipated opposition to the program from 'dug-in establishmentarians fighting for the status quo'.[65] Revenue-sharing hit at the power of Congress to direct the allocation of federal funds, and its reduction of red tape in comparison with the complicated application and oversight processes of categorical grants lessened the role of the federal bureaucracy. Nixon viewed it as a means to enhance local decision-making with the support of federal funding. 'Domestic revenue-sharing was like the Nixon Doctrine abroad', he told Theodore White in 1973, 'The American government helps, but local governments have got to do it on their own'.[66] Nixon was not out to diminish government at home. Instead, his goal was to redistribute power from Congress and the bureaucracy to the presidency and the states and localities. To this end there was a clear nexus between executive reorganization and the New Federalism. As Nixon put it, 'Bringing power to the White House [was necessary] in order to dish it out.'[67]

Nixon's grand vision of the New American Revolution was a casualty of the scandal that destroyed his presidency. With his resignation on 30 April 1973, John Ehrlichman exchanged the role of the man charged with converting his boss's dream of the administrative presidency into reality for that of sacrificial lamb offered up in the vain hope of ending Nixon's Watergate nightmare. Soon afterwards, in the face of a resurgent Congress, the supersecretaries lost their title and functions. Revenue-sharing's association with a wounded president also hurt its cause. The Comprehensive Employment and Training Act of 1973 that provided stringless grants for state-local workforce training programs represented the administration's solitary second-term advance in this area. In Bob Haldeman's estimation, Nixon's administrative reorganizations, including revenue-sharing, constituted the 'hidden story of Watergate'.[68] In this scenario, the Washington power blocs seized on Nixon's unexpected vulnerability over the scandal to cripple his assault on their bailiwicks. The trouble with this analysis is that it implictly presents Nixon as a victim, when in truth he was the architect of his own downfall.

Though initially coined in reference to White House involvement with the burglary of the Democratic headquarters, the term Watergate has become a convenient historical label for all Nixon's illegal actions. Nixon's ruin had its seeds in his contempt for democracy. His imperial presidency entered a terrain of illegality unexplored by his predecessors. His need for secrecy, his need to defeat his enemies, his need to ensure his hold on office against the democratic chance of the election process all propelled him into abuse of power. He then resorted to obstruction of justice as a shield against public exposure of his wrongdoing.

Unauthorized government leaks were the enemy of imperialis-

tic secrecy that Nixon required in order to bring the Vietnam war
to a satisfactory conclusion and conduct back-channel diplomacy
with the Communist powers. In May 1969 a *New York Times*
story revealing the secret bombing of Cambodia prompted a
search for leakers within the NSC. In vain pursuit of the perpe-
trator, the FBI wiretapped eleven officials and four journalists.
NSC aide Morton Halperin later sued Nixon for violation of his
civil rights, winning a judgment that compelled a president for the
first time in history to pay damages ($5) for acts committed in
office. The FBI was not always so pliant, nor would it cooperate
with the rival CIA against the President's enemies. Accordingly, in
June 1970, Nixon attempted to centralize intelligence operations
in the White House through establishment of a special inter-
agency committee. This was to be coordinated by presidential aide
Tom Huston, who devised a secret plan whereby the intelligence
agencies received indirect presidential authorization to conduct
illegal wiretaps, buggings and break-ins in defense of national
security. Hoover's opposition to illegal espionage forced Nixon to
abandon the scheme, but he never acknowledged that it was
immoral. He later told David Frost that any presidential decision
taken to safeguard national security or internal order 'is one that
enables those who carry it out to carry it out without violating a
law'.[69] This mindset had legitimized not only the Huston plan but
also the operations of the White House Special Investigations
Unit – better known as the 'plumbers'.

In creating the plumbers, Nixon was giving vent to his dark
side, which some observers believe was encouraged by White
House aides. H. R. Haldeman was seemingly condemned out of
his own mouth as the unscrupulous mandarin who pandered to
the emperor's evil inclinations. One of the most quoted remarks
of the Nixon era is his own evaluation of his role: 'Every president needs a son of a bitch, and I'm Nixon's. I'm his buffer, I'm
his bastard.'[70] The President himself anointed Haldeman his 'lord
high executioner', empowered to deal mercilessly with any
Cabinet officer who failed to stop leaks from his department.[71]
The Haldeman character was portrayed brilliantly as a saturnine,
amoral, menacing Svengali by the actor Robert Vaughn in
Washington behind Closed Doors. Together Haldeman and John
Ehrlichman became known to journalists as 'the Berlin Wall',
because it was thought they blocked off Nixon from the real
world of Washington politics. With the exception of Kissinger
and Colson, no one got to see the President without Haldeman's

authorization. Nixon himself encouraged a post-Watergate view
of his chief of staff as a misguided zealot who gained too much
power that 'allowed him to isolate me'. He even told David Frost
that Haldeman and Ehrlichman had run the Watergate cover-up
without telling him and that his only guilt in the affair was not
having fired his aides early enough because of misguided loyalty
to them.[72]

The truth was somewhat different from the rationalizations
Nixon subsequently offered. In the estimate of Leonard
Garment, 'Because he knew a great deal about himself, his
strengths and his weaknesses, he also knew how to manage those
who worked for him.'[73] Some aides, like Garment himself, Pat
Buchanan and Bill Safire, did not suffer from association with
Nixon and continued distinguished careers after his fall because
he did not involve them in his unsavory activities. To others
Nixon was more willing to unveil his darker side. Haldeman and
Ehrlichman, in particular, knew about his vices but had committed to him out of a belief in his greatness. In his memoirs
Haldeman reasserted his conviction that Nixon's 'dark spots'
were 'overwhelmingly over-ridden' by his capacity to do great
things and that his own mission became to exercise power 'for
the purpose which I felt would do the most good for President
Nixon'.[74]

At times, Haldeman and Ehrlichman delayed execution of
orders Nixon fired off in anger 'to make sure he really wanted to
do them'.[75] Once he had calmed down, the President often
expressed relief that unreasonable commands had not been carried out. One case involved Haldeman stalling on an order that
every State Department employee – there were thousands –
should be given a lie detector test to find out who had been leaking about Kissinger's secret peace negotiations with the North
Vietnamese.[76] Also, far from isolating Nixon, Haldeman and
Ehrlichman tried to make sure that he heard all sides on an issue,
but found that he preferred solitude. As Ehrlichman remarked,
'The fact is he was down under his desk saying "I don't want to
see those fellows," and we were trying to drag him out.'[77] Yet
there were limits to how far Haldeman and Ehrlichman could
save Nixon from himself because they were ultimately willing to
do whatever was necessary to 'protect his weakness against
exploitation by his political rivals'. According to Haldeman, their
lack of moral scruple 'only fed off Nixon . . . [who] provided the
output which all of us . . . were ordered to put into action'.[78]

It was the White House's response to the leak of the Pentagon Papers that set in motion the unstoppable train of illegal operations. Though an exposure of the deceitful way Democratic presidents had embroiled the nation in Vietnam, these documents posed a threat to the Nixonian imperial presidency. Firstly, they vindicated those who questioned the necessity, wisdom and morality of the ongoing war that Nixon insisted was vital to America's credibility as a great power. Equally important, they created a precedent for other leakers to embarrass Nixon by revealing his dealings with the Communist powers. As the President told Melvin Laird, 'The era of negotiations can't succeed w/o [without] secrecy.'[79] Egged on by Henry Kissinger, Nixon was determined to make an example of Pentagon Papers whistleblower Daniel Ellsberg to discourage other leakers. A plan was hatched to discredit Ellsberg by leaking unfavorable material about his private life to the media. When the FBI refused to undertake surveillance of Ellsberg, Nixon authorized the creation of the plumbers. The task was delegated to John Ehrlichman. He put one of his aides, Egil Krogh, in charge of the unit with Kissinger aide David Young as deputy, and they hired Gordon Liddy and Howard Hunt, respectively former FBI and CIA agents, as operatives.

From the start, the unit fell under the influence of the ruthless Charles Colson, who had previously employed Hunt as a consultant. Absolutely dedicated to Nixon, Colson had been the youngest Marine company commander in history and was known around the White House as the administration's 'evil genius'. Unlike Haldeman and Ehrlichman, he never said 'No' to the President. 'If Nixon said "Go blow up the Capitol"', Ehrlichman avowed, 'Colson would salute and buy a load of dynamite'.[80] Nixon was well aware of this. 'Colson would do anything', he once said. 'He's got the balls of a brass monkey.'[81]

Colson's craziest scheme was the planned burglary of the Brookings Institution, a liberal Washington think-tank suspected of holding classified Johnson administration foreign policy documents whose release would embarrass the Democrats. On 17 June 1971, Nixon had exhorted Haldeman and Kissinger, 'Goddamit, get in and get those files. Blow the safe and get it.'[82] Shortly afterwards Colson produced a plan to fire-bomb the Brookings, but Ehrlichman vetoed this. Another proposal for the plumbers to stage a fire at the Brookings and pose as firefighters to get access to its safes was also rejected.[83]

A plan to break into the Los Angeles office of Ellsberg's psychiatrist to photograph his file went ahead on 3 September 1971 – only to find nothing. It is possible that Nixon himself authorized this operation, about which Ehrlichman had no advance knowledge. In his memoirs, Nixon stated, 'I do not believe I was told about the break-in at the time.'[84] The Watergate tape of 8 September records Ehrlichman telling Nixon of 'one little operation . . . which I think is better that you don't know about'.[85] According to the Watergate testimony of White House counsel John Dean, however, Krogh told him that Nixon had authorized the operation and Haldeman later claimed that the president told him in 1976, 'maybe I did order that break-in.'[86] The extent of Nixon's involvement cannot be conclusively proven, but there is no doubt that Colson believed he had presidential authorization for any action to discredit Ellsberg. In his memoirs, he quotes Nixon telling him, 'We've got a countergovernment here and we've got to fight it. I don't give a damn how it is done, do whatever has to be done to stop these leaks and prevent further unauthorized disclosures.'[87]

Alarmed about the Los Angeles break-in, Ehrlichman henceforth kept the plumbers on mundane tasks and wound up the unit in late 1971. By then the hunt for leakers had taken second place to the task of reelecting the president. Few would have predicted Nixon's 1972 landslide a year before. Having won narrowly against a divided Democratic Party in 1968, he now faced a united opposition. George Wallace was seeking the Democratic nomination, so there would be no third party to split the non-Republican vote. Nixon's intervention in the 1970 midterm campaign offered little reassurance that he could build a new Republican majority. Vietnam was now his albatross, rather than the cross borne by the Democrats, and his diplomatic triumphs were still in the future. With little to be gained from his Republican identity, Nixon disassociated himself from his party by establishing the Committee to Reelect the President. Speechwriter William Safire, who created the title, expected it to be abbreviated to CRP, but this body became known instead as CREEP, a far more suitable appellation for such a sleazy organization. CREEP's misdeeds ran the gamut from illegal fundraising through political subversion to criminal surveillance activities in its efforts to reelect Nixon.

CREEP, which collected more than $60 million in political contributions, marked the climax of Nixon's quarter-century-long association with funny money. Many donations came in cash delivered by suitcase. Though it was illegal to accept money from foreign governments or their agents, the Shah of Iran, President Marcos of the Phillipines and Arab businessmen like Adnan Khashoggi stumped up big funds for Nixon. Corporate donations to political campaigns were also illegal, but this did not stop the President's fund-raisers tapping businesses for cash with the promise of a friendly climate in Washington if he was reelected. Cash-for-favors was another ploy – an order canceling McDonald's unauthorized price increase on a quarter-pound cheeseburger was reversed after its chairman donated $255,000. Ambassadorships were sold quite shamelessly, but the planned minimum going-rate of $250,000 proved too optimistic. The 13 non-career ambassadors appointed after Nixon's reelection contributed only $700,000 in aggregate to his campaign, with the largest donation of $250,000 coming from Walter Annenberg, who got the London embassy.[88]

The dirty tricks of the Nixon campaign also went far beyond the customary rough-and-tumble of American elections. If Nixon did not know of every misdeed his subordinates perpetrated, he broadly approved their operations. The White House had already set the tone with its surveillance of Senator Edward Kennedy, which included placing a mole on his Secret Service detail, in the hope of catching him in a compromising sexual situation. Kennedy's decision not to run in 1972 did not save him from the President's vindictiveness. 'We might just get lucky and catch this son of a bitch', Nixon told aides. 'Ruin him for 76'.[89] With Kennedy out of the race, CREEP's own dirty tricks campaign was directed at the centrist candidates for the Democratic presidential nomination, who were seen as the main threat to Nixon. Some activities were prankish, like ordering thousands of pizzas delivered to Democratic headquarters, but others were plain nasty. The latter included sending out campaign literature in the name of early front-runner Senator Edmund Muskie that spread lies about personal misconduct by his rivals, Senators Hubert Humphrey and Henry Jackson. Muskie himself suffered falsehoods about his wife and the covert leaking of campaign strategy documents by a CREEP mole in his team.[90] To White House delight, the Democrats ended up nominating Senator George McGovern, the most liberal candidate who worried Nixon the least. Party reform of the selection process was mainly responsible for this outcome. The dirty tricks probably had little impact in engineering the defeat of McGovern's rivals, but this does not mitigate their immorality.

Even more sinister were CREEP's political surveillance schemes. With help from Howard Hunt and another former CIA man, James McCord, Gordon Liddy ran what was in effect CREEP's intelligence branch. Nixon knew of its existence and throughout the first half of 1972 would impatiently ask of Haldeman, 'When are they going to *do* something over there?'[91] In fact, Liddy was having difficulty persuading CREEP chairman John Mitchell to support his grandiose plan for electronic eaves-dropping, kidnapping of political opponents, disrupting Democratic gatherings and deploying prostitutes to compromise Democratic convention delegates. But instead of his scheme being dismissed as dangerous fantasy, the former plumber was bidden to come up with something less expensive than the one million dollars he originally asked for. Through Hunt, Liddy enlisted Charles Colson to let the CREEP hierarchy know that 'the president wanted . . . to get this thing off the dime'.[92] On 30 March a scaled-down plan for disruption, espionage and wire-tapping costing a mere $250,000 was finally approved by Mitchell and his deputy, Jeb Magruder.[93] In line with this, illegal entries were twice effected into the Democratic National Committee (DNC) headquarters for the purpose of intelligence gathering. The second break-in, on the night of 17 June, was dis-covered. The five burglars – McCord and four Cuban-Americans who had worked for the CIA – were arrested, as were Liddy and Hunt, discovered in an adjacent building coordinating the opera-tion by walkie-talkie.

In 1990, Nixon claimed that whoever ordered the break-in 'evidently knew little about politics' because the DNC was 'a pathetic target' for a political intelligence operation.[94] Presidential campaign strategy was set by the candidate and his staff, not the party bureaucracy. So what was the purpose of the break-in? There is no shortage of theories.[95]

One explanation centers on the CIA connections of Hunt and McCord. It contends that the break-in was deliberately botched as part of a CIA plot to undo a president whose second-term executive reorganization would trim its power. However, none of the journalistic or congressional investigations of Watergate turned up any proof for this theory. Moreover, the CIA was hardly likely to set in train the investigative culture that eventu-ally intruded on its own cherished secrecy. Another theory focuses on the paranoid politics of Colson and Hunt, claiming that they instigated the break-in to find or plant evidence linking the Democrats to radical groups. Their next step would have been to arrange for violence at the Republican convention and blame it on these radicals in the belief that Nixon would declare martial law in retaliation. John Mitchell did once tell Len Garment, 'That fucking Colson is going to kill us all.'[96] However, the man who once would have done anything for Nixon has always disclaimed responsibility for ordering the break-in, a denial that has the ring of truth given his apparent willingness to tell all in his new persona as a born-again Christian. An even more implausible theory contends that John Dean ordered the break-in to get hold of a DNC official's little black book holding the names of high-priced call girls, among whom was mistakenly listed his fiancée. It also identifies Dean as the author of the cover-up in which Nixon became entangled.[97] The notion that a relative tyro like Dean could have directed veteran operatives to undertake not one but two break-ins and then manipulated a White House damage-limitation operation defies belief.

The most likely explanation is the common-sense one, though it is not definitively documented. Magruder later told Ehrlichman, 'We were really after everything.'[98] This meant sweeping the entire DNC files, photographing sensitive material and tapping phones. The particular target of the second burglary was DNC chair Larry O'Brien, a veteran political operative whom Nixon had long suspected of having the dirt on him, especially about his involvement in the Castro assassination plots in 1959–60 and his dealings with Howard Hughes. Having originally snared Nixon in the 1950s, the eccentric billionaire continued to give him secret donations as president. In 1968, Hughes informed aides that 'he [Nixon], I know for sure, knows the facts of life'. John Mitchell's favorable ruling, over the objections of Justice Department anti-trust lawyers, on the acquisition by Hughes of yet another Las Vegas hotel apparently justified this confidence.[99]

In retrospect it is amazing that the CREEP operation was launched against a party whose only viable presidential candidates – Muskie, through his early defeat in Florida, and Wallace, because of attempted assassination – were no longer in the race. Partly it was a matter of hubris. As Colson recalled, 'We wanted a coronation; we wanted the power that went with the greatest landslide in history.'[100] Partly it was insecurity – the White House was nervous that the Democrats might have embarrassing information that would turn the election into another close race. The burglary took place because Nixon and his closest aides had an insatiable thirst for campaign intelligence, which they considered vital to crushing their opponents. The results they demanded could be achieved only by breaking the laws. As Leonard Garment observed, 'In the environment of this particular campaign, such lawbreaking seemed not only necessary but natural.'[101]

If this was the case, it begs the question famously posed by Senator Howard Baker: 'What did the president know and when did he know it?' Did Nixon authorize the break-in? A recent biography implicitly infers from largely circumstantial evidence that he had advance knowledge of CREEP's intelligence plans from untaped private meetings with Mitchell that were held in the presidential living quarters. A later comment by Mitchell apparently bore this out: 'I never did anything without his permission.'[102] Bob Haldeman suggests that Nixon may have known in advance from a different source, Charles Colson, whom some suspected of then having a blackmail hold over the President.[103] All this is speculation. The newly released White House tapes, which provide explicit proof of Nixon's culpability in other matters, offer no support for this particular contention.

Whatever doubts surround the issue of what Nixon knew in advance, there is no question that he was intimately involved from the start in a criminal conspiracy to cover up the White House's association with the burglars. Within days of the break-in the FBI had tracked money in the possession of Liddy's men back to CREEP's fund-raising operations. On 23 June Nixon and Haldeman conducted what became known as the 'smoking gun' conversations wherein they conspired to obstruct justice. Their plan was to get the CIA to advise the FBI to halt its investigation on grounds that it threatened secret CIA sources.[104] Almost certainly they would never have contemplated this had not J. Edgar Hoover's death on 2 May opened the way for the appointment as acting FBI director of White House loyalist Patrick Gray. The outcome of the scheme was the worst of all worlds for Nixon. CIA deputy director Vernon Walters, another Nixon loyalist, delivered the message but then withdrew it for fear that his agency's integrity was being compromised.[105]

With the FBI investigation back on course, Nixon recognized that the burglars' silence would have to be bought. 'Well . . .

they have to be paid', he told Haldeman. 'That's all there is to that.'[106] This ploy contained the investigation until the start of his second term. Between 6 July 1972 and 22 March 1973 some $430,000 found its way to the indicted conspirators to pay for bail, lawyers' fees and 'income replacement'. The money came from three sources – CREEP, Haldeman's separate slush fund and contributions raised from unwitting donors by presidential lawyer Herb Kalmbach. In late January 1973 the conviction of the seven Watergate burglars without revelation that others were involved in the conspiracy offered Nixon hope that the affair was behind him. On 21 March, he told John Dean that it would be possible to raise another million dollars in cash – 'I know where it could be gotten' – to alleviate the pain of prison for the burglars.[107] On 23 March, however, it was revealed that James McCord had agreed to come clean about the existence of a widespread conspiracy. A week later McCord implicated Magruder, Mitchell, Dean, Haldeman and Colson in the surveillance plot. MacGruder and Dean quickly signified their willingness to testify. Nixon compelled Haldeman and Ehrlichman to offer their resignations on 30 April, but it was only a matter of time before the net closed in on him.

The investigation that unraveled the tangled skein of Watergate involved various institutions and individuals. The *Washington Post*'s Bob Woodward and Carl Bernstein became the paladins of modern investigative journalism for exposing the links between the burglars, CREEP and the White House. Though other reporters from the *New York Times* and *Los Angeles Times* broke important stories, this duo did much to keep the Watergate pot boiling in the six months after the break-in when the White House cover-up was at its most effective. However, Woodward and Bernstein's endeavors were soon overtaken in significance as the momentum of investigation passed to other bodies in the summer of 1973. By then they were engaged in writing their bestselling book, *All the President's Men*, published in early 1974 and later turned into a film starring Robert Redford and Dustin Hoffman. It is fair to say that the appeal of the book and movie lay in how the reporters got their stories, particularly from administration whistleblower 'Deep Throat', rather than the significance of their revelations.

The Watergate cover-up was instigated to hide the truth not from the media but from the FBI, which had quickly established that the burglars were bankrolled by CREEP. Another influential actor in the investigation was US District Court Chief Judge John J. Sirica, a tough law-and-order Republican who presided over the trial of the Watergate burglars. His decision not to hear the case until after the election helped Nixon, but thereafter he proved a doughty adversary. Sirica's instinct that the burglars knew more than they were telling wore down McCord, and his stiff sentences to the others were leavened by the promise of clemency if they too spilled the beans. Only Liddy held out. Later, in August 1973, Sirica was the judge who first ruled that Nixon had to surrender the White House tapes.

In February 1973 the Senate established the bipartisan Select Committee on Presidential Campaign Activities under the chairmanship of Sam Ervin of North Carolina, a conservative Democrat. This body did much to expose the extent of the Watergate conspiracy and unearthed the existence of the crucial evidence pointing to Nixon's guilt. After a slow start, it hit the headlines when White House and CREEP staff eventually appeared before it. Between 17 May and 7 August, it held 37 days of hearings, during which the television networks covered more than 300 hours of testimony. Witness after witness who had supporting roles in the White House's darker operations piled up damning testimony about what had gone on. However, the man who did Nixon most damage was John Dean, who had effectively run the Watergate cover-up before resigning as presidential counselor on 30 April. He delivered a 246-page statement at the start of his five-day appearance on 25 June. His words put Nixon at the heart of the conspiracy. This was hotly contested by Haldeman, Ehrlichman and Mitchell in their testimony. Nixon himself had issued a 4,000-word public statement of his innocence on 22 May, in which he declared, 'I took no part in, nor was I aware of, any subsequent efforts that may have been made to cover up Watergate.'[108] The committee investigation appeared to revolve around one question – whether to believe the President or John Dean. The means to answer this were provided when White House aide Alexander Butterfield testified on 16 July about the White House taping system, whose existence had hitherto been a closely guarded secret known only to a handful of Nixon's men.

As well as creating the Ervin Committee, Congress twisted Nixon's arm to appoint through the Attorney General the first special prosecutor in American history in May 1973. The post went to Archibald Cox, a distinguished Harvard Law School professor. It was a supreme irony that his great-grandfather had a century earlier successfully defended Andrew Johnson in the only presidential impeachment trial in American history. More pertinently, the blue-blooded Cox – a Kennedy man, to boot – was a representative of the Eastern Establishment that Nixon had spent his political life fighting. He vowed that if necessary he would pursue his investigation into the Oval Office. Profiting from the Ervin Committee's work and that of Justice Department investigators, Cox focused on securing release of the Nixon tapes. Eventually his refusal to withdraw a subpoena on nine tapes and limit the scope of his investigation led Nixon to order his sacking and the abolition of the special prosecutor's office on 20 October 1973. Attorney General Elliot Richardson and his deputy, William Ruckelshaus, resigned rather than carry out the order, which was eventually implemented by Solicitor General Robert Bork.

The so-called Saturday Night Massacre was the last gesture of Nixon's imperial presidency. Facing simultaneous confrontation with the Soviets in the Middle East, he told Richardson, 'Brezhnev would never understand it if I let Cox defy my instructions.'[109] Cox, however, saw the issue differently: the question now at stake was 'whether we shall continue to be a government of laws and not of men'.[110] Nixon could not delude himself that the common people were on his side. His Gallup approval rating plummeted to 17 percent. Within ten days of Cox's dismissal, the White House and Congress had received 450,000 telegrams, the largest traffic in Western Union history and almost entirely opposed to the Presidsent. On 31 October, a chastened Nixon reestablished the special prosecutor's office. Leon Jaworski, a Nixon Democrat and eminent Texas lawyer, was named to the post. The previous day the House Judiciary Committee approved broad subpoena powers and a $1 million budget to hire 106 staff (among them recent Yale Law School graduate and future First Lady Hillary Rodham) for an impeachment investigation. For all the apparent power at his disposal, Nixon himself could only muster a legal team of 15 to deal with both the Judiciary Committee and Jaworski.

On 1 March 1974 the special prosecutor's case against seven of the president's former aides resulted in their indictment for involvement in the Watergate cover-up. Nixon was named unindicted co-conspirator, but this was not made public. Meanwhile Jaworski and the House Judiciary Committee worked in tandem to subpoena more White House tapes. Nixon had surrendered the first batch of seven on 26 November 1973, an act that did not lessen suspicion about him. The seven tapes contained nothing damning, but there was a gap of $18^{1}/_{2}$ minutes on the tape of the 20 June conversation between the President and Haldeman and two other tapes of the nine subpoenaed were claimed not to exist. In April 1974 Nixon agreed to supply the Judiciary Committee with edited transcripts of further tapes that had been requested. These ran to 1,254 pages and were full of embarrassing material – the scores of 'expletives deleted' were a shocking revelation to most Americans of their President's foul mouth – but they contained nothing incriminating.

The only way of proving Nixon's guilt was through the actual tapes not selectively edited transcripts. Accordingly, Jaworski asked the Supreme Court in an 'imperative public importance' brief to hear the subpoena case without it first going to a lower appeal court. Agreeing to do so for only the third time since 1945, the court on 24 July handed down an unopposed ruling in the case of *United States of America* v. *Richard M. Nixon, President* that the tapes should be released. On the same day the House Judiciary Committee began hearings that quickly approved three articles of impeachment dealing with obstruction of justice, abuse of power and contempt of Congress. It rejected two articles dealing with the secret bombing of Cambodia and the president's personal tax violations. The vote went on partisan lines that offered Nixon hope that he would avoid impeachment by the necessary two-thirds majority in the Senate if Republican ranks held firm. However, the release on 5 August of the tape of his 'smoking gun' conversation with Haldeman on 23 June 1972 loaded the scales inexorably against him.

Nixon wavered between fighting on and resigning. Why did the man whose proud boast was that he never gave up choose the latter option? Partly his decision was driven by monetary concerns. If he was impeached, he had told Colson in December 1973, 'I'll be wiped out financially.'[111] He would lose his $60,000 presidential pension and $100,000 for staff expenses and face a huge bill for unpaid taxes. Nixon had paid virtually no federal or state income tax since becoming president, had claimed a large tax write-off for the donation of his vice-presidential papers to the National Archives and had made questionable untaxed capital gains in selling some real estate to businessmen friends Robert Abplanalp and Bebe Rebozo.

Determined to assert his financial probity, Nixon made a statement on 17 November 1973 to a group of newspaper managing editors that no American president had ever had to make before: 'People have got to know whether or not their President is a crook. Well, I am not a crook'.[112] As he soon realized, this was a mistake. It became a staple of comedians' jokes as the Watergate scandal progressed towards its denouement. The injury that was added to insult was the announcement by Congress in April 1974 that he owed $432,787.13 in back taxes, a sum he would never fully repay.

Nixon's resignation was also motivated by fear of criminal proceedings if he was impeached. Anxious to avoid further national anguish, House Judiciary Committee chairman Peter Rodino got a message to the White House on 6 August that Nixon would face no further charges if he resigned. 'If he quits', he promised, 'that's the end of it'.[113] It was also evident that Nixon could not count on Republican senators to avoid impeachment. When chief of staff Alexander Haig rang Barry Goldwater to ask how many votes Nixon had, the answer was 12 – he needed 34. The Arizonan made it clear that the smoking gun tape had changed everything. 'Dick Nixon has lied to me for the very last time', he snapped. 'And to a hell of a lot of others in the Senate and House. We're sick to death of it all'.[114] Nor was there any hope that a Checkers-style television appeal to the American people would work. One poll showed support for impeachment running by an overwhelming margin of 66 to 27 percent. When Nixon did go on television on 8 August, it was to announce that he would resign the presidency at noon the next day.

Could Nixon have avoided this fate? It is evident that the cover-up was doomed from the start. Too many people knew that the White House was involved for the secret to be kept. Might an admission of guilt before the cover-up started have saved Nixon? Such a step was impossible for a man so concerned with his historical reputation. Nixon could never admit his guilt after leaving office let alone during it. Even had he done so, the ploy could not have worked because the illegal operations he was involved with were so extensive and hence unforgivable. If Richard Nixon was more than Watergate, so too was Watergate more than just a botched burglary. In his defense, Victor Lasky wrote a book entitled *It Didn't Start with Watergate*, detailing examples of how other presidents had sanctioned illegal wiretapping and used federal agencies for political intelligence.[115] James Roosevelt, son of

FDR, told Nixon secretary Rose Woods that 'everything they ever accuse him of, Father did twice as much of'.[116] A more recent example of misconduct was LBJ's bugging of Martin Luther King's sexual trysts. However, as Melvin Small asserts, other presidents may have participated in illegal acts, but 'none of them committed all the illegal acts that constituted Watergate all the time'.[117]

To some wags, Nixon's best hope of salvation disappeared with the resignation of Spiro Agnew, because no one would have wanted him to succeed as president. The Vice-President was a wholly innocent party in Watergate because Nixon's disdain for him had ruled out his involvement. Instead, Agnew came under Justice Department investigation for having accepted kickbacks on public-works contracts as Baltimore county executive and then Maryland governor. As a result of a complex plea-bargain arrangement, he became on 10 October 1973 the first vice-president in US history to resign. Gerald Ford, the Republican minority leader in the House of Representatives, was appointed to take his place. Agnew might have fought his case if Nixon had given him support, but the President did not want him indicted for fear of the precedent it would create regarding his own case. It is intriguing to speculate that, had he urged Agnew to go down the time-consuming route of impeachment, this might have taken the heat off his own investigation and provided breathing space to marshal his defense of the tapes.

Another possible escape route was getting rid of the evidence. Nixon could have destroyed the unsubpoenaed tapes once Cox had requested nine specific conversations. In July 1973, Henry Kissinger, Nelson Rockefeller and John Connally all advised that he could do this because they were his private property. 'For heaven's sake', Connally told Haldeman, 'tell the President to go on and burn the rest of these tapes'.[118] At this time, however, Nixon still believed that the tapes would exonerate him of wrongdoing, a hope shared by Haldeman. Even had he thought differently, the actual number of tapes was so great that their destruction in secret would have been well nigh impossible. Would any one have carried out a presidential order to do so in public in the face of likely criminal prosecution? Nixon could never have managed it himself: this was a man who, in Leonard Garment's words, 'could not even open an aspirin bottle'.[119] Ironically the Oval Office taping system was voice-activated because Nixon was too clumsy to operate it manually – otherwise he might have been able to switch it off to prevent recording of incriminating conversations.

In the end, of course, it was not the tapes in themselves that led to Nixon's downfall but the wrongdoings that they recorded. The release of the smoking gun tape of 23 June 1972 sealed his fate, but it only revealed his involvement in the obstruction of justice as a participant in the Watergate cover-up. It is for this wrongdoing that he is chiefly remembered in the public's memory of history. By resigning, Nixon avoided an impeachment trial, and Ford's pardon spared him from having to undergo any criminal prosecution. As a result, what was arguably his more serious misconduct – the abuse of power delineated in the second of the articles of impeachment – is much less remembered and understood. The use of the Watergate label as a convenient shorthand for Nixon's misdeeds has reinforced this amnesia. The word most commonly linked with Watergate is 'scandal', which obscures its significance as a constitutional crisis.

If Watergate were merely a scandal, it would be possible to dismiss it as a personal aberration and the fitting culmination of the low career in high politics of Tricky Dick. Nixon was certainly distinctive and unprecedented, but the growth of executive power had made possible someone like him. Watergate was as much a constitutional crisis of the presidency as an ethical scandal to do with Nixon. The imperial presidency's thirst for power had put it on a collision course with the Constitution from the moment of its birth in the Roosevelt era. The combination of Nixon's resentments, insecurities and lack of moral scruple drove him to cross the line between the exercise of power and the abuse of power. Nixon wanted to go down in history as a great president, but his historical significance was that he embodied the dangers of the imperial president. America's experience with Nixon resurrected the question that had troubled the Founders and still remains unanswered: how can presidential leadership be exerted effectively but also effectively restrained?

|8|

Conclusion

When Herbert Butterfield revealed the existence of the Oval Office tapes to the Ervin Committee, he remarked, 'The President is very history-oriented and history-conscious about the role he is going to play'.[1] It was ironic that the recordings intended to help him write his version of history became instrumental in the downfall that has defined his place in history. Instead of enjoying a splendid Churchillian retirement, Nixon spent the final twenty years of his life trying to rebuild his reputation. The greatest enemies he faced in his last battle were historians. Nixon's campaign for his version of history challenged the very ethos of the historical profession. In reaction it became an article of faith for many historians to ensure that Nixon remained saddled with the reputation of villain lest he recast himself as geopolitical maestro and world statesman. 'Richard Nixon has struggled mightily for the soul of history and historians', warned Stanley Kutler. 'Historians *ought* to worry about theirs.'[2]

Central to many historians' assessment of Nixon's place in history is the sense that memory of his misdeeds must be highlighted and preserved. Historical guilt somehow makes up for the fact that Nixon was never tried for, let alone found guilty of, an impeachable offense or criminal misdemeanor. Even the pardon granted him by Gerald Ford did not specify what he was being pardoned for but gave broad immunity for crimes he 'committed or may have committed' as president. This act of clemency became to all intents and purposes part of the Watergate cover-up. History was denied the cleansing effect of a judicial procedure that would have pronounced Nixon innocent or guilty of a particular charge.

Henry Kissinger may not be so lucky now that 'sovereign immunity' for state crimes has been voided in cases like Chile's

Augusto Pinochet and Serbia's Slobodan Milosevic. Journalist Christopher Hitchens recently advocated that Kissinger should be tried for 'war crimes' in which Nixon was also implicated. These include: deliberate mass killings of civilan populations in Indochina; deliberate collusion in mass murder and later assassination in Bangladesh; and involvement in the plot to overthrow and murder the democratically elected head of state in Chile.[3] Whether any charges will be brought against Kissinger remains to be seen, but Nixon can only be tried in the dock of history.

Many historians have an understandable desire to see Nixon punished in history for the abuse of power and obstruction of justice that he escaped being found guilty of in 1974. This is probably why he has long occupied bottom or near-bottom place in scholarly rankings of presidential greatness below such undistinguished presidents as John Tyler, Millard Fillmore, Rutherford Hayes, Benjamin Harrison and Calvin Coolidge. Yet history's judgments are rarely final. For most historians who have written about Nixon, Watergate was history lived through. With the passage of time and the emergence of a new generation of scholars, Nixon will be looked at anew as history examined rather than experienced.

Nixon was a multi-faceted and multi-layered figure who contained within him many contradictions. How should he be remembered: the arch anti-Communist or the dean of détente; the opponent of a presidential cover-up in the Hiss case or the proponent of one over Watergate; the heir of Roosevelt or the forerunner of Reagan; the mad bomber or the peacemaker; the anti-semite or the ally of Israel; the practitioner of desegregation or the rhetorician of race; the man of honor who conceded to Kennedy in 1960 to spare his country a constitutional crisis or the Tricky Dick of 1946, 1950, 1968 and 1972; the rock-ribbed Republican or the planner of a new party; the imperial president who broke the law or the constitutional president who surrendered his tapes in obedience to the Supreme Court?

The historian is best advised to accept that there were many sides to Nixon and move on from there to determine which are of most importance for judging his historical reputation. This is not to downplay his abuse of power and obstruction of justice as president, but Nixon's place in history cannot be determined entirely by his misdeeds. There is a danger that concern to keep Watergate in the center of history's lens obscures Nixon's importance in other regards.

Nixon's vision in foreign policy was on a grand scale virtually from the moment he entered politics. The Herter Committee experience in postwar Europe enabled him to rise above the parochial concerns of a new congressman. He was one of the first American politicians to recognize the significance of Asia in the Cold War. He acquired prodigious knowledge of international affairs as vice-president. Nevertheless he could not break free from some of the dominant orthodoxies of Cold War doctrine regarding the monolithic nature of world Communism and the efficacy of military power as an instrument of containment in the third world. Having consistently advocated a military solution to the Indochina problem in the 1950s, he found himself presiding over America's disengagement from Vietnam in the 1970s. The peace with honor that he promised was an impossible goal and his slow retreat from the conflict was one of his greatest mistakes. Over 20,500 Americans and a vastly greater number of Vietnamese, Cambodians and Laotians lost their lives during his four-year prolongation of US involvement in a war that ultimately failed to preserve Southeast Asia from Communism. Nixon's insistence that this was a necessary price to shore up the credibility of US power as a prerequisite for the establishment of détente was at best a dubious premise.

Nixon's handling of the Vietnam war would be enough to ensure that his foreign policy record as president was adjudged to fall short of greatness. Nor was the strategy of détente as significant or innovative as he made out. As his Vietnam policy indicated, Nixon always remained a Cold Warrior at heart. Détente did not end Soviet–American competition but established a process for managing it. The new foreign policy prevented the rivalry of the superpowers escalating to dangerous levels and fostered cooperation where possible. It did not lay the foundations for Cold War victory that a combination of developments within the Soviet Union and its satellites and of Ronald Reagan's huge defense budgets eventually delivered. Nixon's most signal contribution to this outcome was the rapprochement with China, which helped to keep the Communist powers apart when the Cold War intensified in the late 1970s. He is also significant for showing that peaceful relations between the Soviets and Americans were possible. The Nixon détente established the precedent for the final incarnation of détente in the late 1980s. In contrast, it did not provide a model to help policymakers deal with the disorder and diversity of the post-Cold War era. Nixon's world vision was rooted in superpower relations. His disdain for black Africa, his underestimation of nationalism in Asia and the Middle East and his support for military dictators in Latin America testified to lack of interest in and understanding of the third world.

Nixon's achievements in the domestic sphere were greater than he was wont to brag. The centrist course that he steered from 1954 to 1960 helped to keep his party away from the rocks of electoral disaster on which it sank in 1964. His eventual election as president in 1968 was a vindication of his middle-way strategy. At one juncture, it looked as if he might engineer a political realignment to create a new Republican majority. Had he succeeded, the history books might have spoken of a Nixon coalition as they do of the Roosevelt coalition, but this possibility became a casualty of Watergate. This failure does not relegate Nixon to unimportance in American electoral history. He was instrumental in the disintegration of the New Deal voter coalition. If there was no Nixon realignment, it is certainly feasible to speak of the Nixon dealignment whose fissures have shaped American electoral politics down to the present. There may not have been a Republican majority in the last third of the twentieth century, but neither was there a Democratic one. Nixon's Southern strategy laid the foundations for the Republicans to make the once solidly Democratic South their new bailiwick, and his courting of the blue-collar vote marked the end of its automatic inclusion in the Democratic column.

Nixon also had substantial accomplishments in domestic policy. Among all presidents only Franklin D. Roosevelt and, arguably, Lyndon Johnson could claim a superior record of reform. The fact that Nixon was often a reluctant reformer and had to share credit with a Democratic Congress does not diminish his achievement. In the age of the toxic Texan, environmentalists in particular have good cause to look back with affection on Nixon as the first green president. His record on civil rights, particularly in desegregating Southern public schools and the development of affirmative action, also merits greater historical plaudits than it has yet received. Though Nixon's polarizing rhetoric on race justifiably counts against him, Lyndon Johnson was the only president who did more in substantive terms to advance African-American rights in the twentieth century. Even Nixon's unsuccessful attempts to enact welfare reform and health insurance were bold failures. Economic management was the only real area of domestic policy failure for Nixon, but this was because he had to deal with unprecedented problems.

Without Watergate, Nixon could well be rated one of the best modern presidents. However, such a judgment is not worth debating because Watergate has to be factored into any evaluation of him. The more relevant issue is whether his misconduct should be personalized as peculiar to him or viewed more as the product of broader forces. According to Tom Wicker, Nixon was 'one of us', typically American in 'working and scheming without let to achieve his dreams' and whose misconduct reflected 'the national rush to get ahead'.[4] Irwin Gellman's study of Nixon's congressional career shows that he did not start out the way he became but quickly learned how guile, sharp practice and vitriolic rhetoric constituted the way to get ahead in American politics.[5] In Joan Hoff's estimate, Nixon was 'a normal product of the aprincipled American political system' and Watergate was 'a disaster waiting to happen' because of the decline in political ethics and practices during the Cold War.[6]

The notion that Nixon was somehow a typical American politician does not ring true. While he must be contextualized within the reality of American politics, equally his distinctiveness – both positive and negative – must be acknowledged. Nixon was *both* much better *and* much worse than the norm. He had exceptional ability, exceptional intelligence and exceptional vision. Yet no other leading figure of postwar politics was as lacking in moral scruple as Nixon, lied as often as he did or matched his determination to win at any cost. No one else was so subject to the allure of power nor so prone to misuse it. Watergate may have been a disaster waiting to happen, but it is difficult to believe it would have happened in the early 1970s if Hubert Humphrey rather than Nixon had been elected president in 1968.

Nixon's legacy has been defined hitherto not by his many achievements but by the consequences of Watergate: the popular distrust of leaders and government that was a defining feature of late-twentieth-century America; the ethos of investigative journalism always on the look-out for political scandal; the culture of the special prosecutor investigating presidential wrongdoing; and the reforms enacted to prevent future Watergates, such as the Budget and Impoundment Control Act of 1974, the 1974 amendment to the Federal Elections Campaign Act, the Presidential Materials and Preservation Acts of 1974 and 1978 and the Ethics in Government Act of 1978.

It is indisputable, however, that there was more to Nixon than Watergate. He left a deep imprint on the second half of the twentieth century, not all of it bad. With time, his accomplishments will receive more consideration, but it is doubtful that his misdeeds can ever be discounted. Just as Nixon polarized political opinion throughout his career, his Shakespearean complexity is likely to divide future historical opinion as to the relative weighting his virtues and his vices should have in the assessment of his reputation and place in history.

Notes

Chapter 1   Nixon and reputation

1. Quoted in Melvin Small, *The Presidency of Richard Nixon* (Lawrence, Kan., 1999), p. 311.
2. Stanley I. Kutler, *The Wars of Watergate: The Last Crisis of Richard Nixon* (New York, 1992), p. 576.
3. Gerald Ford, *A Time to Heal: The Autobiography of Gerald R. Ford* (New York, 1979), p. 178.
4. Bob Woodward, *Shadow: Five Presidents and the Legacy of Watergate* (New York, 1999), pp. 37–8.
5. Stephen Ambrose, *Nixon: Vol. III: Ruin and Recovery, 1973–1990* (New York, 1991), p. 545.
6. Quoted in Richard Maidment, 'A Crook who was Good at his Job', *Times Higher Education Supplement*, 29 July 1994.
7. Peter Biskind, *Easy Riders, Raging Bulls* (New York, 1998), p. 342.
8. *The Times*, 25 Apr. 1994.
9. US Congress, *Memorial Services in the Congress of the United States* (Washington: US Government Printing Office, 1996), pp. 5, 11–12.
10. Jonathan Aitken, *Nixon: A Life* (London, 1993), p. 535.
11. Michael Schudson, *Watergate in American Memory: How We Remember, Forget, and Reconstruct the Past* (New York, 1992), p. 187.
12. Joan Hoff, *Nixon Reconsidered* (New York, 1994), p. 341.
13. Richard Nixon, *RN: The Memoirs of Richard Nixon* (New York, 1978).
14. David Frost, *'I Gave Them a Sword': Behind the Scenes of the Nixon Interviews* (New York, 1978).
15. Aitken, *Nixon*, p. 547.
16. Richard Nixon, *The Real War* (New York, 1980), esp. pp. 279–306.
17. Robert Sam Anson, *Exile: The Unquiet Oblivion of Richard Nixon* (New York, 1985), p. 235.
18. Stanley I. Kutler, ed., *Watergate: The Fall of Richard M. Nixon* (Westbury, Conn., 1997), p. 213.
19. Anson, *Exile*, p. 167.
20. Ambrose, *Nixon III*, p. 566.
21. Richard Nixon, *In the Arena: A Memoir of Victory, Defeat and*

Renewal (New York, 1990), p. 40.

22. Aitken, *Nixon*, pp. 552–60.
23. Wilfred Sheed, *Essays in Disguise* (New York, 1990), p. 155.
24. See, for example: Muriel Spark, *The Abbess of Crewe* (New York, 1974); Richard Condon, *Death of a Politician* (New York, 1978); John Hunt with Martin Kaplan, 'Knights Errant', in Otis L. Guernsey Jr, ed., *Best Plays of 1982–1983* (New York, 1983); Donald Freed and Arnold Stone, *Secret Honour: A Political Myth*, one-act play (1984) and film, dir. Robert Altman (1984).
25. *Nixon in China: An Opera in Two Acts*, music by John Adams and libretto by Alice Goodman (1987). For a review of the latest London production of this, see Fiona Maddocks, 'Mao is Making Eyes at me', *Observer*, 11 June 2000.
26. 'Katherine Graham 1917–2001: An American Original', *Newsweek*, 30 July 2001, p. 38.
27. For an excellent assessment of media mythology, see Schudson, *Watergate*, pp. 103–26.
28. Woodward, *Shadow*, p. 515.
29. Bob Woodward, 'The Last Prosecutor: Special Watergate Force is Going out of Business', *Washington Post*, 19 June 1977, p. A1; see too, Woodward, *Shadow*, p. 513.
30. Robert K. Murray and Tim H. Blessing, 'The Presidential Performance Study: A Progress Report', *Journal of American History*, 70 (Dec. 1983), pp. 540–1; Arthur Schlesinger Jr, 'Rating the Presidents: Washington to Clinton', *Political Science Quarterly*, 112 (Summer 1997), pp. 179–80. Nixon rose to the dizzy heights of 25th of 41, his best ever, in a presidential ranking poll conducted by the public affairs television channel C-Span in early 2001. This put him close to almost all his successors, Gerald Ford (23rd), Jimmy Carter (22nd), Bill Clinton (21st) and George Bush (20th) – with only Ronald Reagan (11th) well ahead. See 'From Great to Ghastly – all the US presidents', *Guardian*, 22 Feb. 2000; Center for the Study of the Presidency – home page: **www.cspresidency.org**
31. Nixon, *Arena*, p. 75.
32. Nixon, *Arena*, p. 249.
33. Jon Wiener, 'Inside the Nixon Liebrary', *Nation*, 10 Sept. 1990, pp. 242–5.
34. For the legal and procedural problems over release of the Nixon papers and records, see Joan Hoff, 'Researcher's Nightmare: Studying the Nixon Presidency', *Presidential Studies Quarterly*, 26 (Winter 1996) pp. 259–75. In 1996, a lawsuit brought by historian Stanley Kutler and *Public Citizen* resulted in a binding agreement for the release of the more than 3,700 hours of Nixon presidential tapes. For transcripts of the first 201 hours of released tapes, which focus on Watergate, see Stanley I. Kutler, ed., *Abuse of Power: The New Nixon Tapes* (New York, 1997). In 1998 the Nixon estate won a battle to compel the National Archives to remove all private conversations from the tapes and deposit these with the Nixon Library. It also sued the government for $213 million for the tapes, photographs and papers seized in 1974.

35. Hoff, *Nixon*, p. 342.
36. Quoted in Herbert Parmet, *Richard Nixon and his America* (Boston, 1990), p. 19.
37. Richard Nixon, *Six Crises* (Garden City, NY, 1962), p. 1.
38. 'Interview: Paying the Price', *Time*, 2 Apr. 1990, p. 46.

Chapter 2   The Nixon character

1. Quoted in High Sidey, 'Perspectives on Richard Nixon', in Leon Friedman and William F. Levantrosser, eds, *Politician, President, Administrator: Richard M. Nixon* (Westport, Conn., 1991), p. 9.
2. Stephen Ambrose, *Nixon: Vol. II: Triumph of a Politician, 1962–1972* (New York, 1989), p. 10.
3. Richard Nixon, *RN: The Memoirs of Richard Nixon* (New York, 1978), p. 3.
4. See, for example, Fawn M. Brodie, *Richard Nixon: The Shaping of his Character* (New York, 1981), pp. 36–63.
5. Tom Wicker, *One of Us: Richard Nixon and the American Dream* (New York, 1991), p. 31.
6. Stephen Ambrose, *Nixon: Vol. I: The Education of a Politician, 1913–1962* (New York, 1987), p. 24; Richard Nixon, *In the Arena: A Memoir of Victory, Defeat and Renewal* (New York, 1990), p. 87.
7. Ambrose, *Nixon II*, p. 176.
8. Henry Kissinger, *Years of Upheaval* (Boston, 1982), p. 1213.
9. Wicker, *Nixon*, p. 28.
10. Jonathan Aitken, *Nixon: A Biography* (London, 1993), p. 339.
11. Herbert Parmet, *Richard Nixon and his America* (Boston, 1990), p. 55.
12. Wicker, *Nixon*, p. 28.
13. Stewart Alsop, *Nixon and Rockefeller: A Double Portrait* (New York, 1960), pp.185–6.
14. Nixon, *Arena*, pp. 83, 86.
15. Nixon, *RN*, pp. 12–13.
16. Lewis Chester, Godfrey Hodgson and Bruce Page, *An American Melodrama* (New York, 1969), p. 224.
17. Kenneth Clawson, 'A Loyalist's Memoir', *Washington Post*, 9 Aug. 1979, p. D1.
18. A. James Reichley, *Conservatives in an Age of Change: The Nixon and Ford Administrations* (Washington, 1981), p. 206.
19. Aitken, *Nixon*, p. 314.
20. Roger Morris, *Richard Milhous Nixon: The Rise of an American Politician* (New York, 1990), p. 341.
21. Nixon, *Arena*, p. 203.
22. Brodie, *Nixon*, p. 414.
23. Raymond Price, *With Nixon* (New York, 1977), pp. 138–48.
24. William Safire, *Before the Fall: An Inside View of the Pre-Watergate White House* (Garden City, NY, 1975), pp. 97–104.

25. H. R. Haldeman with Joseph Di Mona, *The Ends of Power* (New York, 1978), p. 62.
26. Haldeman, *Ends*, p. 64.
27. Nixon, *Arena*, p. 41.
28. Nixon, *RN*, p. 247.
29. Morris, *Nixon*, p. 584.
30. Ambrose, *Nixon I*, p. 223.
31. Nixon, *Arena*, p. 203.
32. Earl Mazo, *Richard Nixon: A Political and Personal Portrait* (New York, 1959), p. 26.
33. Aitken, *Nixon*, pp. 83–4.
34. Nixon, *RN*, p. 101.
35. Richard Nixon, *Six Crises* (Garden City, NY, 1962), p. xii.
36. Herbert Klein, *Making It Perfectly Clear* (Garden City, NY, 1980), p. 371.
37. Leonard Garment, *In Search of Deep Throat: The Greatest Political Mystery of our Time* (New York, 2000), p. 263.
38. Nixon, *Arena*, p. 197.
39. Nixon, *RN*, p. 717.
40. Henry Kissinger, *White House Years* (Boston, 1979), p. 1406.
41. Melvin Small, *The Presidency of Richard Nixon* (Lawrence, Kan., 1999), p. 262.
42. H. R. Haldeman, *The Haldeman Diaries: Inside the Nixon White House* (New York, 1994), p. 277.
43. Nixon, *Arena*, p. 103
44. Wicker, *Nixon*, p. 99.
45. Parmet, *Nixon*, p. 62.
46. Wicker, *Nixon*, p. 33.
47. Stanley I. Kutler, ed., *Abuse of Power: The New Nixon Tapes* (New York, 1997), pp. 8, 6.
48. Nixon, *Arena*, pp. 191, 252–62; Nixon, *Six Crises*, pp. 469–71; Wicker, *Nixon*, pp. 436–46 (quotation p. 438).
49. Nixon, *RN*, p. 17; Alsop, *Nixon*, p. 194.
50. Parmet, *Nixon*, pp. 22–3.
51. Small, *Nixon*, pp. 40–1; Haldeman, *Ends*, pp. 174–5.
52. Kevin Phillips, *The Emerging Republican Majority* (New Rochelle, NY, 1969), p. 470.
53. Brodie, *Nixon*, p. 306
54. Stanley I. Kutler, *The Wars of Watergate: The Last Crisis of Richard Nixon* (New York, 1992), p. 68.
55. Nixon, *Six Crises*, p. 344.
56. Haldeman, *Diaries*, p. 333.
57. Bruce Oudes, ed., *From: The President: Richard Nixon's Secret Files* (New York, 1989), p. xv.
58. Haldeman, *Diaries*, p. 331.
59. Stephen Ambrose, *Nixon: Vol. III: Ruin and Recovery, 1973–1990* (New York, 1991), pp. 147–8.
60. Brodie, *Nixon*, p. 34. See too pp. 25–8, 30–5, 57–8.
61. Bela Kornitzer, *The Real Nixon: An Intimate Biography* (Chicago, 1960), p. 120; Brodie, *Nixon*, pp. 130–1; Haldeman, *Ends*, p. 170.

62. Bob Woodward, *Shadow: Five Presidents and the Legacy of Watergate* (New York, 1999).
63. Joan Hoff, *Nixon Reconsidered* (New York, 1994), p. 3.
64. Leonard Garment, *Crazy Rhythm* (New York, 1997), p. 117.
65. Wicker, *Nixon*, p. 26.
66. Richard Nixon, *Leaders: Profiles and Reminiscences of Men who have Shaped the Modern World* (New York, 1982), p. 333.
67. Haldeman, *Diaries*, p. 292. See too Kutler, ed., *Abuse*, pp. 31, 172.
68. Wicker, *Nixon*, p. 26.
69. Quoted in Wicker, *Nixon*, pp. 658–9.
70. Brodie, *Nixon*, p. 307.
71. Mazo, *Nixon*, p. 21.
72. Theodore White, *The Making of the President 1972* (New York, 1973), p. 355.
73. Aitken, *Nixon*, p. 375. Moynihan chose: John Adams, *Autobiography* (1802); Lord Charnwood, *Abraham Lincoln* (1917); Henry Adams, *The Education of Henry Adams* (1918); Duff Cooper, *Talleyrand* (1932); Lord David Cecil, *Melbourne* (1939); Allan Bullock, *Hitler: A Study in Tyranny* (1952); John Blum, *The Republican Roosevelt* (1961); Robert Blake, *Disraeli* (1966); and John Womack, *Zapata and the Mexican Revolution* (1969).
74. Haldeman, *Diaries*, p. 256.
75. Haldeman, *Diaries*, p. 352.
76. Kornitzer, *Nixon*, pp. 65–6.
77. Aitken, *Nixon*, p. 54.
78. Ambrose, *Nixon I*, p. 72.
79. Nixon, *RN*, p. 13.
80. Nixon, *RN*, p. 14.
81. Haldeman, *Diaries*, p. 672.
82. Nixon, *RN*, pp. 16, 26. For Nixon's Quakerism, see: Ambrose, *Nixon I*, pp. 31, 57–8; Parmet, *Nixon*, pp. 71–3.
83. Aitken, *Nixon*, p. 42. See too Nixon, *RN*, p. 15.
84. Aitken, *Nixon*, pp. 41–2; Ambrose, *Nixon I*, p. 59
85. Nixon, *RN*, pp. 19–20; Nixon, *Arena*, pp. 104–5, 241.
86. Wicker, *Nixon*, p. 650.
87. John Robert Greene, *The Limits of Power: The Nixon and Ford Administrations* (Bloomington, Ind., 1992), p. 16.
88. Theodore White, *Breach of Faith: The Fall of Richard Nixon* (New York, 1975), p. 272.
89. Anthony Summers, *The Arrogance of Power: The Secret World of Richard Nixon* (London, 2000). There are 24 entries in the index under 'Nixon . . . drinking by'.
90. Haldeman, *Ends*, p. 45 (both quotations).
91. Quoted in Lester David, *The Lonely Lady of San Clemente: The Story of Pat Nixon* (New York, 1978), p. 186.
92. Summers, *Nixon*, pp. 232–6, 464. For a rebuttal, see Jonathan Aitken, 'Assassination of a President', *Daily Mail*, 9 Sept. 2000, pp. 12–13.
93. Ambrose, *Nixon III*, pp. 312–13, 400, 472–3.
94. Garment, *Deep Throat*, p. 265.
95. Clawson, 'Loyalist', p. D1.

Chapter 3   Elephant man

1. Patrick Buchanan, *Right from the Beginning* (Boston, 1988), p. 321.
2. William Safire, *Before the Fall: An Inside View of the Pre-Watergate White House* (Garden City, NY, 1975), p. 135.
3. Herbert Parmet, *Richard Nixon and his America* (Boston, 1990), pp. 62, 78–9.
4. Earl Mazo, *Richard Nixon: A Political and Personal Portrait* (New York, 1959), p. 26.
5. Richard Nixon, *RN: The Memoirs of Richard Nixon* (New York, 1978), p. 35.
6. Ronald Reagan, *My Early Life: or Where's the Rest of me?* (London, 1980), p. 139.
7. Gary Wills, *Nixon Agonistes: The Crisis of the Self-Made Man* (Boston, 1970), p. 79.
8. Nixon, *RN*, pp. 17–18.
9. Roger Morris, *Richard Milhous Nixon: The Rise of an American Politician* (New York, 1990), p. 176.
10. Mazo, *Nixon*, p. 26.
11. Mazo, *Nixon*, p. 25.
12. Jonathan Aitken, *Nixon: A Life* (London, 1993), p. 76.
13. Morris, *Nixon*, p. 200; Julie Nixon Eisenhower, *Pat Nixon: The Untold Story* (New York, 1986), p. 58.
14. Mazo, *Nixon*, p. 32.
15. Stephen Ambrose, *Nixon: Vol. I: The Education of a Politician 1913–1962* (New York, 1987), p. 114.
16. Aitken, *Nixon*, p. 102.
17. Parmet, *Nixon*, pp. 295–6.
18. Nixon, *RN*, p. 35.
19. Anthony Summers, *The Arrogance of Power: The Secret World of Richard Nixon* (London, 2000), pp. 45–8.
20. Morris, *Nixon*, p. 309, also pp. 366–7.
21. Parmet, *Nixon*, pp. 105–14; Tom Wicker, *One of Us: Richard Nixon and the American Dream* (New York, 1991), pp. 34–48
22. For contrasting views of the Nixon–Chotiner relationship, see Ambrose, *Nixon I*, pp. 124–5, 220, and Summers, *Nixon*, pp. 42–3, 50–9.
23. Summers, *Nixon*, p. 44.
24. Nixon, *RN*, p. 39.
25. Parmet, *Nixon*, pp. 102–14; James Keogh, *This is Nixon* (New York, 1956), esp. pp. 34–7, 80–102.
26. Fawn M. Brodie, *Richard Nixon: The Shaping of his Character* (New York, 1981), p. 228.
27. Wicker, *Nixon*, p. 66.
28. Allen Weinstein, 'Nixon vs. Hiss', *Esquire* (Nov. 1975), p. 152.
29. Aitken, *Nixon*, p. 174.
30. Nixon, *RN*, p. 70.
31. Ambrose, *Nixon I*, p. 205.
32. Wicker, *Nixon*, p. 68.
33. Brodie, *Nixon*, p. 291.

34. Stanley I. Kutler, *The Wars of Watergate: The Last Crisis of Richard Nixon* (New York, 1992), p. 44.
35. Morris, *Nixon*, p. 615.
36. Nixon, *RN*, p. 76.
37. For the campaign, see Morris, *Nixon*, pp. 538–621, and Greg Mitchell, *Tricky Dick and the Pink Lady: Richard Nixon vs. Helen Gahagan Douglas – Sexual Politics and the Red Scare* (New York, 1997).
38. Morris, *Nixon*, p. 584.
39. Summers, *Nixon*, p. 85.
40. Mazo, *Nixon*, pp. 84–5.
41. Nixon, *RN*, p. 93.
42. Mazo, *Nixon*, pp. 126–8, 130.
43. Mazo, *Nixon*, pp. 129–31.
44. Wicker, *Nixon*, pp. 108, 107.
45. Nixon, *RN*, p. 106.
46. Kutler, *Watergate*, pp. 44–5.
47. Kutler, *Watergate*, p. 45.
48. Melvin Small, *The Presidency of Richard Nixon* (Lawrence, Kan., 1999), p. 15.
49. Nixon, *RN*, pp. 149–50; Dwight D. Eisenhower, *Mandate for Change* (Garden City, NY, 1963), pp. 330–1.
50. Nixon, *RN*, p. 149.
51. Ambrose, *Nixon I*, p. 337.
52. Wicker, *Nixon*, p. 201; Parmet, *Nixon*, p. 262.
53. Nixon, *RN*, p. 161.
54. Parmet, *Nixon*, p. 201; Brodie, *Nixon*, p. 314.
55. Parmet, *Nixon*, p. 262.
56. Wicker, *Nixon*, p. 251.
57. Arthur Larson, *A Republican Looks at his Party* (New York, 1956).
58. Ambrose, *Nixon I*, p. 230.
59. David W. Reinhard, *The Republican Right since 1945* (Lexington, Mass. 1983), pp. 75–158; Nicol Rae, *The Decline and Fall of the Liberal Republicans: From 1952 to the Present* (New York, 1989), pp. 25–77.
60. Alonzo Hamby, *Liberalism and its Challengers: Roosevelt to Reagan* (New York, 1985), pp. 115–28.
61. Ambrose, *Nixon I*, p. 365.
62. Iwan Morgan, *Eisenhower versus 'The Spenders': The Eisenhower Administration, the Democrats and the Budget, 1953–60* (London, 1990), p. 169.
63. Theodore White, *The Making of the President 1960* (New York, 1961), p. 242.
64. Nixon, *RN*, p. 163.
65. Wicker, *Nixon*, pp. 214–15.
66. Wicker, *Nixon*, p. 243.
67. Reinhard, *Republican Right*, p. 152.
68. Arthur M. Schlesinger Jr, *A Thousand Days: John F. Kennedy in the White House* (Boston, 1965), pp. 58–9.
69. Richard Nixon, *Six Crises* (Garden City, NY, 1962), p. 102.
70. Morgan, *Eisenhower*, p. 161.
71. Theodore Sorensen, *Kennedy* (London, 1965), p. 217.

72. Nixon, *Six Crises*, pp. 340–1. For debate transcripts, see Sidney Kraus, ed., *The Great Debates: Kennedy vs. Nixon 1960* (Bloomington, Ind., 1962)
73. Parmet, *Nixon*, p. 356.
74. William B. Ewald, *Eisenhower the President: Crucial Days, 1953–1960* (Englewood Cliffs, NJ, 1981), p. 313.
75. Nixon, *RN*, pp. 237–40.
76. Brodie, *Nixon*, pp. 435–41.
77. Aitken, *Nixon*, p. 306.
78. Nixon, *RN*, p. 260.
79. Allen J. Matusow, *The Unraveling of America: A History of Liberalism in the 1960s* (New York, 1984), pp. 131–52; and Iwan W. Morgan, *Beyond the Liberal Consensus: A Political History of the United States since 1965* (London, 1994), pp. 41–57.
80. Mary Brennan, *Turning Right in the Sixties: The Conservative Capture of the GOP* (Chapel Hill, NY, 1995), pp. 122–3.
81. Leonard Garment, *In Search of Deep Throat: The Greatest Political Mystery of our Time* (New York, 2000), p. 265.
82. Safire, *Before the Fall*, pp. 49–50.
83. Nixon, *RN*, pp. 304–5.
84. Stephen Ambrose, *Nixon: Vol. II: The Triumph of a Politician, 1962–1972* (New York, 1989), p. 161.

Chapter 4   American Disraeli

1. Joan Hoff, *Nixon Reconsidered* (New York, 1994), p. 17.
2. Tom Wicker, *One of Us: Richard Nixon and the American Dream* (New York, 1991), p. 674.
3. Hoff, *Nixon*, p. 20.
4. Robert Blake, *Disraeli* (New York, 1966).
5. Rowland Evans Jr and Robert D. Novak, *Nixon in the White House: The Frustration of Power* (New York, 1971), p. 213.
6. Hoff, *Nixon*, p. 17.
7. John C. Whitaker, 'Nixon's Domestic Policies: Both Liberal and Bold in Retrospect', *Presidential Studies Quarterly,* 26 (Winter 1996), p. 131.
8. Hugh Davis Graham, *The Civil Rights Era: Origins and Development of National Policy, 1960–1972* (New York, 1990), pp. 302, 308, 313, 475.
9. See, for example, James Patterson, *Grand Expectations: The United States, 1945–1974* (New York, 1996), p. 719.
10. Hoff, *Nixon*, p. 18.
11. Melvin Small, *The Presidency of Richard Nixon* (Lawrence, Kan., 1999), p. 214.
12. H.R. Haldeman, *The Haldeman Diaries: Inside the Nixon White House* (New York, 1994), p. 298.
13. Wicker, *Nixon*, p. 517.
14. Richard M. Scammon and Benjanim J. Wattenberg, *The Real Majority: An Extraordinary Examination of the American Electorate* (New York, 1970), p. 21.

15. Hoff, *Nixon*, p. 28 and pp. 27–44.
16. Richard Nixon, *In the Arena: A Memoir of Victory, Defeat and Renewal* (New York, 1990), pp. 168–71.
17. Small, *Nixon*, p. 192.
18. Richard Nixon, *RN: The Memoirs of Richard Nixon* (New York, 1978), p. 426.
19. Barbara Kellerman, *The Political Presidency: Practice of Leadership* (New York, 1984), p. 136.
20. Vincent J. Burke with Vee Burke, *Nixon's Good Deed: Welfare Reform* (New York, 1974).
21. Wicker, *Nixon*, pp. 530–1.
22. Stephen Ambrose, *Nixon: Vol. II: The Triumph of a Politician, 1962–1972* (New York, 1989), p. 269.
23. Haldeman, *Diaries*, p. 53.
24. Kellerman, *Political Presidency*, pp. 133–55; A. James Reichley, *Conservatives in an Age of Change: The Nixon and Ford Administrations* (Washington, 1981), pp. 144–51.
25. Small, *Nixon*, p. 188.
26. Haldeman, *Diaries*, p. 181.
27. Reichley, *Conservatives*, p. 143.
28. Nixon, *RN*, p. 428.
29. Alex Waddan, 'A Liberal in Wolf's Clothing: Nixon's Family Assistance Plan in the Light of 1990s Welfare Reform', *Journal of American Studies*, 32 (Aug. 1998), pp. 203–18.
30. For the best assessment, see J. Brooks Flippen, *Nixon and the Environment* (Albuquerque, NM, 2000).
31. Hoff, *Nixon*, p. 23.
32. Small, *Nixon*, p. 198.
33. Hoff, *Nixon*, pp. 24–7.
34. William Safire, *Before the Fall: An Inside View of the Pre-Watergate White House* (Garden City, NY, 1975), p. 592.
35. Wicker, *Nixon*, p. 513; Small, *Nixon*, p. 199.
36. Wicker, *Nixon*, pp. 515–16.
37. Iwan W. Morgan, *Beyond the Liberal Consensus: A Political History of the United States since 1965* (London, 1994), p. 98.
38. Reichley, *Conservatives*, p. 220.
39. Herbert Stein, *Presidential Economics: The Making of Economic Policy from Roosevelt to Reagan and Beyond* (New York, 1985), p. 187.
40. Allen J. Matusow, *Nixon's Economy: Booms, Busts, Dollars, & Votes* (Lawrence, Kan., 1998), pp. 214–302.
41. Matusow, *Nixon's Economy*, p. 181.
42. Matusow, *Nixon's Economy*, p. 307.
43. Hebert Parmet, *Richard Nixon and his America* (Boston, 1990), p. 262.
44. Kenneth O'Reilly, *Nixon's Piano: Presidents and Racial Politics from Washington to Clinton* (New York, 1995), p. 311; John Ehrlichman, *Witness to Power: The Nixon Years* (New York, 1982), p. 223.
45. Hoff, *Nixon*, p. 113; Small, *Nixon*, p. 183.
46. Ehrlichman, *Witness*, p. 227.

47. Small, *Nixon*, p. 163.
48. Harry S. Dent, *The Prodigal South Returns to Power* (New York, 1978), p. 136.
49. Ehrlichman, *Witness*, pp. 229, 233.
50. Ehrlichman, *Witness*, p. 235.
51. Dan T. Carter, *The Politics of Rage: George Wallace, the Origins of the New Conservatism, and the Transformation of American Politics* (New York, 1995), p. 423.
52. Small, *Nixon*, p. 168.
53. Michael Genovese, *The Nixon Presidency: Power and Politics in Turbulent Times* (Westport, Conn., 1990), p. 42.
54. Wicker, *Nixon*, pp. 498–9.
55. Dent, *Prodigal South*, p. 212.
56. Maurice Stans, *One of the President's Men: Twenty Years with Eisenhower and Nixon* (Washington, 1995), p. 69.
57. See Graham, *Civil Rights*, pp. 278–97, 322–45.
58. Ehrlichman, *Witness*, p. 229.
59. Thomas Byrne Edsall with Mary D. Edsall, *Chain Reaction: The Impact of Race, Rights and Taxes on American Politics* (New York, 1992), p. 97.
60. Patrick J. Buchanan, *Conservative Votes, Liberal Victories: Why the Right has Failed* (New York, 1975), p. 49.
61. Daniel Patrick Moynihan, *The Politics of a Guaranteed Income: The Nixon Administration and the Family Assistance Plan* (New York, 1973), p. 157.
62. Edsall, *Chain Reaction*, p. 98.
63. Kevin Phillips, *The Emerging Republican Majority* (New Rochelle, NY, 1969).
64. Quoted in Michael Kazin, *The Populist Persuasion: An American History* (New York, 1995), p. 251.
65. Rochelle Gatlin, *American Women since 1945* (New York, 1987), p. 212.
66. Small, *Nixon*, pp. 177–8.
67. Kazin, *Populist Persuasion*, p. 251.
68. Hywel Williams, 'What Tories have Become', *Guardian*, 18 Jan. 2001.
69. *Time*, 5 Jan, 1970, pp. 10–17.
70. Bruce Oudes, ed., *From: The President: Richard Nixon's Secret Files* (New York, 1989), p. 53.
71. Jonathan Aitken, *Nixon: A Life* (London, 1993), p. 357.
72. Gary Orfield, *Must We Bus?* (Washington, 1978), pp. 103–4.
73. Ambrose, *Nixon II*, p. 376.
74. Ambrose, *Nixon II*, p. 637.
75. Small, *Nixon*, p. 258.
76. Kazin, *Populist Persuasion*, p. 255.
77. Haldeman, *Diaries*, p. 546.
78. Haldeman, *Diaries*, p. 397.
79. Small, *Nixon*, p. 243.
80. John Robert Greene, *The Limits of Power: The Nixon and Ford Administrations* (Bloomington, Ind., 1992), pp. 56–8.

81. Haldeman, *Diaries*, p. 275.
82. Ambrose, *Nixon II*, p. 589.
83. Nixon, *RN*, pp. 674–5.
84. Stanley I. Kutler, *The Wars of Watergate: The Last Crisis of Richard Nixon* (New York, 1992), pp. 577–8.
85. Norman Podhoretz, 'The New American Majority', in Seymour Martin Lipsett, ed., *Party Coalitions in the 1980s* (San Francisco, 1981), pp. 405–13.
86. Aitken, *Nixon*, p. 549.

Chapter 5　　Cold Warrior

1. Stephen Ambrose, *Nixon: Vol. I: The Education of a Politician, 1913–1962* (New York, 1987), p. 616.
2. Tom Wicker, *One of Us: Richard Nixon and the American Dream* (New York, 1991), p. 657.
3. Marvin Kalb, *The Nixon Memo: Political Responsibility, Russia, and the Press* (Chicago, 1994).
4. Ambrose, *Nixon I*, p. 617.
5. Richard Nixon, *Six Crises* (Garden City, NY, 1962).
6. Ambrose, *Nixon I*, pp. 289–90.
7. Henry Kissinger, *White House Years* (Boston, 1979), p. 247.
8. Richard Nixon, *RN: The Memoirs of Richard Nixon* (New York, 1978), p. 71.
9. Allen Weinstein, *Perjury: The Hiss–Chambers Case* (New York, 1978). For the critical response, see the *Nation*, 8 Apr. and 17 June. 1978, and *Newsweek*, 17 Apr. 1978.
10. Monica Crowley, *Nixon in Winter* (New York, 1998), p. 304.
11. Anthony Summers, *The Arrogance of Power: The Secret World of Richard Nixon* (London, 2000), pp. 75–8. See too the updated version of Allen Weinstein, *Perjury: The Hiss–Chambers Case* (New York, 1997).
12. Nixon, *RN*, p. 45.
13. Jonathan Aitken, *Nixon: A Life* (London, 1993), p. 141.
14. Nixon, *RN*, p. 49.
15. Ambrose, *Nixon I*, p. 213.
16. Burton I. Kaufman, *The Korean War* (New York, 1986), p. 24.
17. Ambrose, *Nixon I*, p. 239.
18. Nixon, *RN*, p. 126.
19. Nixon, *RN*, pp. 126–9.
20. Nixon, *RN*, pp. 125–6.
21. Richard Nixon, *No More Vietnams* (New York, 1985), p. 31.
22. Jeffrey Kimball, *Nixon's Vietnam War* (Lawrence, Kan., 1998), p. 24.
23. Nixon, *RN*, p. 155.
24. Stephen Ambrose, *Eisenhower the President, 1952–1969* (New York, 1984), p. 184.
25. Nixon, *RN*, p. 155.
26. Kimball, *Nixon's Vietnam*, p. 25.
27. Ambrose, *Nixon I*, p. 347.

28. Herbert Parmet, *Richard Nixon and his America* (Boston, 1990), p. 316.
29. Nixon, *RN*, p. 205.
30. Nikita S. Khrushchev, *Khrushchev Remembers*, ed. Strobe Talbott (New York, 1970), pp. 398, 458.
31. Ambrose, *Nixon I*, p. 518.
32. Aitken, *Nixon*, p. 146; Nixon, *RN*, pp. 134–5.
33. Nixon, *RN*, p. 52.
34. Nixon, *RN*, p. 52.
35. Nixon, *RN*, p. 50.
36. Parmet, *Nixon*, p. 314.
37. Nixon, *RN*, pp. 121–2.
38. Nixon, *RN*, pp. 128, 129.
39. Wicker, *Nixon*, p. 135.
40. H. R. Haldeman with Joseph DiMona, *The Ends of Power* (New York, 1978), p. 83.
41. Aitken, *Nixon*, p. 146.
42. Nixon, *RN*, p. 131.
43. Summers, *Nixon*, pp. 288–92; Parmet, *Nixon*, p. 452.
44. Ambrose, *Nixon I*, p. 468; Nixon, *Six Crises*, p. 202; Vernon Walters, *Silent Missions* (Garden City, NY, 1978), p. 323.
45. Nixon, *Six Crises*, p. 207.
46. Earl Mazo and Stephen Hess, *President Nixon: A Political Portrait* (London, 1968), pp. 165–87.
47. Fawn M. Brodie, *Richard Nixon: The Shaping of his Character* (New York, 1981), p. 373.
48. Nixon, *Six Crises*, pp. 208–9.
49. Nixon, *Six Crises*, p. 245.
50. Ambrose, *Nixon I*, p. 520.
51. Nixon, *Six Crises*, p. 283.
52. Seymour Hersh, *The Dark Side of Camelot* (Boston, 1997), p. 178.
53. Nixon, *RN*, p. 202.
54. Summers, *Nixon*, pp. 181–99.
55. Summers, *Nixon*, p. 190.
56. Haldeman, *Ends*, pp. 25–7; Summers, *Nixon*, pp. 176–8.
57. According to Seymour Hersh, Kennedy learned of the plan from CIA officials, Mafia boss Sam Giancana and Alabama's Governor John Patterson, whose Air National Guard was involved in training the exiles. See *Camelot*, pp. 169–78.
58. Nixon, *Six Crises*, p. 352.
59. Nixon, *RN*, p. 221.
60. Nixon, *RN*, p. 226.
61. William Safire, *Before the Fall: An Inside View of the Pre-Watergate White House* (Garden City, NY, 1975), pp. 36–40.
62. Summers, *Nixon*, p. 306.
63. William Bundy, *A Tangled Web: The Making of Foreign Policy in the Nixon Presidency* (New York, 1998), p. 47.
64. The fullest accounts of what happened are: Summers, *Nixon*, pp. 297–307, Bundy, *Tangled Web*, pp. 20–48, and Kimball, *Nixon's Vietnam*, 56–61.

65. Nixon, *RN*, p. 343.
66. H. R. Haldeman, *The Haldeman Diaries: Inside the Nixon White House* (New York, 1994), p. 96; Haldeman, *Ends*, p. 81.
67. Kimball, *Nixon's Vietnam*, p. 371.
68. Stephen Ambrose, *Rise to Globalism: American Foreign Policy since 1938* (New York, 1991), p. 240; and *Nixon: Vol. II: The Triumph of a Politician, 1962–1972* (New York, 1989), p. 278.
69. Nixon, *No More Vietnams*, p. 165.
70. Kissinger, *White House*, p. 965.
71. Nixon, *No More Vietnams*, p. 100.
72. Kimball, *Nixon's Vietnam*, pp. 87–102.
73. Summers, *Nixon*, p. 294. Never at any time did Nixon claim to have a 'secret plan' to end the war, which some critics have alleged. For this controversy, see Parmet, *Nixon*, p. 506.
74. Kimball, *Nixon's Vietnam*, pp. 63–86.
75. Haldeman, *Ends*, p. 83.
76. Nixon, *RN*, pp. 393–4, 397.
77. Kissinger, *White House*, p. 305.
78. Leonard Garment, *Crazy Rhythm* (New York, 1997), p. 174.
79. Bundy, *Tangled Web*, p. 65.
80. Nixon, *RN*, p. 499.
81. Nixon, *No More Vietnams*, p. 141.
82. Christopher Hitchens, *The Trial of Henry Kissinger* (London, 2001), pp. 34–40.
83. Bundy, *Tangled Web*, pp. 221–2, 498.
84. William Shawcross, *Sideshow: Kissinger, Nixon and the Destruction of Cambodia* (London, 1979), pp. 394, 396.
85. Melvin Small, *The Presidency of Richard Nixon* (Lawrence, Kan., 1999), 69.
86. Nixon, *RN*, pp. 409, 410.
87. Melvin Small, *Johnson, Nixon and the Doves* (New Brunswick, NJ, 1988).
88. The episode is recounted in Wicker, *Nixon*, pp. 634–5.
89. Nguyen Tien Hung and Jerold Schecter, *The Palace File* (New York, 1986), p. 146.
90. Hung and Schecter, *Palace File*, p. 392.
91. Small, *Nixon*, p. 93.
92. John Ehrlichman, *Witness to Power: The Nixon Years* (New York, 1982), p. 316.
93. Bundy, *Tangled Web*, p. 500.

Chapter 6   World statesman

1. Leonard Garment, *Crazy Rhythm* (New York, 1997), p. 85; Tom Wicker, *One of Us: Richard Nixon and the American Dream* (New York, 1991), pp. 13–14.
2. Richard Nixon, *RN: The Memoirs of Richard Nixon* (New York, 1978), pp. 280–1.
3. Jonathan Aitken, *Nixon: A Life* (London, 1993), p. 1.

4. Melvin Small, *The Presidency of Richard Nixon* (Lawrence, Kan., 1999), p. 107.

5. Seymour Hersh, *The Price of Power: Kissinger in the Nixon White House* (New York, 1983), p. 456.

6. Nixon, *RN*, p. 132; William Costello, *The Facts about Nixon: An Unauthorized Biography* (New York, 1960), p. 250.

7. See, for example, Seymour Hersh, *The Dark Side of Camelot* (Boston, 1997), pp. 268–93.

8. Stephen Ambrose, *Nixon: Vol II: The Triumph of a Politician, 1962–1972* (New York, 1989), p. 383.

9. William Bundy, *A Tangled Web: The Making of Foreign Policy in the Nixon Presidency* (New York, 1998), pp. 191–7, 506.

10. Keith L. Nelson, *The Making of Détente: Soviet–American Relations in the Shadow of Vietnam* (Baltimore, 1995), pp. 102–3.

11. Robert Bothwell, *Canada and the United States: The Politics of Partnership* (New York, 1992), p. 113.

12. Nixon, *RN*, p. 559.

13. Anatoly Dobrynin, *In Confidence* (New York, 1995), p. 245.

14. Aitken, *Nixon*, pp. 380–1.

15. Joan Hoff, *Nixon Reconsidered* (New York, 1994), pp. 149, 155.

16. For good assessments of their relationship, see: Hoff, *Nixon*, pp. 149–157; Ambrose, *Nixon II*, pp. 231–4, 488–91, 654–5; and Walter Isaacson, *Kissinger: A Biography* (New York, 1992), pp. 139–46.

17. Hoff, *Nixon*, p. 153. For the offending interview, see 'Kissinger: An Interview with Oriana Fallaci', *New Republic*, 16 Dec. 1972, pp. 17–22.

18. Small, *Nixon*, p. 98.

19. Donald White, *The American Century: The Rise and Decline of the United States as a World Power* (New York, 1996), p. 341.

20. John L. Gaddis, *Strategies of Containment: A Critical Appraisal of Postwar American National Security Policy* (New York, 1982), p. 284.

21. *Time*, 3 Jan 1972, p. 15, quoted in Gaddis, *Containment*, p. 280.

22. For détente, see: Gaddis, *Containment*, pp. 274–344; Raymond L. Garthoff, *Détente and Confrontation: American–Soviet Relations from Nixon to Reagan* (Washington, 1985); and Robert S. Litwak, *Détente and the Nixon Doctrine: American Foreign Policy and the Pursuit of Stability, 1969–1976* (New York, 1984).

23. Gaddis, *Containment*, p. 280.

24. Small, *Nixon*, p. 63.

25. Nixon, *RN*, p. 562.

26. Nixon, *RN*, p. 562.

27. Andrei Gromyko, *Memoirs* (New York, 1989), p. 283.

28. Walter LaFeber, *The American Age: United States Foreign Policy at Home and Abroad since 1750* (New York, 1989), p. 605.

29. See Gaddis, *Containment*, pp. 289–301

30. Henry Kissinger, *White House Years* (Boston, 1979), p. 136.

31. Hedrick Smith, *The Power Game: How Washington Works* (New York, 1988), p. 600.
32. Kissinger, *White House*, p. 39.
33. Monica Crowley, *Nixon in Winter* (New York, 1998), p. 293; Kissinger, *White House*, p. 841.
34. Garthoff, *Détente*, p. 70.
35. Franz Schurmann, *The Foreign Politics of Nixon: The Grand Design* (Berkeley, 1987), p. 118.
36. Nixon, *RN*, p. 602.
37. William Shawcross, *Sideshow: Kissinger, Nixon and the Destruction of Cambodia* (New York, 1979), p. 145.
38. Nixon, *RN*, p. 452.
39. Nixon, *RN*, p. 395.
40. Nguyen Tien Hung and Jerold Schecter, *The Palace File* (New York, 1986), p. 31.
41. Nixon, *RN*, pp. 382–5; Hoff, *Nixon*, pp. 173–9.
42. Nixon, *RN*, p. 602.
43. Ilya V. Gaiduk, *The Soviet Union and the Vietnam War* (Chicago, 1996), p. 25.
44. Nixon, *RN*, p. 407.
45. Nixon, *RN*, pp. 405–7.
46. Wicker, *Nixon*, p. 454.
47. Cyrus L. Sulzberger, *The World and Richard Nixon* (New York, 1987), p. 44.
48. Gerard Smith, *Doubletalk: The Story of the First Arms Limitation Talks* (New York, 1980), p. 468.
49. Ambrose, *Nixon II*, p. 276.
50. Kissinger, *White House*, p. 525.
51. Smith, *Doubletalk*, p. 154.
52. Hoff, *Nixon*, p. 202.
53. Small, *Nixon*, p. 111.
54. John Newhouse, *War and Peace in the Nuclear Age* (New York, 1989), p. 243.
55. Kissinger, *White House*, p. 1269.
56. Roger B. Porter, *The U.S.–U.S.S.R. Grain Agreement* (Cambridge, 1984), p. 6.
57. Arkady N. Shevchenko, *Breaking with Moscow* (New York, 1985), p. 164.
58. Bruce Oudes, ed., *From: The President: Richard Nixon's Secret Files* (New York, 1989), p. 601.
59. Nixon, *RN*, pp. 562, 564.
60. Kissinger, *White House*, p. 1066.
61. Ambrose, *Nixon II*, p. 115.
62. Richard Nixon, 'Asia after Viet Nam', *Foreign Affairs*, 46 (Oct. 1967), pp. 111–25.
63. H. R. Haldeman, *The Haldeman Diaries: Inside the Nixon White House* (New York, 1994), p. 274.
64. Haldeman, *Diaries*, p. 275.
65. Robert J. Art, 'Bureaucratic Politics and American Foreign Policy: A Critique', *Policy Sciences: An International Journal*, 4 (1973) p. 482.

66. Hoff, *Nixon*, p. 197.
67. Kissinger, *White House*, p. 194, and pp. 163–94.
68. Kissinger, *White House*, p. 182.
69. Robert D. Schulzinger, *Henry Kissinger: Doctor of Diplomacy* (New York, 1989), p. 86.
70. Hoff, *Nixon*, p. 200.
71. Kissinger, *White House*, p. 1067.
72. Bundy, *Tangled Web*, pp. 304–6.
73. Alexander M. Haig Jr. with Charles McCarry, *Inner Circles: How America Changed the World* (New York, 1982), p. 260.
74. Hoff, *Nixon*, p. 244.
75. Small, *Nixon*, p. 64.
76. Bundy, *Tangled Web*, pp. 269–92.
77. Hersh, *Price of Power*, p. 458.
78. Nixon, *RN*, p. 527.
79. Barry Rubin, *Paved with Good Intentions: The American Experience and Iran* (New York, 1980), pp. 125–7.
80. Small, *Nixon*, p. 139.
81. Isaacson, *Kissinger*, p. 564.
82. Haldeman, *Diaries*, p. 53.
83. Kenneth O'Reilly, *Nixon's Piano: Presidents and Racial Politics from Washington to Clinton* (New York, 1995), p. 229.
84. Mohamed A. El-Khawas and Barry Cohen, eds, *The Kissinger Study of Southern Africa: National Security Study Memorandum 39* (Westport, Conn., 1976), pp. 105–6.
85. Anthony Lake, *The 'Tar Baby' Option: American Policy toward Southern Rhodesia* (New York, 1976), pp. 123–57.
86. Gaddis, *Containment*, p. 330.
87. Schulzinger, *Kissinger*, p. 132.
88. Anthony Summers, *The Arrogance of Power: The Secret World of Richard Nixon* (London, 2000), p. 337.
89. Paul E. Sigmund, *The United States and Democracy in Chile* (Baltimore, 1993), pp. 56–84.
90. For US policy in the Middle East, see: William B. Quandt, *Decade of Decisions: American Policy towards the Arab–Israeli Conflict, 1967–1976* (Berkeley, 1977); and Stephen L. Spiegel, *The Other Arab–Israeli Conflict: Making America's Middle East Policy from Truman to Reagan* (Chicago, 1985).
91. Nixon, *RN*, p. 483.
92. Nixon, *RN*, pp. 483–5.
93. Bundy, *Tangled Web*, pp. 337–8.
94. Small, *Nixon*, pp. 134–5.
95. Kissinger, *Years of Upheaval* (Boston, 1982), p. 580.
96. Haig, *Inner Circles*, p. 415.
97. For a highly critical account, see Summers, *Nixon*, pp. 459–62.
98. Hoff, *Nixon*, pp. 269–70.
99. Hoff, *Nixon*, p. 269.
100. Summers, *Nixon*, p. 462.
101. Dobrynin, *In Confidence*, p. 195.
102. Hoff, *Nixon*, p. 273.

103. Bundy, *Tangled Web*, pp. 514–16.
104. Richard Nixon, *Six Crises* (Garden City, NY, 1962), p. xiii.

Chapter 7   Imperial president

1. H. R. Haldeman, *The Haldeman Diaries: Inside the Nixon White House* (New York, 1994), p. 372.
2. Arthur M. Schlesinger Jr, *The Imperial Presidency* (New York, 1974), p. 216.
3. Richard Nixon, *Leaders: Profiles and Reminiscences of Men who have Shaped the Modern World* (New York, 1982), p. 348.
4. Stephen Ambrose, *Nixon: Vol. I: The Education of a Politician, 1913–1962* (New York, 1987), pp. 228–9.
5. Schlesinger, *Imperial Presidency*, p. 206.
6. Nixon, *Leaders*, pp. 43, 70–1.
7. Stephen Ambrose, *Nixon: Vol. III: Ruin and Recovery, 1973–1990* (New York, 1991), p. 590.
8. Stanley I. Kutler, *The Wars of Watergate: The Last Crisis of Richard Nixon* (New York, 1992), p. 131.
9. Richard Nixon, *RN: The Memoirs of Richard Nixon* (New York, 1978), p. 769.
10. Nixon, *RN*, p. 770.
11. H. R. Haldeman with Joseph DiMona, *The Ends of Power* (New York, 1978), pp. 181, 172.
12. Charles W. Colson, *Born Again* (Old Tappan, NJ, 1976), p. 41.
13. Godfrey Hodgson, *All Things to All Men: The False Promise of the Modern American Presidency* (London, 1980), p. 190.
14. Bruce Oudes, ed., *From: The President: Richard Nixon's Secret Files* (New York, 1989), p. 88.
15. Anthony Summers, *The Arrogance of Power: The Secret World of Richard Nixon* (London, 2000), p. 338.
16. Melvin Small, *The Presidency of Richard Nixon* (Lawrence, Kan., 1999), p. 228.
17. Small, *Nixon*, p. 234.
18. James Keogh, *President Nixon and the Press* (New York, 1972), pp. 2–3.
19. Haldeman, *Ends*, p. 184.
20. Nixon, *RN*, pp. 411–12.
21. Haldeman, *Diaries*, p. 297.
22. Haldeman, *Diaries*, p. 293.
23. Haldeman, *Diaries*, p. 476.
24. Quoted in Michael A. Genovese, *The Power of the American Presidency, 1789–2000* (New York, 2000), p. 194.
25. Haldeman, *Diaries*, p. 326.
26. Nixon, *RN*, p. 467.
27. William Safire, *Before the Fall: An Inside View of the Pre-Watergate White House* (Garden City, NY, 1975), p. 331.
28. Haldeman, *Diaries*, p. 205.
29. Kutler, *Watergate*, p. 126.

30. Bob Woodward, *Shadow: Five Presidents and the Legacy of Watergate* (New York, 1999), pp. 34–5.
31. Ralph Huitt, 'White House Channels to the Hill', in Harvey C. Mansfield Sr, *Congress against the President* (New York, 1975), p. 71.
32. James MacGregor Burns, *Leadership* (New York, 1978), pp. 4, 19.
33. Summers, *Nixon*, p. 330.
34. Summers, *Nixon*, p. 329.
35. Richard Neustadt, *Presidential Power* (New York, 1960).
36. David McClelland, *Power: The Inner Experience* (New York, 1975), p. 253.
37. John Robert Greene, *The Limits of Power: The Nixon and Ford Administrations* (Bloomingto n, Ind., 1992), p. 36.
38. Nixon, *RN*, p. 418.
39. Kutler, *Watergate*, p. 132.
40. Greene, *Limits*, p. 61.
41. Louis Fisher, *Constitutional Conflicts between Congress and the President* (Princeton, 1985), p. 236.
42. Kutler, *Watergate*, p. 133.
43. Schlesinger, *Imperial Presidency*, p. 240.
44. Joan Hoff, *Nixon Reconsidered* (New York, 1994), pp. 26–7.
45. James L. Sundquist, *The Decline and Resurgence of Congress* (Washington, 1981), p. 1.
46. William Bundy, *A Tangled Web: The Making of Foreign Policy in the Nixon Presidency* (New York, 1998), pp. 407–9.
47. Richard Nixon, *In the Arena: A Memoir of Victory, Defeat and Renewal* (New York, 1990), pp. 205–6.
48. Richard P. Nathan, *The Plot that Failed: Nixon and the Administrative Presidency* (New York, 1975), p. 69.
49. Arthur M. Schlesinger Jr, *A Thousand Days: John F. Kennedy in the White House* (Boston, 1965), p. 413.
50. Haldeman, *Diaries*, p. 309.
51. Joel Aberbach and Bert Rockman, 'Clashing Beliefs within the Executive Branch', *American Political Science Review*, 70 (June 1976), pp. 456–68.
52. Nixon, *RN*, p. 338.
53. Nixon, *RN*, p. 339; Small, *Nixon*, p. 269.
54. Henry Kissinger, *White House Years* (Boston, 1979), p. 32.
55. Small, *Nixon*, p. 38; Stanley I. Kutler, ed., *Abuse of Power: The New Nixon Tapes* (New York, 1997), p. 8.
56. Safire, *Before the Fall*, p. 644.
57. Kissinger, *White House*, p. 951.
58. Haldeman, *Diaries*, p. 289.
59. Hoff, *Nixon*, p. 58.
60. Peri E. Arnold, *Making the Managerial Presidency: Comprehensive Reorganization Planning, 1905–1980* (Princeton, 1986), pp. 293–364.
61. Harold Seidman, *Politics, Position and Power: The Dynamics of Federal Organization*, 2nd edn. (New York, 1975), p. 106.
62. Nathan, *Plot*, pp. 61–95.

63. Nixon, *RN*, p. 769.
64. A. James Reichley, *Conservatives in an Age of Change: The Nixon and Ford Administrations* (Washington, 1981), p. 166.
65. Hoff, *Nixon*, p. 71.
66. Theodore White, *The Making of the President 1972* (New York, 1973), p. 358.
67. Hoff, *Nixon*, p. 67.
68. Haldeman, *Ends*, pp. 167–88.
69. David Frost, *'I Gave Them a Sword': Behind the Scenes of the Nixon Interviews* (New York, 1978), p. 183.
70. Jeb Stuart Magruder, *An American Life: One Man's Road to Watergate* (New York, 1974), p. 61.
71. Haldeman, *Diaries*, p. 309.
72. Small, *Nixon*, p. 43; Haldeman, *Ends*, p. 65.
73. Leonard Garment, *In Search of Deep Throat: The Greatest Political Mystery of our Time* (New York, 2000), p. 263.
74. Haldeman, *Ends*, pp. xx-xxi.
75. John Ehrlichman, quoted in Fred I. Greenstein, *The Presidential Difference: Leadership Style from FDR to Clinton* (New York, 2000), p. 107.
76. Haldeman, *Ends*, pp. 111–12.
77. Kenneth W. Thompson, ed., *The Nixon Presidency – Twenty-Two Intimate Perspectives of Richard M. Nixon* (Lanham, Md, 1987), p. 132.
78. Haldeman, *Ends*, p. 61.
79. Kutler, *Watergate*, p. 109.
80. Greenstein, *Presidential Difference*, p. 107.
81. 'Watergate', *Vanity Fair* (June 1992), p. 69.
82. Kutler, ed., *Abuse*, p. 3.
83. Summers, *Nixon*, p. 387.
84. Nixon, *RN*, p. 514.
85. Kutler, ed., *Abuse*, p. 28.
86. Haldeman, *Ends*, p. 114.
87. Colson, *Born Again*, p. 59.
88. Summers, *Nixon*, pp. 395–8.
89. Small, *Nixon*, p. 251.
90. Summers, *Nixon*, pp. 380–2.
91. Haldeman, *Ends*, p. 11.
92. Summers, *Nixon*, p. 402.
93. Fred Emery, *Watergate: The Corruption of American Politics and the Fall of Richard Nixon* (London, 1994), pp. 101–2.
94. Nixon, *Arena*, p. 41.
95. For a review of these theories, see Hoff, *Nixon*, pp. 304–12.
96. Garment, *Deep Throat*, p. 71.
97. Len Colodny and Robert Gettlin, *Silent Coup: The Removal of a President* (New York, 1991).
98. Summers, *Nixon*, p. 423.
99. Summers, *Nixon*, pp. 279–82.
100. Summers, *Nixon*, p. 402.
101. Garment, *Deep Throat*, p. 77.

102. Summers, *Nixon*, pp. 402–3.
103. Haldeman, *Ends*, pp. 162–4.
104. Kutler, ed., *Abuse*, pp. 67–70
105. Garment, *Deep Throat*, pp. 83–6.
106. Kutler, ed., *Abuse*, p. 111.
107. Kutler, ed., *Abuse*, p. 254.
108. Ambrose, *Nixon III*, pp. 147–8.
109. Elliot Richardson, *The Creative Balance: Government, Politics and the Individual in America's Third Century* (New York, 1976), p. 39.
110. Emery, *Watergate*, p. 399.
111. Colson, *Born Again*, p. 179.
112. Nixon, *RN*, p. 957.
113. Small, *Nixon*, p. 295.
114. Ambrose, *Nixon III*, p. 420.
115. Victor Lasky, *It Didn't Start with Watergate* (New York, 1977).
116. Leon Friedman and William F. Levantrosser, eds, *Watergate and Afterward: The Legacy of Richard M. Nixon* (Westport, Conn., 1993), p. 249.
117. Small, *Nixon*, p. 273.
118. John Connally with Mickey Herskowitz, *In History's Shadow: An American Odyssey* (New York, 1993), p. 266.
119. Garment, *Deep Throat*, p. 106.

Chapter 8   Conclusion

1. Stanley I. Kutler, ed., *Abuse of Power: The New Nixon Tapes* (New York, 1997), p. xiv.
2. Quoted in Melvin Small, *The Presidency of Richard Nixon* (Lawrence, Kan., 1999), p. xiv.
3. Christopher Hitchens, *The Trial of Henry Kissinger* (London, 2001), p. x.
4. Tom Wicker, *One of Us: Richard Nixon and the American Dream* (New York, 1991), p. 687.
5. Irwin F. Gellman, *The Contender: Richard Nixon: The Congress Years, 1946–1952* (New York, 1999).
6. Joan Hoff, *Nixon Reconsidered* (New York, 1994), p. 341.

Further reading

This is a selective guide for those wishing to learn more on one of the most written-about figures in American history. For other studies, consult the notes.

The most authoritative biography is Stephen Ambrose's three-volume *Nixon: Vol. I: The Education of a Politician, 1913–1962*, *Nixon: Vol. II: The Triumph of a Politician, 1962–1972*, and *Nixon: Vol. III: Ruin and Recovery, 1973–1990* (New York, 1987, 1989 and 1991). The most critical biography is Anthony Summers, *The Arrogance of Power: The Secret World of Richard Nixon* (London, 2000), which focuses on Nixon's dark side without much consideration of his achievements. By contrast, Jonathan Aitken, *Nixon: A Life* (London, 1993), offers recognition for Nixon's virtues. Herbert Parmet, *Richard Nixon and his America* (Boston, 1990), Roger Morris, *Richard Milhous Nixon: The Rise of an American Politician* (New York, 1990), and Tom Wicker, *One of Us: Richard Nixon and the American Dream* (New York, 1991), portray Nixon as a product of his nation and his times. A new resource category produced by Graphix Zone, *Nixon: The CD-Rom*, features photographs, essays and 70,000 pages of documents.

Nixon's own writings are an essential source that reveal far more than he intended. *RN: The Memoirs of Richard Nixon* (New York, 1978) covers his life up to his resignation and is complemented by *Six Crises* (Garden City, NY, 1962) and *In the Arena: A Memoir of Victory, Defeat and Renewal* (New York, 1990). Nixon's mindset is also revealed in: *The Real War* (New York, 1980); *Leaders: Profiles and Reminiscences of Men who have Shaped the Modern World* (New York, 1982); *Real Peace: A Strategy for the West* (New York, 1984); and *No More Vietnams* (New York, 1985). For further reflections on his career and times, see Monica Crowley, *Nixon off the Record: His Candid Commentary on People and Politics* and *Nixon in Winter* (New York, 1996 and 1998).

Most psychobiographical assessments of Nixon's personality are negative. The best of these is Fawn M. Brodie, *Richard Nixon: The Shaping of his Character* (New York, 1981). See too David Abrahamsen, *Nixon vs. Nixon: An Emotional Tragedy* (New York, 1977), and Vamik D. Volkan *et al.*, *Richard Nixon: A Psychobiography* (New York, 1997). Garry Wills, *Nixon Agonistes: The Crisis of the Self-Made Man* (Boston, 1970), is a more sympathetic pre-Watergate analysis.

A number of studies cover Nixon's role in the Republican party up to 1968. Irwin F. Gellman, *The Contender: Richard Nixon: The Congress Years, 1946–1952* (New York, 1999), is definitive on his early career. For Nixon's role in the Red Scare, see: Allen Weinstein, *Perjury: The Hiss–Chambers Case* (New York, 1978 and rev edn, 1997); Richard Gid Powers, *Not without Honor: The History of American Anti-Communism* (New York, 1995); and Greg Mitchell, *Tricky Dick and the Pink Lady: Richard Nixon vs. Helen Gahagan Douglas – Sexual Politics and the Red Scare* (New York, 1997). Republican factionalism is covered by: David W. Reinhard, *The Republican Right since 1945* (Lexington, 1983); Nicol Rae, *The Decline and Fall of the Liberal Republicans: From 1952 to the Present* (New York, 1989); and Mary Brennan, *Turning Right in the Sixties: The Conservative Capture of the GOP* (Chapel Hill, NY, 1995). For Nixon's vice-presidential efforts to promote more expansionary fiscal measures, see Iwan Morgan, *Eisenhower versus 'The Spenders': The Eisenhower Administration, the Democrats and the Budget, 1953–60* (London, 1990). Theodore White, *The Making of the President 1960, The Making of the President 1964* and *The Making of the President 1968* (New York, 1961, 1965 and 1969), provide a good chronicle of the 1960s elections. Also useful is Christopher Matthews, *Kennedy and Nixon: The Rivalry that Shaped Postwar America* (New York, 1996). For Nixon's comeback, see Jules Witcover, *The Resurrection of Richard Nixon* (New York, 1970).

A number of studies cover Nixon's presidency in its many facets. The best is Melvin Small, *The Presidency of Richard Nixon* (Lawrence, Kan., 1999), which has the added benefit of a superb annotated bibliography. Joan Hoff's *Nixon Reconsidered* (New York, 1994) underplays Watergate but is path-breaking on

Nixon's domestic policy. Michael Genovese, *The Nixon Presidency: Power and Politics in Turbulent Times* (Westport, Conn., 1990), and John Robert Greene, *The Limits of Power: The Nixon and Ford Administrations* (Bloomington, Ind., 1992), are also valuable. For useful commentaries see: Leon Friedman and William F. Levantrosser, eds, *Politician, President, Administrator: Richard M. Nixon, Cold War Patriot and Statesman: Richard M. Nixon* and *Watergate and Afterward: The Legacy of Richard M. Nixon* (Westport, Conn., 1991, 1992, and 1993).

Nixon's public addresses are published in *Public Papers of the Presidents of the United States, Richard Nixon*, 5 vols (Washington, 1970–5). Joan Hoff, ed., *Papers of the Nixon White House* (Bethesda, Ind., 1988–) is an ongoing microfiche series of newly released records. Some of these papers can be found in Bruce Oudes, ed., *From: The President: Richard Nixon's Secret Files* (New York, 1989).

Memoirs by administration insiders are also an important source. The most significant is H. R. Haldeman, *The Haldeman Diaries: Inside the Nixon White House* (New York, 1994), a unique daily record that reveals Nixon's thoughts and his interactions with top aides. Still useful is Haldeman's earlier memoir, co-written with Joseph DiMona, *The Ends of Power* (New York, 1978). The more critical John Ehrlichman's *Witness to Power: The Nixon Years* (New York, 1982) is vital for domestic policy in particular. Also valuable are: William Safire, *Before the Fall: An Inside View of the Pre-Watergate White House* (Garden City, NY, 1975); Ray Price, *With Nixon* (New York, 1977); and Leonard Garment, *Crazy Rhythm: My Journey from Brooklyn, Jazz, and Wall Street to Nixon's White House, Watergate, and Beyond* . . . (New York, 1997). Kenneth W. Thompson, ed., *The Nixon Presidency – Twenty-Two Intimate Perspectives of Richard M. Nixon* (Lanham, Ind., 1987) and Gerald S. Strober and Deborah Hart Strober, eds, *Nixon: An Oral History of his Presidency* (New York, 1994), contain useful interviews.

For Nixon's domestic policy, a good starting point is A. James Reichley, *Conservatives in an Age of Change: The Nixon and Ford Administrations* (Washington, 1981). Allen J. Matusow, *Nixon's Economy: Booms, Busts, Dollars & Votes* (Lawrence, Kan., 1998), and J. Brooks Flippen, *Nixon and the Environment* (Albuquerque, NM, 2000), are first-rate monographs. See too: Vincent J. Burke with Vee Burke, *Nixon's Good Deed: Welfare*

Reform (New York, 1974); Hugh Davis Graham, *The Civil Rights Era: Origins and Development of National Policy, 1960–1972* (New York, 1990); Dean Kotlowski, 'Richard Nixon and the Origins of Affirmative Action', *Historian,* 60 (Spring 1998), pp. 523–41; and Alex Waddan, 'A Liberal in Wolf's Clothing: Nixon's Family Assistance Plan in Light of 1990s Welfare Reform', *Journal of American Studies,* 32 (Aug. 1998), pp. 203-18. Kevin Phillips, *The Emerging Republican Majority* (New Rochelle, NY, 1969), and Richard M. Scammon and Benjamin J. Wattenberg, *The Real Majority: An Extraordinary Examination of the American Electorate* (New York, 1970), both influenced Nixon's electoral strategy. Harry S. Dent, *The Prodigal South Returns to Power* (New York, 1978), is a memoir of the Southern strategy. For Nixon's new populism, see Thomas Byrne Edsall with Mary D. Edsall, *Chain Reaction: The Impact of Race, Rights and Taxes on American Politics* (New York, 1992), and Michael Kazin, *The Populist Persuasion: An American History* (New York, 1995).

For understanding the Cold War, see: Stephen Ambrose, *Eisenhower the President, 1952–1969* (New York, 1983); Thomas J. McCormick, *America's Half-Century: US Foreign Policy in the Cold War* (Baltimore, 1989); John Lewis Gaddis, *We Know Now: Rethinking Cold War History* (New York, 1997); and John White, *Still Seeing Red: How the Cold War Shapes the New American Politics* (Boulder, Colo., 1997). For Vietnam, consult George Herring, *America's Longest War: The United States and Vietnam, 1950–1975* (New York, 1996), and Robert Schulzinger, *A Time for War: The United States and Vietnam, 1950–1975* (New York, 1997). Jeffrey Kimball's excellent *Nixon's Vietnam War* (Lawrence, Kan., 1998) is definitive. William Shawcross, *Sideshow: Kissinger, Nixon and the Destruction of Cambodia* (London, 1979), is highly critical.

For Nixon's foreign policy as president, a balanced but ultimately critical study is William Bundy, *A Tangled Web: The Making Foreign Policy in the Nixon Presidency* (New York, 1998). Excellent on geopolitics is John Lewis Gaddis, *Strategies of Containment: A Critical Appraisal of Postwar American National Security Policy* (New York, 1982). Raymond L. Garthoff, *Detente and Confrontation: American–Soviet Relations from Nixon to Reagan* (Washington, 1985), and Keith L. Nelson, *The Making of Detente: Soviet–American Relations in the Shadow of Vietnam* (Baltimore, 1995), are insightful on Nixon's Soviet policy. For nuclear issues, consult Gerard Smith's bitter memoir, *Doubletalk: The Story of the First Arms Limitation Talks* (New York, 1980), and Terry Terriff's scholarly *The Nixon Administration and the Making of US Nuclear Strategy* (Ithaca, NY, 1995). Gordon H. Chang, *Friends and Enemies: The United States, China, and the Soviet Union, 1948–1972* (Stanford, 1990), and Robert S. Ross, *Negotiating Cooperation: the United States and China, 1969–1989* (Stanford, Calif., 1995), cover the China opening.

Henry Kissinger's *White House Years* and *Years of Upheaval* (Boston, 1979, 1982) are indispensable. They must be supplemented by more balanced scholarly studies, notably Robert Schulzinger, *Henry Kissinger: Doctor of Diplomacy* (New York, 1989), and Walter Isaacson, *Kissinger: A Biography* (New York, 1992). For critical journalistic appraisals, see Seymour Hersh, *The Price of Power: Kissinger in the Nixon White House* (New York, 1983), and Christopher Hitchens, *The Trial of Henry Kissinger* (London, 2001).

For understanding Nixon within the context of the modern presidency, begin with Arthur M. Schlesinger Jr, *The Imperial Presidency* (New York, 1974), and Richard Neustadt, *Presidential Power: The Politics of Leadership from FDR to Carter* (New York, 1980). On Nixon's relations with Congress, see James L. Sundquist, *The Decline and Resurgence of Congress* (Washington, 1981), and Louis Fisher, *Constitutional Conflicts between Congress and the President* (Princeton, 1985). For his battles with the media, see William E. Porter, *Assault on the Media* (Ann Arbor, 1976), and Joseph Spear, *Presidents and the Press: The Nixon Legacy* (Cambridge, Mass., 1984). Richard P. Nathan, *The Plot that Failed: Nixon and the Administrative Presidency* (New York, 1975), and Peri E. Arnold, *Making the Managerial Presidency: Comprehensive Reorganization Planning, 1905–1980* (Princeton, 1986), are excellent on administrative reform.

For Watergate, the best study remains Stanley I. Kutler, *The Wars of Watergate: The Last Crisis of Richard Nixon* (New York, 1992). The same author has also edited two valuable collections, *Abuse of Power: The New Nixon Tapes* (New York, 1997), transcripts of newly released tapes, and *Watergate: The Fall of Richard M. Nixon* (Westbury, Conn., 1997). For a solid, journalistic study, see Fred Emery, *Watergate: The Corruption of American Politics and the Fall of Richard Nixon* (London, 1994). An intriguing memoir is Leonard Garment, *In Search of Deep Throat: The Greatest Political Mystery of our Time* (New

York, 2000). John Dean, whose congressional testimony helped destroy Nixon, tells his tale in *Blind Ambition: The White House Years* (New York, 1976). Nixon's 'evil genius', Charles W. Colson, also tells all in *Born Again* (Old Tappan, NJ, 1976). The most famous book on Watergate is Carl Bernstein and Bob Woodward, *All the President's Men* (New York, 1974), a riveting tale that implicitly overplays its authors' role in Nixon's downfall. Less impressive is their much disputed account of Nixon's resignation, *The Final Days* (New York, 1976). Victor Lasky argues that Nixon's misdeeds had plentiful precedents in *It Didn't Start with Watergate* (New York, 1977). Bob Woodward, *Shadow: Five Presidents and the Legacy of Watergate* (New York, 1999), shows how Nixon's successors have not always been faithful to the truth. Finally, Michael Schudson's *Watergate in American Memory: How We Remember, Forget, and Reconstruct the Past* (New York, 1992) is excellent.

Index